Photo Restoration and Retouching Using Corel® PaintShop Pro® X5,
Fourth Edition

D1371873

Robert Correll

Course Technology PTR

A part of Cengage Learning

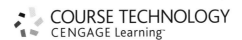

COURSE TECHNOLOGY
CENGAGE Learning

Australia, Brazil, Japan, Korea, Mexico, Singapore, Spain, United Kingdom, United States

COURSE TECHNOLOGY
CENGAGE Learning™

Photo Restoration and Retouching Using Corel® PaintShop Pro® X5, Fourth Edition
Robert Correll

**Publisher and General Manager,
Course Technology PTR:** Stacy L. Hiquet

Associate Director of Marketing:
Sarah Panella

Manager of Editorial Services:
Heather Talbot

Senior Marketing Manager:
Mark Hughes

Acquisitions Editor:
Heather Hurley

Project and Copy Editor:
Marta Justak

Technical Reviewer:
Lori Davis

Interior Layout:
Shawn Morningstar

Cover Designer:
Mike Tanamachi

Indexer and Proofreader:
Kelly Talbot Editing Services

For product information and technology assistance, contact us at

**Cengage Learning Customer and Sales Support,
1-800-354-9706**

For permission to use material from this text or product, submit all requests online at
cengage.com/permissions

Further permissions questions can be emailed to
permissionrequest@cengage.com

Library of Congress Control Number: 2012948825
ISBN-13: 978-1-285-19656-5
ISBN-10: 1-285-19656-2

Course Technology, a part of Cengage Learning
20 Channel Center Street
Boston, MA 02210
USA

Cengage Learning is a leading provider of customized learning solutions with office locations around the globe, including Singapore, the United Kingdom, Australia, Mexico, Brazil, and Japan. Locate your local office at:
international.cengage.com/region

Cengage Learning products are represented in Canada by Nelson Education, Ltd.

For your lifelong learning solutions, visit **courseptr.com**
Visit our corporate website at **cengage.com**

Printed in the United States of America
1 2 3 4 5 6 7 14 13 12

To our family—
past, present, and future

Foreword

FOR PEOPLE WHO LOVE to take photographs, the pure enjoyment of capturing and crafting an image is often enough to warrant the effort it takes to do so. But there's another kind of happiness photographers take out of their work—the act of sharing a meaningful image can spread the joy of photography and delight viewers of all ages.

The new Corel PaintShop Pro X5 has been designed recognizing the importance of sharing. People inspire us, not as subjects of our craft, but as participants in enjoying the results of our efforts. Once the capture, enhancement, and editing of our photos is over, sharing with others can give us a unique sense of fulfillment.

PaintShop Pro X5 includes new features that reflect this. From Face recognition to Places, our new Photo Mapping tools to our new level of social media integration, PaintShop Pro X5 accelerates a photographer's ability to share his or her craft. And other new tools, such as the Instant Effects palette, let us make and enhance photos faster than ever, so we can get on with the sharing!

In his excellent book, *Photo Restoration and Retouching Using Corel PaintShop Pro X5, Fourth Edition,* Robert Correll reveals his deep grasp of what a photo means to others. The thought of restoring a cherished family photo for our loved ones to enjoy is what motivates the people at Corel to keep pushing PaintShop Pro forward and invent new ways to enhance and share our—or our forebears'—photographs.

This book is a fantastic guide to help you uncover the possibilities of what you can do with your photos—both new and old—taking you step-by-step through the process of restoring and enhancing your precious memories.

Photo Restoration and Retouching Using Corel PaintShop Pro X5 will provide you with the skills you need to make subtle enhancements or dramatic artistic embellishments to your photographs.

Happy reading, happy editing, and we wish you all the best in making and sharing your photographs.

Craig Copley
Senior Product Manager,
Corel PaintShop Pro X5
Corel Corporation

Acknowledgments

I HAVE MANY PEOPLE TO THANK. Publishing this book was a team effort from start to finish.

Thanks to David Fugate, my agent and the founder of LaunchBooks Literary Agency. Thank you for your tireless efforts, wisdom, expertise, and friendship!

Many thanks to all the great people I met and worked with at Course Technology. Thank you to Heather Hurley for your wonderful support as you have shepherded the book through the process; Marta Justak, for your excellent editing and encouragement; Shawn Morningstar, for your great layouts; Mike Tanamachi, for your work on the cover; and Mark Hughes, for your marketing efforts.

Tremendous thanks go to Lori Davis, the technical reviewer.

Thank you to many people at the Corel Corporation. It's been a pleasure using PaintShop Pro to show people how to restore and retouch their photos. Thank you for your support and help, which was consistent and enthusiastic since the beginning of this project. Special thanks go to Craig Copley (Senior Product Manager, Corel PaintShop Photo Pro X5), Greg Wood (Product Marketing Manager), and Sara Chesiuk (Public Relations Manager).

Thanks to my family for their support, ideas, encouragement, and love.

About the Author

ROBERT CORRELL is an author, photographer, and artist with a lifetime of film and digital photography experience. He is a longtime expert in photo editing and graphics software, such as Corel PaintShop Pro (formerly Paint Shop Pro), Adobe Photoshop, and Adobe Photoshop Elements.

Other than this book, his latest published works focus on digital photography and showing people how to use their cameras. These include *Digital SLR Photography All-in-One For Dummies, Canon EOS 5D Mark III For Dummies, Sony Alpha SLT-A65/77 For Dummies,* and *Sony Alpha SLT-A35/55 For Dummies.* He has also written *Canon EOS Rebel T3/1110D For Dummies* and *Canon EOS 60D For Dummies* (both with Julie Adair King), *High Dynamic Range Digital Photography For Dummies, HDR Photography Photo Workshop* (Second Edition, with Pete Carr), *Your Pro Tools Studio,* and earlier editions of this book. Robert has authored creative tutorials for Corel Corporation and the Virtual Training Company on subjects like PaintShop Pro, music production software, and HDR. He contributed to every issue of the now defunct *Official Corel PaintShop Pro Photo Magazine* as the resident photo-retouching expert.

When not writing, Robert enjoys family life, photography, playing the guitar and bass, recording music, and grilling. Robert graduated from the United States Air Force Academy and resides in Indiana.

You can reach Robert at *www.robertcorrell.com.*

Table of Contents

Chapter 5   Sharpness, Noise, and Distortion. 117

Chapter 8   Moving, Adding, or Removing Objects . . . 225

Chapter 10   The Good, the Bad, and the Artistic 307

Introduction

WELCOME TO *Photo Restoration and Retouching Using Corel PaintShop Pro X5, Fourth Edition*. Follow along with me as I retouch and restore over 50 "real-world" photos from my own print and digital photo collection. I'll address a wide range of problems that many photos have, whether they are new or old, digital or print, color or black-and-white. I'll show you different techniques for problems with lighting, color and contrast, tears, scratches, and other blemishes. You'll learn what works, along with what doesn't, and discover how to judge for yourself. I'll also cover photo-retouching topics that range from retouching people, adding, moving, or deleting objects, to retouching good photos and very bad photos.

Photo Restoration and Retouching Using Corel PaintShop Pro X5, Fourth Edition is focused, comprehensive, practical, and effective at showing photo-retouching and restoration techniques. It is not a general PaintShop Pro tutorial/reference.

This book is meant to accompany the latest version of PaintShop Pro, version X5, but you can use virtually all of the techniques with the older versions of the program.

Download the (slightly downsized) "before" versions of each photo study from *www.courseptr.com/downloads*.

Paint Shop Pro Naming Conventions

The official name of the latest version of this product is Corel PaintShop Pro X5. I often refer to it as PaintShop Pro or more simply "X5" for the latest version.

What You'll Find in This Book

Photo Restoration and Retouching Using Corel PaintShop Pro X5, Fourth Edition, contains over 50 practical photo studies, each aimed at a specific photo restoring and retouching element. Each study is fully restored or retouched. The book is filled with empowering, practical examples that cover the following topics:

▶ What's new in PaintShop Pro X5

▶ PaintShop Pro tips and tricks

▶ Removing specks and dust

▶ Reducing noise

▶ Retouching shots for online auctions

▶ Improving brightness and contrast

▶ Correcting distortion

▶ Making color corrections

▶ Making colors more vibrant

▶ Repairing borders, scratches, creases, holes, and missing corners

▶ Erasing pen, pencil, marker, spots, and other marks

▶ Moving things

▶ Adding people

▶ Creating montages

▶ Removing red eye

▶ Performing face makeovers

▶ Glamorous retouching

▶ Introducing full-body makeovers

▶ Retouching hair

▶ Restoring very badly damaged photos

▶ Making good photos better

▶ Using your photos as the basis of artistic retouching

Whom This Book Is For

Photo Restoration and Retouching Using Corel PaintShop Pro X5, Fourth Edition is for anyone who wants to restore or retouch photographs. I love restoring old photos and retouching digital ones. It's a passion of mine, and this book is designed and created to share that passion with you. It's not rocket science. All you need are the photos, PaintShop Pro, the desire, and time. Want to learn more? Read this book and look at the sample photos. Everything you see on these pages has been done in PaintShop Pro.

Restoring and retouching photos complements many other activities. The restored and retouched photos you use will enhance whatever you're doing. If you're involved in any of the following activities (to list just a few), you'll get a lot out of this book:

▶ Everyday life (taking digital photos and retouching them for your family and friends)

▶ Amateur and professional photography (retouching new digital photos)

▶ Scrapbooking (restoring or retouching new and old photos, artistic retouching)

▶ Family history/genealogy (restoring and preserving family photos)

▶ Art (artistic retouching)

▶ Publishing (retouching new photos for Internet and traditional media)

▶ Small businesses (using photography to augment your business)

▶ Home businesses like direct sales (retouching your product photos)

My focus is to show you how to restore and retouch photos—not provide a ground-up tutorial on PaintShop Pro. If you're a beginner to computing or graphics programs, you will want to spend time outside of this book learning how to use the basics of the program.

How This Book Is Organized

Photo Restoration and Retouching Using Corel PaintShop Pro X5, Fourth Edition is organized into 10 chapters. The first two chapters focus on PaintShop Pro X5, describing the program and illustrating many of my photo-retouching tips. The next eight chapters feature photo studies that each addresses a specific aspect of photo restoration or retouching.

▶ **Chapter 1, "Getting Started with Corel PaintShop Pro X5":** This chapter introduces you to PaintShop Pro X5 and shows you around the interface. You'll learn about the Manage, Adjust, and Edit tabs and how to use them. You'll also learn how to update the program.

▶ **Chapter 2, "Retouching Techniques and Methods":** This action-packed chapter contains a number of different retouching methods and PaintShop Pro X5 tips and tricks, including duplicating windows, using adjustment layers, cloning on a separate layer, and masking.

▶ **Chapter 3, "Improving Brightness and Contrast":** Learn how to make brightness and contrast adjustments to your photos in this chapter, which has seven photo studies. You'll compare and contrast the results of several different techniques as you search for the best method to use.

▶ **Chapter 4, "Solving Color Problems":** Old and new photos alike can benefit from the proper color balance and intensity. Follow along with seven photo studies in this chapter. Multiple techniques are again compared, including Curves, Levels, White Balance, Saturation, Vibrancy, Fade Correction and the Histogram Adjustment tool (and that's not all).

▶ **Chapter 5, "Sharpness, Noise, and Distortion":** Learn how to sharpen out-of-focus or blurry photos, reduce noise, correct distortion, and correct perspective in these six photo studies.

▶ **Chapter 6, "Removing Specks and Dust":** This chapter has four photo studies, each looking at a different aspect of removing specks and dust. Techniques range from using the Clone brush to different types of smoothing and noise removal to fix backgrounds.

▶ **Chapter 7, "Repairing Scratches, Tears, Creases, and Holes":** These eight photo studies tackle the difficult job of repairing damaged photos. You'll learn how to repair borders, scratches, creases, cracks, holes, and missing pieces of photos, mostly with the Clone brush.

▶ **Chapter 8, "Moving, Adding, or Removing Objects":** Follow along with seven photo studies as you learn how to erase writing, move a teddy bear, add a person to a photo, create montages, and move or remove other objects. Multiple techniques are analyzed, ranging from simply copying and pasting to using the Clone brush and Object Remover.

▶ **Chapter 9, "Retouching People":** This powerful chapter features eight photo studies that walk you through the important skill of retouching people. Learn how to eliminate red eye, smooth skin, whiten teeth, remove distracting blemishes, perform makeovers, and hide hair loss.

▶ **Chapter 10, "The Good, the Bad, and the Artistic":** These six photo studies cover a range of photos, from good to very bad. They will show you how to critically analyze photos that you may not think need retouching and to get the most out of them, rescue photos you think may be impossible to restore, and use photos for more artistic purposes.

What's New in This Edition

You'll find several new photos and a few new studies sprinkled throughout this edition of the book. Some are techniques and ideas that were not in the previous editions, such as "Repairing a Mounted Photo" and "Mending a Partial Tear." Others are brand new photos for existing studies, such as "Dusting Off Digital Shots for eBay." In those cases, the main thrust of the study remained unchanged.

Every other photo study in the book has been reviewed and updated in PaintShop Pro X5.

Companion Website Downloads

You may download the companion website files from *www.courseptr.com/downloads.* You'll find the "before" shots of all the photo studies (slightly downsized) for you to practice on and use as you follow along with the book.

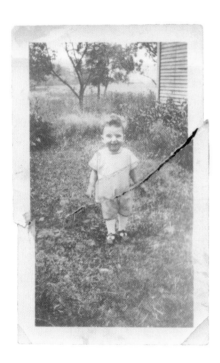

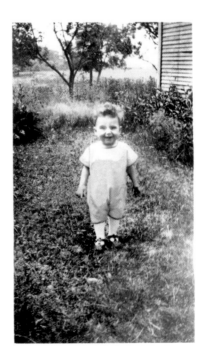

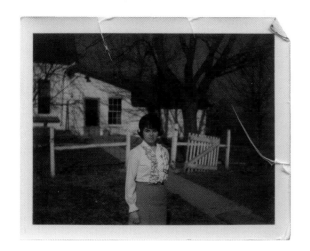
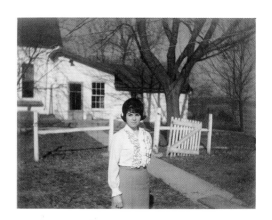
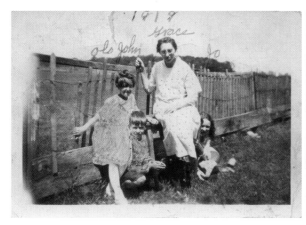
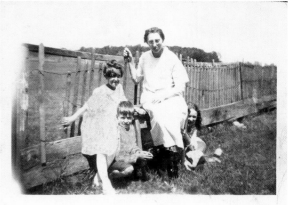
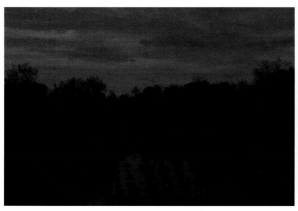
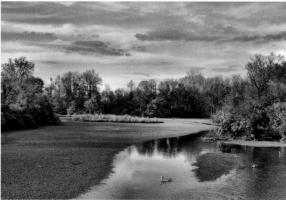

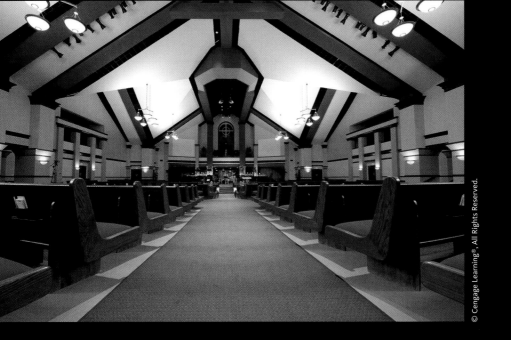

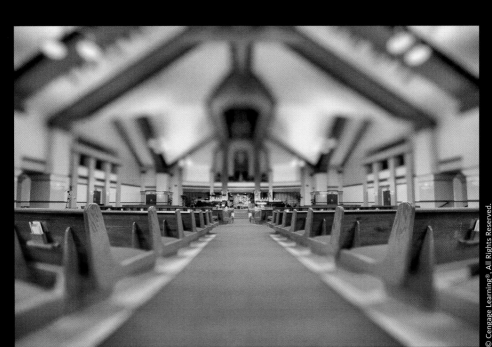

Getting Started with Corel PaintShop Pro X5

1

T HIS CHAPTER GETS YOU STARTED DOWN THE PATH
of photo restoration and retouching using Corel PaintShop Pro. I'll
cover some general aspects of restoration and retouching, introduce
PaintShop Pro, review the new features of PaintShop Pro X5, and take a
look at the different interface elements of the program.

Photo Restoration and Retouching

THIS BOOK IS ABOUT PHOTO RESTORATION and retouching.

When I say "photo restoration," I am referring to repairing scanned photo prints—the prints that have been converted to digital files on your computer. You'll run into a number of problems as you retouch these photos. They may have dust, cracks, scratches, tears, blemishes, color problems, brightness, contrast, sharpness, or other issues. They may have been poorly handled, improperly stored, torn, worn, or are just plain old.

Boxes of photos and photo albums are steadily deteriorating as I type this sentence. They take up a lot of space and are prone to loss and damage from acid (from your hands as you handle them), humidity, fire, water, light, mold, and other dangers. Photo restoration saves, restores, and preserves these memories in a modern form that you can back up and store for hundreds of years.

You don't have to be an art expert or have a degree in antiquities conservation to start restoring photos.

Photo retouching is more of a digital exercise. We've all pretty much got at least one digital camera now. Digital pictures (normally JPEG files, but you could have a camera that stores photos in a RAW format) are stored on memory cards, optical discs, and hard disk drives, so they won't have torn corners or faded colors. Common problems are poor lighting, color, sharpness, and composition. Photo retouching corrects, adjusts, and enhances digital photos.

One of the biggest lessons I've learned with digital photos is that even good ones need our helping hand to look their best. Don't think of photo retouching as only making bad photos better. It's not. You don't have to be a professional photographer to start retouching photos.

Photo restoration and retouching don't take place in a vacuum. In this case, our tool is Corel PaintShop Pro, which is what the rest of this chapter is about.

Getting Acquainted with PaintShop Pro X5

PAINTSHOP PRO IS A POWERFUL PHOTO, image, and graphics editing program that has been available in one form or another since 1992. PaintShop Pro (its original name) began life in 1992 as a shareware program and was owned by Jasc Software Inc. PaintShop Pro was enthusiastically embraced from the beginning because of its low cost and practical feature set. (People were beginning to create Web pages for the first time in 1992.) PaintShop Pro (as it is now known) continues the tradition of offering tremendous power to amateur and professional photographers and graphic artists at a very reasonable price.

Jasc?

Jasc stands for Jets and Software Company, two of the passions of Robert Voit, PaintShop Pro's inventor and the founder of Jasc Software, Inc.

If you have PaintShop Pro installed, go ahead and fire it up as I take you on a quick tour around the interface. You'll learn about the elements of the program that make it particularly useful for photo restoration and retouching.

Learning PaintShop Pro

I don't have room to start at the beginning and show you everything you need to know about installing, running, and working with PaintShop Pro. To get the most out of this book, you should be familiar with things like how to use the Selection tools, the Layers palette, the Materials palette, and so forth. My purpose is to show you how to use elements of the program in the context of photo retouching and restoration. Having said that, I will try to ease you into many of the tools I use and tell you how to get started with them.

What's New in X5

PaintShop Pro X5 has several new features that make the program even more exciting to use for photo restoration and retouching. This section summarizes the major changes from the previous version.

Location Information

PaintShop Pro X5 can now display location information in the Manage tab (which is covered later). If you have a camera that stores the latitude and longitude where you take each photo in the photo's EXIF data, PaintShop Pro can place it on the map. All you have to do is switch to Map mode, as shown in Figure 1.1. I took the photo shown in the Organizer right beside the fountain on Belle Isle, which is right by downtown Detroit. As you can see from the map, the red locator points at the location on the map that corresponds to the photo's internal coordinates. I love the fact that the map and satellite views are provided in the program.

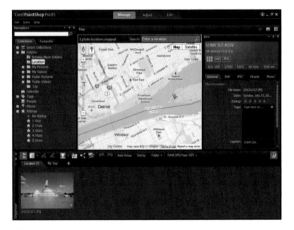

Figure 1.1

The fountain at Belle Isle.

If you have an older camera or one that doesn't receive GPS (Global Positioning Signals), you can enter the location information yourself and map photos (even .pspimage files) to your heart's content.

Face Tagging

Face Tagging is a new PaintShop Pro feature that enables you to identify people in your photos. As you identify new people, PaintShop Pro builds a database of faces that appear in the Navigation palette. You can click a person's name and see all the photos they are in.

I am tagging my family in Figure 1.2. We went to a local air show on Labor Day, and I took a photo of them posing in front of one of our unit's A-10s. You can manually tag faces or rely on the program's automatic face recognition routine. All you need to do in that case is name the person PaintShop Pro has identified. I have typed in "Anne." As you can see from the list of people on the left, I have already identified the kids.

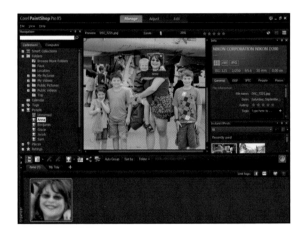

Figure 1.2

Face tagging creates a database of people in your photos.

HDR From a Single RAW Exposure

High Dynamic Range (HDR) photography has become more popular than ever. Normally, digital cameras have a hard time capturing really bright lights or reflections and really dark shadows at the same time. What happens is that the bright areas become washed out and turn white. This is called being "blown out." Darker areas lose detail as well when they turn black.

HDR involves taking more than one photo of a scene, each with a different exposure. One is normally dark, which reveals details that would otherwise be too bright. Another is in the middle. A third is brighter than it should be, which reveals details that would otherwise be too dark. PaintShop Pro merges the photos together and lets you fiddle with a number of settings (see the HDR example in Chapter 10, "The Good, the Bad, and the Artistic") that control properties like brightness, contrast, and color.

What's new in this version is being able to work from a single RAW photo instead of a number of shots. Select a RAW image in your Organizer and then select File ❯ HDR ❯ Single RAW Photo. Next, split the shot into separate images. PaintShop Pro will use them just as if you took more than one photo. Figure 1.3 illustrates a single photo of an aircraft on static display that I split into three parts and am now "tone mapping" to make it look cool.

Retro Lab

The Retro Lab (Effects ❯ Photo Effects ❯ Retro Lab) combines a number of cool effects into a single large dialog box. I'm working on a photo of the business end of the A-10's GAU-8/A Avenger gun in Figure 1.4.

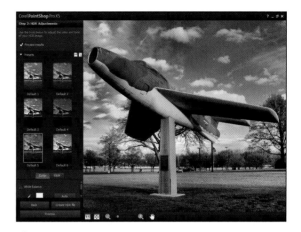

Figure 1.3
Single-exposure HDR opens a new world of processing options.

As you can see from the figure, I've selected the Contrast preset. This has identified an area to keep sharp and an area to blur, adjusted the color, and loaded a curve that enhances the photo's contrast. There are quite a few presets to explore. If none suits your needs, experiment with the settings on your own.

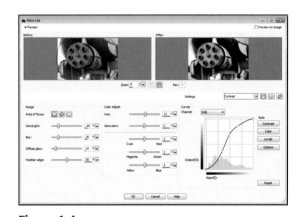

Figure 1.4
Making a good shot look even better.

Graduated Filter Effect

The Graduated Filter effect is like applying a gradient fill layer on top of your photo. There are a number of settings involved, which work just like gradients in the Materials palette. I recommend creating a new raster layer, applying the graduated filter, and then experimenting with Blend modes, opacity, and masking, in order to maximize the precision by which you can target the effect. However, if you want to apply what amounts to a duotone or color layer effect, you can't beat its speed and simplicity.

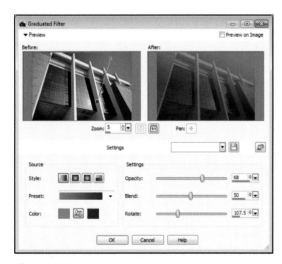

Figure 1.5

Exploring an artistic effect.

Instant Effects Palette

The Instant Effects palette, new to PaintShop Pro X5, is shown in Figure 1.6. You can use this feature to quickly decide what effect you want to try out on a photo. Apply it by double-clicking the effect's name. Scroll down to see more effects. You can also display effects by categories.

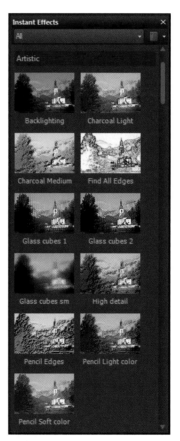

Figure 1.6

The Instant Effects palette is a convenient location from which you can apply effects.

Share My Trip

Share My Trip is a new feature that's really cool, but more involved than I have space to show you here. Basically, you identify a number of photos, and PaintShop Pro collects and organizes them into a Web page with cool thumbnails and navigation buttons. You can upload the package and show it off online or keep it on your computer.

I am starting the process in Figure 1.7. I have named the trip as "Our Trip to Detroit" and have loaded several photos. If you select a photo in this dialog box and it has location information, you'll see it appear on the map to the right.

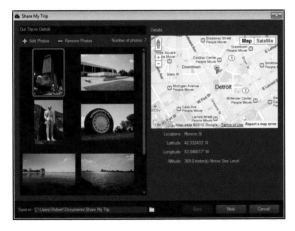

Figure 1.7
Use Share My Trip to showcase trips you take.

You might use this feature to show how your family migrated from one place to another over time. You could also show where people lived in a single town. The possibilities are pretty exciting.

New and Improved Sharing

The Sharing option has been improved in version X5. In addition to some minor menu and dialog box changes to streamline your workflow, you can now upload Google+ in addition to Facebook and Flickr.

Workspace Color

If you don't like the dark gray, you can now change PaintShop Pro's interface color. Select View > Workspace Color and choose your color. There are four options: Dark Gray, Medium Gray, Light Gray, and Blue. As soon as you do, PaintShop Pro dynamically changes to the new appearance you have selected.

Rationale

I've made the decision not to extend coverage of some elements of PaintShop Pro (new and old) that automate tasks, such as removing things from photos or blending elements from different photos together. That's not an editorial comment on my part. Given a fixed amount of space, I want to teach you how to perform tasks such as these manually. I encourage you to experiment with all the features included in PaintShop Pro on your own to see if they work with your photos.

Enhancements

PaintShop Pro X5 features several enhancements from X4. Here is a quick summary of them:

▶ **HDR:** There have been several improvements made to the Exposure Merge feature, which is located under the File ❯ HDR menu. You can preview the alignment before you process it and adjust your settings if things don't look right. As you adjust your HDR image, you can now choose between using the Color or B&W tabs. What's more, you can now assign a preset when using HDR ❯ Batch Merge, and as already mentioned, process a single RAW photo as HDR.

▶ **Text tool:** Some improvements to the Text tool have been made. These appear to be improvements that make selecting and editing text easier, as well as making the Text and Pick tools work better together. If this has been a problem for you, you may see an improvement. Otherwise, this may be a transparent upgrade.

▶ **Sharing options:** Sharing your files online has never been easier. Select the photos you want to share from the Organizer palette and then press the Share button. Select what sites you want to upload to (Facebook, Flickr, or Google); then choose an album or create a new one. Add or change photo information, choose a quality option, and upload.

▶ **Crop tool:** This Crop tool has a few improvements. In addition to the standard set of predefined crop sizes and aspect ratios, you can keep the original proportions or select a square. Take a look at the Tool Options toolbar with the Crop tool selected. You can crop the current photo as a new image, change the crop rectangle by entering new pixel dimensions, specify a print size, and numerically change the rotation angle and pivot point.

▶ **Layer styles:** Although they remain the same, there is a dedicated Layer Styles button on the Layers palette. Click it to open the selected layer's Layer Properties dialog box with the Layer Styles tab preselected.

▶ **Multi-Script support:** If you're into running scripts, you can run more than one now, consecutively. Select File ❯ Script ❯ Run Multiple Scripts to get started.

What's the Same

What's the same between PaintShop Pro X4 and X5? Quite a bit, actually, especially when it comes to the program interface and specific support for photo retouching and restoration. The program tabs work the same, HDR works pretty much the same, the Camera RAW Lab is the same, and the Edit workspace remains fundamentally unchanged (with regard to the essence of editing photos). There are differences, of course, but the tools are the same, most of the menus are the same, and layers, masks, selections, effects, most palettes, and so forth are the same. If you have dual monitors, you can expand your work area by choosing View ❯ Dual Monitor. The Manage tab will open on one monitor while the Adjust/Edit tabs open on the other.

If you're used to X4, you should be able to use X5 without any problem.

If you're upgrading from an older version, you will have to get used to the workspace tabs (which, in my opinion, are a great improvement), the new color schemes, the Learning Center palette being on the right side of the screen, the drop cues you get when dragging and dropping palettes, a slightly different Camera RAW Lab, the HDR Exposure Merge, and other new features.

The Adjust workspace takes the place of the Express Lab. If you liked working in the Express Lab, you should find yourself comfortable in the Adjust workspace.

Likewise, although the name has changed to the Manage workspace, most of the functionality was present in X3. It was simply called the *Organizer*.

In the end, there's not much to worry about if you love working in X3 or earlier versions and are thinking of upgrading to X5.

Working with the Manage Workspace

THE MANAGE WORKSPACE ENABLES YOU to track all your files, organize them, rate photos, browse thumbnails of your collection, and add other tags and captions to your files and photos. It's a built-in management and organization tool.

When you're working with thousands of digital photos or working with a number of scanned photos that you're restoring, being able to organize them automatically is a wonderful timesaver.

Unless you're working with dual monitors, you can't use the Manage workspace at the same time as the other two (Adjust and Edit). You can, however, switch back and forth using the tabs at the top of the program interface (see Figure 1.8).

Notice the folder list on the left of the window. This is where you manage the folders and where PaintShop Pro watches for new pictures and keeps them organized. In the center, there is a large space to preview a single photo at a good size.

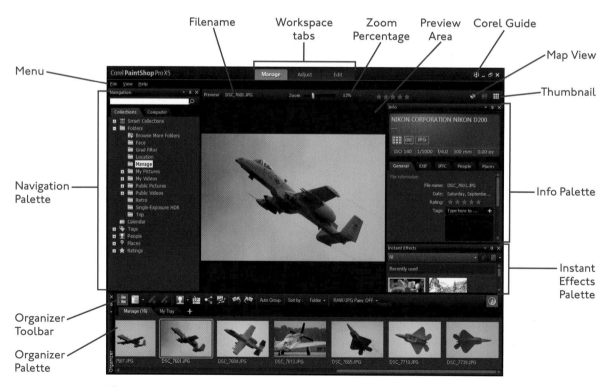

Figure 1.8

The Manage workspace.

© Corel® Corporation, All Rights Reserved. © 2013 Cengage Learning®, All Rights Reserved.

The area to the right is where you can see information about the photo, such as its name, the date you took it, the file size, and other EXIF info. You can also tag photos, rate them, and create captions here.

Finally, the bottom window has thumbnails of the photos in the folder you've selected from the Collections or Computer tab at the top left. When in Preview mode, the thumbnails occupy the bottom of the screen. When in Thumbnail mode, they take up the entire central part of the window. The preview area shrinks and is put below the Navigation palette.

Notice the buttons at the top-right portion of the screen, just above the General Info area (see Figure 1.9). This is where you can change between Map mode (new to X5), Preview, and Thumbnail modes for the Organizer. The button beside the minimize button at the top of the screen is for the Corel Guide.

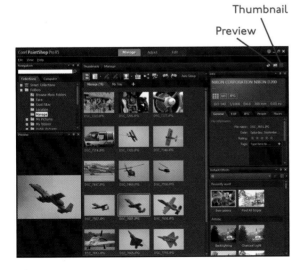

Figure 1.9
Change from Preview to Thumbnail mode here.
© Corel® Corporation, All Rights Reserved. © 2013 Cengage Learning®, All Rights Reserved.

PaintShop Pro X5 starts out in the Manage workspace. If you would prefer to start in the Edit or Adjust workspace, or launch in whatever mode you last used, change the Default Launch workspace preference from File ❯ Preferences ❯ General Program Preferences (see Figure 1.10) to whatever you want. Since there is no Adjust option, however, you will need to switch to Keep Last View and then exit the program from the Adjust workspace.

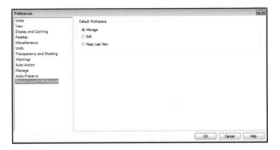

Figure 1.10
Choose your default workspace.
© Corel® Corporation, All Rights Reserved. © 2013 Cengage Learning®, All Rights Reserved.

The main components of the Manage workspace are the following:

▶ **Title bar:** This area contains the Manage, Adjust, and Edit tabs. On the right are the window controls, and to the left of them is the Corel Guide icon. Click it to launch Corel Guide, which contains additional helpful information.

▶ **Menu bar:** There are only three menus in the Manage workspace: File, View, and Help.

▶ **Navigation palette:** Think "search and organize." You can navigate folders on the left by clicking a folder in the list. It works just like Windows Explorer. The Collections tab is a hierarchical way to present the folders and photos on your system. Create Smart Collections, add folders, and organize files by date, tag, or rating. Use the Computer tab to find things on your computer.

Photos in the folder you have selected in the Navigation palette show up in the Organizer as thumbnails.

▶ **Preview palette:** This is where you see your photos and files. The default setting shows the Preview palette in large form. You can change this so that thumbnails take up most of the space and the Preview palette is shown smaller and to the right.

▶ **Info palette:** This palette shows you camera information, exposure parameters, general photo information, and EXIF data. You can tag and rate photos and add captions here.

▶ **Organizer:** Think "thumbnails and sorting." After you have selected a folder from the Navigation palette, photo thumbnails show up in the Organizer. PaintShop Pro scans select folders when you start it up and creates resizable thumbnails of the files in those folders. This allows you to access photos quickly, sort, tag and categorize, print, and edit them.

The Organizer is available in all three workspaces.

▶ **Trays:** Trays are customizable collections. Use them to further organize photos without moving the files around. For example, if you have several photos to retouch, add them to a "To Do" tray. Remove them when you're done working on them. Trays are workflow helpers and time-savers.

Trays are also available in all three workspaces.

Using the Adjust Workspace

THE ADJUST WORKSPACE IS A HANDY place to adjust photos quickly. You'll find it most helpful for working with digital photos. After you transfer the files to your computer, use the Adjust workspace to tweak brightness, contrast, color, and perform other fairly straightforward photo-editing operations.

The big thing to remember when working with the Adjust workspace is that changes you make with tools on the left are applied when you change tools and "stick" immediately. In other words, you can't press Cancel as if you were in a dialog box and make the changes go away. You have to use Undo or set the controls back to their defaults (before changing tools) to back out of changes. When you're done with the photo, you'll have a chance to save everything to the file.

Figure 1.11 shows the interface with everything labeled.

▶ **Adjust palette:** This is where it's located. At the top of the Adjust palette is a histogram, which shows you the photo's distribution of pixels by brightness and color. Beneath that is an area that shows the exposure data taken from the camera, then a mini-toolbar with Crop, Straighten, Red Eye, Makeover, and Clone tools.

Beneath those tools are several adjustment areas. They are the Smart Photo Fix, Color Balance, Brightness/Contrast, Fill Light/Clarity, Local Tone Mapping, High Pass Sharpen, and Digital Noise Removal.

Click the adjustment name to switch to that control, and then make changes to the options as you would an ordinary dialog box. The other controls minimize. You can't save or load settings from preset files.

You have everything you need here to spruce up most digital photos.

▶ **Toolbar:** The toolbar has a collection of handy tools such as Save, Save As, Rotate, Delete, and viewing controls for easy access.

▶ **Preview window:** This is where you see your photo. It's pretty self-explanatory. You can zoom in and out and rate the photo. The file name appears on the bottom left.

▶ **Instant Effects:** By default, the Instant Effects palette is visible on the Adjust tab. It sits right next to the Preview window.

▶ **Organizer palette:** This works the same as in the Manage workspace. It's handy.

The only downside to the Adjust workspace is that it doesn't have the complete toolset of the Edit workspace. Then again, it's not supposed to. You can't create or work with levels, masks, and perform other complex editing tasks. If you need those, switch to the Edit workspace and continue working.

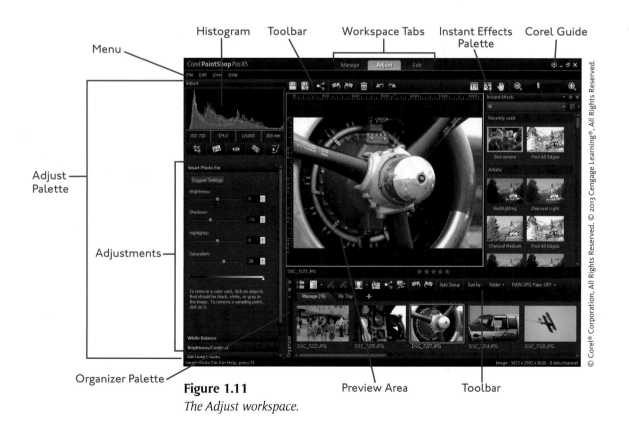

Figure 1.11
The Adjust workspace.

Using the Edit Workspace

THE EDIT WORKSPACE IS WHERE I spend most of my time when I am working in PaintShop Pro to retouch and restore photos. I have all the power of the program at my fingertips.

It is well structured, and once you learn where things are, it is easy to use. And if that's not enough for you, you can customize it by turning palettes on and off, dragging them around the workspace, and docking them to various sides—you can even change the menus and toolbars. Figure 1.12 shows PaintShop Pro X5 in Edit mode with several of the palettes turned on.

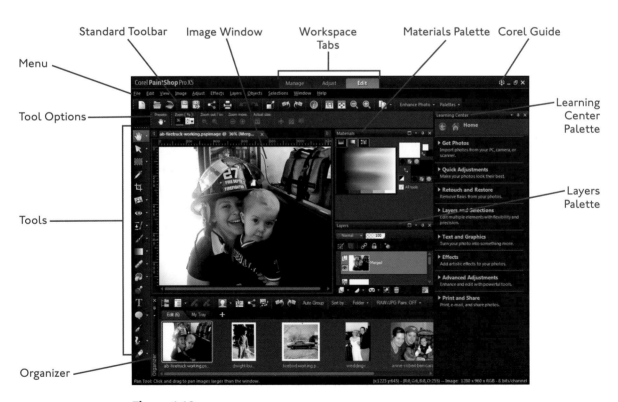

Figure 1.12
The Edit workspace is powerful and flexible.
© Corel® Corporation, All Rights Reserved. © 2013 Cengage Learning®, All Rights Reserved.

I've annotated the interface elements in order to provide a quick overview of what each piece does.

▶ **Menu bar:** Most commands and many options are located here.

▶ **Standard toolbar:** The toolbar that has many common commands within easy reach, such as New, Open, File Save, Undo Last Command, Resize, Palettes, and so forth.

Reclaiming Space

I turn off the Learning Center palette, Organizer, and Photo Trays but keep the Materials and Layers palettes visible all times. This gives me more room to work and keeps information I use a lot on-screen. Give yourself even more room to work by turning off the Materials and Layers palettes when you are working on a photo intensely and don't need to change materials or layers quickly.

▶ **Tool Options palette:** Looks like a toolbar, but is really a palette. The Tool Options palette changes, based on what tool you have selected, and it displays the options applicable to that tool. You can select brushes, enter pertinent data (such as the dimensions of a selection box), make adjustments (such as the line thickness of a vector object), and accept or reject an operation here. This is one of the most important interface elements in PaintShop Pro. Master it!

▶ **Learning Center palette:** Gives assistance to quickly lead you through various tasks. It is context sensitive. When you click on different tools, the content changes to match what you are doing.

▶ **Tools toolbar:** Known as the "bad boy" of the entire program. You'll use this to choose and select from the many tools PaintShop Pro has to offer.

▶ **Other palettes:** View the other visible palettes; their importance depends on what you are doing. If you are painting or entering text, for example, you'll need the Materials palette to select the color and material of the object you are creating. The Layers palette is another important interface element to master. I use layers all the time, even when I am working to restore or retouch a photo.

The Menus

The Edit workspace organizes most of the photo retouching and restoration features into several menus. It will help if you know the general organization so you can quickly find things when you need them.

▶ **File:** Open, Close, Save, and that sort of thing. There are a number of other commands here as well: Photo Blend, HDR, Export, Script, Preferences, and Workspace, to name a few.

▶ **Edit:** Cut, Copy, Paste. The Copy Special option is important if you want to use Copy Merged, and there are a number of different Paste options.

▶ **View:** Zoom, Full Screen Preview, Rulers, Grid, Guide. Also, this is where you open toolbars and palettes, change docking options and customize menus, keyboard shortcuts, toolbars, and other options. If you have a dual monitor, select Dual Monitor here.

▶ **Image:** This is a big menu. Rotate, Resize, Canvas size are some of the more important options. You can also launch the Smart Carver and Object Extractor here, view EXIF data from the Image Information command, and change color options. Don't forget that the Split Channel and Combine Channel submenus are also here.

▶ **Adjust:** This is the single most important photo-retouching menu. At the top, you have a few instant options like One Step Photo Fix and One Step Noise Removal, but you also can access Smart Photo Fix and Digital Noise Removal here. Beneath these options are submenus for Color, Brightness and Contrast, and Hue and Saturation adjustments. Beneath that are many more menus like Depth of Field, Add/Remove Noise, Blur, Sharpness (Unsharp Mask is located under the Sharpness submenu), Softness, Skin Smoothing, Backlighting, Fill Flash, Red Eye Removal, and distortion correction tools.

Yes, that's a lot, and I didn't even list them all. Study the Adjust menu and learn it.

▶ **Effects:** The Effects menu has all the different photo and other types of effects. (You may hear them called *filters.*) They are organized by type. Photo Effects are practical and useful. Many others won't be. They are more useful for graphic artists; however, explore and have fun learning what they do.

▶ **Layers:** This is a practical menu that collects all the Layers commands. Create and manage layers here. Don't forget, this is where the Mask commands are as well.

▶ **Objects:** You won't use objects that much, unless you are working with text, shapes, or other vector objects. If you are, then this menu has alignment, grouping, properties, and other important commands.

▶ **Selections:** I use this menu to load and save selections when I am retouching and restoring, as well as creating selections from a mask. Additionally, it's got useful selection commands.

► **Window:** The Window menu is where you go to arrange your windows in the Edit workspace. I like working with Tabbed Documents, but you may prefer working with image windows. Aside from the window and view commands, the Duplicate command is here. That is a very practical command that helps you pursue alternate paths without affecting your original file. Don't forget it's here.

► **Help:** Standard help options. Manually update the program from this menu.

Many of these commands are also located on other toolbars and palettes. Whichever way you choose to access these commands is purely a personal preference.

The Tools

PaintShop Pro sure has a lot of tools, and I've found that I use quite a few of them for many different tasks. Sure, you'll develop your favorites like I have, but you need to be able to use any tool in the arsenal. The Tools toolbar is illustrated in Figure 1.13. You'll notice that many of the tools have a light triangle in the lower-right corner. This indicates that there are tools grouped together to save space. Click on the arrow to show the tool group.

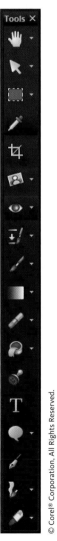

Figure 1.13
PaintShop Pro's tools.

The specific tools are the following:

 Pan: Click and drag around an image that's zoomed in. I rarely use it because most of the time I just zoom out and then back in where I want to see. Lots of people swear by panning, though.

 Zoom: Click in the image to zoom; right-click to zoom out. Another tool I rarely use. I like to use my mouse wheel to zoom in and out quickly. I also use the wheel on my Wacom pen tablet. There are times, however, when the wheels don't want to work so I select this tool to get back to zooming.

 Pick: Click to pick. A finicky tool if there ever was one. Make sure you are picking the right object. There are times when it's a good idea to hide a layer to get at the object you want on another layer. Despite what the name implies, you can move, scale, rotate, and deform objects with this tool. I often use this to resize a layer at the end of the process instead of cropping.

 Move: Seemingly redundant, but I do find myself using it at times. If you have linked layers, this is the only way to move them together. In addition, if you hold the Shift key down when you click and drag, only material on the current layer is moved. That prevents a lot of inadvertent selections in complicated files.

 Selection: Muy importante for a graphic artist. Less so for a photo retoucher. Selections can help you selectively apply effects or modify parts of an image. This tool is "many tools in one" because you can change the type of selection in the Tool Options palette.

 Freehand Selection: Can be Freehand, Point to point, Edge Seeker, or Smart Edge. Each has its advantages. I use Point to point when I want to make a selection quickly where the borders don't need to be exact. Freehand is more exacting, and Edge Seeker and Smart Edge find edges for you. Try each of them out and compare.

 Magic Wand: Selects by matching pixels of an image (can be adjacent, not adjacent, and even on different layers) within a certain tolerance. Most of the time, you'll use color as the criterion, but you can change this.

 Dropper: Loads the color you click in your photo into the Materials palette. Left-click for foreground; right-click for background.

 Crop: Crops an image to the size and aspect ratio you choose. There are a lot of cool little features to the Crop tool, such as "Crop as New Image," which creates a new image with what you're cropping and leaves the original intact. You can also rotate the crop window or rotate the photo upon cropping.

 Straighten: Used after scanning or with digital photos where you accidentally had the camera out of alignment. Straightens an image. Be careful to select the right options. You can straighten individual layers and automatically crop.

 Perspective Correction: Useful in retouching when it's obvious that the perspective is a bit out of whack.

 Red Eye: Pretty self-explanatory. Click to correct someone's red eyes.

Makeover: Five tools in one. The original Makeover tools are the Blemish Fixer, Toothbrush, Eye Drop, Suntan, and Thinnify. Sounds like a pretty good spa treatment to me! I can't wait for Nose Wiper and Waxer.

 Clone: My all-time favorite tool. Take parts of a photo and paint them to another part. You'll use this to cover up things, remove things, clean up dust and specks, and even clone from other photos. Know it. Trust it. Clone it.

 Scratch Remover: Pretty good tool, actually. It's like applying the Clone brush in a straight line.

 Object Remover: I've used this, and it's very good for removing objects quickly. Your mileage may vary, depending on the complexity of the background.

 Paint Brush: Paints what you have in the Materials palette onto the canvas. Lots of options and different choices for brushes.

 Airbrush: To be truthful, I've never really figured out why this is needed. I just use the brushes. However, if you want to get technical, the longer you hold the mouse button down, the more paint is applied with the Airbrush. With the Paint brush, the full amount is applied immediately.

 Lighten/Darken: Very useful when you want some artistic control over what you want to lighten or darken. Change brush properties and opacity to get different effects. Left-click to lighten and right-click to darken.

 Dodge: Not as strong as Lighten, and with different tool options. Very effective when you modify the opacity.

 Burn: Not as strong as Darken, and with different tool options. The terms, Dodge and Burn, come from the photographer's darkroom. Dodging is the technique used to lighten a print by underexposing it, and burning is used to darken the print by exposing it longer. Very effective when you modify the opacity.

 Smudge: Smudge pushes paint around with a brush and smudges it. Try it out for some interesting effects.

 Push: Push smudges paint around with a brush and pushes it. I couldn't resist that. Push is identical to Smudge, except that Smudge picks up new colors as it smudges (like sticking your finger in wet paint), and Push doesn't as it pushes.

 Soften: A very useful tool. I use it when I clone and want to soften the edges of pixels or a border region between where I've cloned and the original photo.

 Sharpen: Another very useful tool for sharpening exactly what you need without applying an effect to the entire photo.

When Selected

My entries in this list assume that you have selected the tool you are reading about at the time, and it is active. I got tired of typing, "When selected...," so I thought one note would do the trick.

Emboss: Cool effect where you brush over parts of the photo and it appears as if they are embossed.

 Saturation Up/Down: Changes the saturation where you brush. Left-click and brush to saturate; right-click and brush to desaturate.

 Hue Up/Down: Changes the hue where you brush. Left-click and brush to change hue in one direction on the color wheel; right-click and brush to go the other direction. This effect is best when it is used very subtly and the opacity is very low.

 Change to Target: Left-click to change where you brush to the foreground color in the Materials palette; right-click to use the background color. My first reaction to this tool was ambivalent, but I've been won over. Make sure to set the mode correctly in the Tools Options palette.

 Color Replacer: Replaces the color where you click with the foreground color.

 Eraser: Erases things. This doesn't work on vector objects or text created as a vector. Until you resize, transform, or warp the layer you erase on, you can right-click with the Eraser and material will be "unerased." This is very nice, but don't count on it as you work your photos. Think of it as a short-term feature that adds convenience.

 Background Eraser: Detects the border between where you click and the edge of the brush and erases the background (which is where you should be clicking).

 Flood Fill: Fills an area with the current foreground color, pattern, or texture. You guessed it: If you right-click, it fills an area with the background color, pattern, or texture.

 Color Changer: This replaces color ranges (as opposed to replacing a single color) pretty realistically. The Color Changer also preserves a photo's details as it changes the color.

 Picture Tube: Allows you to squish preset images out of a Picture Tube onto your canvas.

 Text: If a picture is worth a thousand words, this is where you add the words. I rarely use text when I am restoring or retouching. About the only time I use it is when I want to re-create text in a border, which was a common feature of photos in the 1960s and early '70s, or when I retouch house numbers.

 Preset Shape: Enables you to choose a preset vector shape, such as an arrow or thought balloon, and draw it on your canvas.

 Rectangle: Not surprisingly, this is the tool you should use to draw rectangles (and squares).

 Ellipse: Draws ellipses and circles.

 Symmetric Shape: Draws shapes. You can set the number of sides from 3 (triangle) to 1,000 (who knows what it's called, but it looks like a circle).

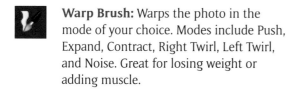

Pen: Creates vector lines and nodes. A very powerful tool. I use it when I want to make a precise selection, most often when I am working with a mask.

Warp Brush: Warps the photo in the mode of your choice. Modes include Push, Expand, Contract, Right Twirl, Left Twirl, and Noise. Great for losing weight or adding muscle.

Mesh Warp: Instead of brushing a warp, use a mesh to drag nodes that warp the photo. This is an easy way to make people skinny.

Oil Brush: Art Media tool that emulates oil painting. You must use this and the subsequent tools on an Art Media layer.

Chalk: Art Media tool that emulates chalk drawing.

Pastel: Art Media tool that emulates pastels.

Crayon: Art Media tool that emulates crayons.

Colored Pencil: Art Media tool that emulates drawing with colored pencils.

Marker: Art Media tool that emulates marking with a marker.

Palette Knife: Art Media tool that emulates using a palette knife to lay down oil paint on a canvas, much like Bob Ross, my favorite PBS personality of all time.

Smear: Art Media tool you should use to smear paint (or the other mediums) around the canvas.

Art Eraser: The tool you use to erase Art Media.

Other Useful Tips

You'll find the Enhance Photo button on the Standard toolbar. Click to expand and choose a command. This is a faster way to select specific menu options than digging down through the menu bar. The available options are the following:

▶ One Step Photo Fix

▶ Smart Photo Fix

▶ One Step Noise Removal

▶ White Balance

▶ Local Tone Mapping

▶ High Pass Sharpen

There are a number of toolbars that you can use that will help you retouch and restore photos. The Photo toolbar, shown in Figure 1.14, is among the most important for photo work (not surprisingly).

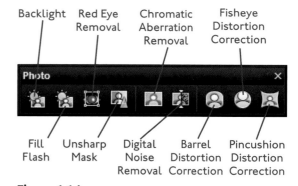

Figure 1.14
The Photo toolbar has some handy buttons.

You can also create your own toolbars. Select the View ❯ Customize menu and select the Toolbars tab, as shown in Figure 1.15.

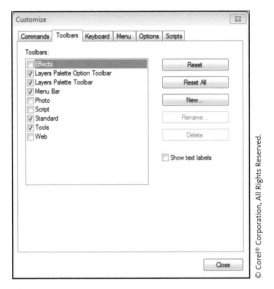

Figure 1.15
Customizing toolbars.

© Corel® Corporation, All Rights Reserved.

Press the New button to create a new toolbar and give it a name, as shown in Figure 1.16.

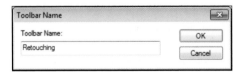

Figure 1.16
Name your toolbar.
© Corel® Corporation, All Rights Reserved.

Now, select the Commands tab and then select the menu you want to choose commands from, as shown in Figure 1.17. The Command list on the right will update to show you what's under each menu choice.

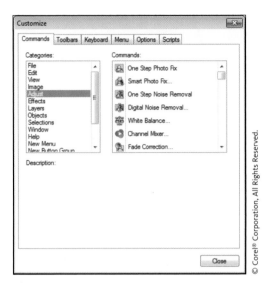

Figure 1.17
Select the menu item first.

© Corel® Corporation, All Rights Reserved.

Drag the specific commands from the Command list to your new toolbar (see Figure 1.18) and enjoy!

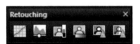

Figure 1.18
Drag and drop on your new toolbar.
© Corel® Corporation, All Rights Reserved.

Updating the Program

COREL CONTINUES TO PROVIDE support for each version of PaintShop Pro after it is released. Their team of developers release updates, called *patches* or *updates*, which continue to improve the program. Take advantage of this free service by keeping your version of PaintShop Pro in tip-top, updated shape. You don't have to obsess over it, but you should consider updating PaintShop Pro whenever there is a patch available.

To manually check for updates, follow these steps:

1. Make sure that your computer has a working, active connection to the Internet.

2. Select the Help menu and choose Check for Updates, as shown in Figure 1.19. PaintShop Pro will connect to Corel and determine whether or not there are new patches available for download. If not, you will see a message box telling you there are no updates available. You can click it away and continue with the knowledge that you've got the latest version of the program.

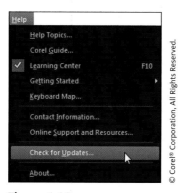

Figure 1.19
Manually checking for updates.

3. If there are updates, you'll see a message from Corel. Download and install the updates to your version of PaintShop Pro.

To turn auto updating on or off, follow these steps:

1. Click the Corel Guide icon to bring up the guide.

2. Click the little gears at the top of the window (it's called Program information and preferences) and choose Message preferences. This opens another dialog box, shown in Figure 1.20.

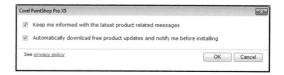

Figure 1.20
Uncheck auto update if you want to handle it yourself.
© Corel® Corporation, All Rights Reserved.

3. Click to uncheck the Automatically download free product updates and notify me before installing (could that be any longer?) option to turn it off.

There you have it. You're ready to start retouching and restoring photos with your fully updated copy of Corel PaintShop Pro X5.

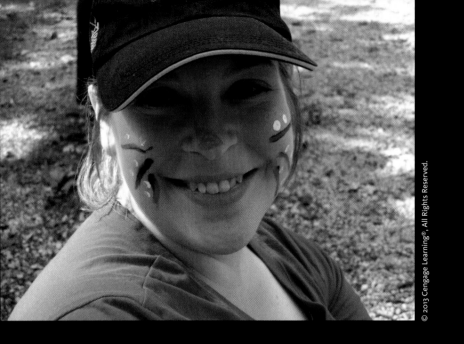

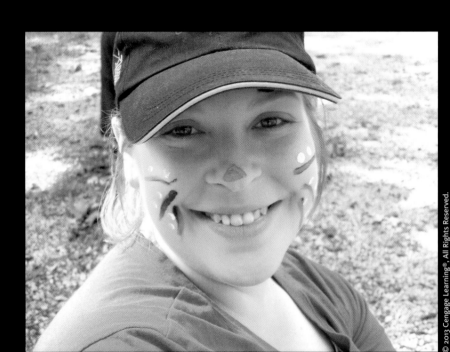

Retouching Techniques and Methods

2

THE GOAL OF THIS CHAPTER IS TO ILLUSTRATE a number of my tips, tricks, and techniques that have more to do with working in PaintShop Pro than correcting specific photos. In other words, the spotlight is on the program and how to optimize your efforts within that context.

You'll learn things like how to preserve your work history in layers, why adjustment layers can be cool, whether you should use masks or the eraser, and why I always try to use a separate layer to clone on. I provide the rationale for why I do things, present alternatives, give you some pros and cons of different methods, and share other interesting tips that might help you if you find yourself in a tough spot.

It's time to get started.

Using the Adjust Versus Edit Workspace

THE ADJUST WORKSPACE (see Figure 2.1) is a fantastic solution for quick photo editing and retouching, but I have rarely used it in this book. In fact, I have used the Edit workspace in all but one photo study.

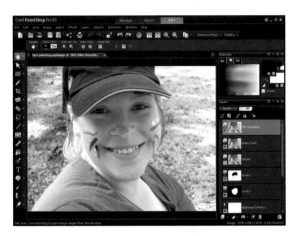

Figure 2.2
The Edit workspace gives you more power.
© Corel® Corporation, All Rights Reserved. © 2013 Cengage Learning®, All Rights Reserved.

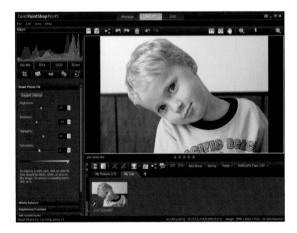

Figure 2.1
Quickly edit shots in the Adjust workspace.
© Corel® Corporation, All Rights Reserved. © 2013 Cengage Learning®, All Rights Reserved.

The reason is not because I don't like the Adjust workspace. On the contrary, it's got great options and a lot of powerful tools. However, the Adjust workspace is optimized for fast retouching work that can be accomplished quickly, simply, and without complicated layers, masks, and other features that are only accessible from the Edit workspace (see Figure 2.2). Notice the plethora of layers and masked adjustment layers in the Layers palette that I've used to work with and organize my approach. That's one of the great strengths of the Edit workspace.

So, if you're working through photos from a birthday party or your latest photo excursion, the Adjust workspace gives you exposure, color, sharpness, noise, and other controls to whip your shots into shape. If you need the additional power that layers, masks, and other Edit workspace features provide, then the Edit workspace is the answer.

Thankfully, PaintShop Pro has both. Use whichever one you prefer to touch up new photos, but the Edit workspace has the power you'll need to tackle photos that require more care and attention.

Preserving a History with Working Layers

I DON'T PERFORM MULTIPLE edits on a single layer. I create working layers at each stage by duplicating the last working layer and renaming it according to what I'm doing (for example, Unsharp Mask), or by performing "Copy Merged" (Edit > Copy Special > Copy Merged), followed by "Paste As New Layer" (Edit > Paste As New Layer). Figure 2.3 shows the Layers palette from one of the finished photo studies, which has several merged layers, adjustment layers, a layer group, and other working layers that hold the results of adjustments like noise reduction.

I also use my own abbreviations. For example, I use "USM" for Unsharp Mark and "Sat," as in "Sat +15." to indicate that I increased the saturation by 15.

I save these working-layer files in .pspimage format for archiving and future use. I can go back and tweak, redo, and improve anywhere in the previous process. When finished, and I need to save the file as a JPEG to put on the Web, I simply use File > Save Copy As, and then save the file as a merged JPEG, or use File > Export > JPEG Optimizer. Saving a copy of the file or exporting it removes the danger of accidentally flattening your working file and then overwriting it. If the file has layers, you'll be told the copy has to be saved as a merged image, as shown in Figure 2.4.

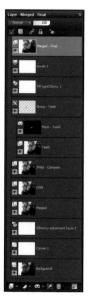

Figure 2.3

Tracking changes with working layers.

© Corel® Corporation, All Rights Reserved. © 2013 Cengage Learning®, All Rights Reserved.

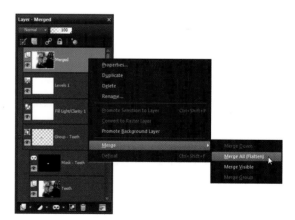

Figure 2.4

Flattening the image to save the copy in a format that doesn't have layers.

© Corel® Corporation, All Rights Reserved. © 2013 Cengage Learning®, All Rights Reserved.

Sometimes, I put the settings I used in the name of the layer so I can keep track of more details. (This isn't necessary when working with adjustment layers because you can pop those open and look at the settings directly.) For example, if I increased the Vibrancy by 30, I might name that layer "Vibrancy +30."

Duplicating Layers Versus Copying and Pasting

IT'S EASIER TO DUPLICATE A LAYER and erase or mask out what you don't need than it is to select what you want (assuming it doesn't fill the canvas), copy it, paste it to a new layer, and then try to align it precisely. That's because a duplicate layer is in perfect alignment with the one beneath it without you having to do a thing.

For example, if you want to brighten someone's face but not the background, duplicate the last working layer, brighten it, and then erase or mask around the face instead of trying to select that person's face, copy, paste it to a new layer, align it, and then brighten it. Aligning things is a major headache when you're working with photos, and it's why I duplicate layers and erase or mask whenever possible.

One technique I use when I have to is to select the Paint brush and dab some obnoxious color at the four corners of the canvas (see Figure 2.5) on a layer that I need to copy and paste and don't want to realign. This sets the boundaries of Select All to the canvas, which means that when you paste what you've copied, it lines up perfectly. The key when you brush is to set the hardness to 0, which keeps the pixels opaque, easy to spot, and well into the corners. Make these helper dabs easy to identify and erase.

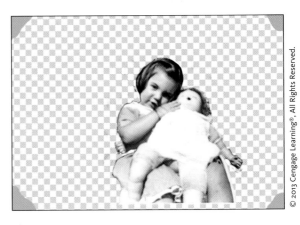

Figure 2.5
Setting corners to copy the entire layer.

You can also promote a selection to a layer. Make the selection and press Ctrl+Shift+P. This works better than duplicating a layer and erasing in many situations, but be careful. You can't promote a selection from more than one layer at a time. (In other words, you can't perform a merged copy and promote the selection at the same time.) You also can't "unerase" material from the layer you promoted because it was never there to begin with. If neither of those situations bothers you, try promoting selections to align them automatically.

Copying Merged Layers and Pasting to Lock in Changes

I USE THE COPY MERGED COMMAND to lock in edits from adjustment layers or layers with transparent areas, such as Mask groups or layers on which I've erased. I use the term "Copy Merged" sometimes as shorthand to indicate this process, or give the basic commands: Copy Merged and Paste As New Layer.

The detailed steps are pretty simple:

1. **Make sure that the layers you want visible are visible.** It doesn't matter what layer you have selected because this technique copies everything that is visible, although I normally select the layer I want to paste above, which is usually the top layer. Figure 2.6 shows a Layers palette with layers ready to be consolidated and changes locked in.

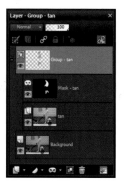

Figure 2.6
Ready to perform a merged copy.
© Corel® Corporation, All Rights Reserved. © 2013 Cengage Learning®, All Rights Reserved.

2. **Choose Edit > Copy Special > Copy Merged (Ctrl+Shift+C).** Your keyboard shortcut might be different for Copy Merged. Older versions use Ctrl+Shift+C, but you may not see any shortcut on the menu. The odd thing is that Ctrl+Shift+C still works, whether the menu has it listed or not.

To change the keyboard shortcut to something else, select the View > Customize menu and then choose the Keyboard tab. Choose Edit from the Category list and then select Copy Merged from the Commands list. Click in the Press New Shortcut Key box and then press the combination of keys you want to assign to the command (see Figure 2.7). Press Assign to assign it; then Close to get out of the dialog box.

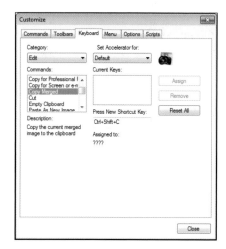

Figure 2.7
Customizing keyboard shortcuts.
© Corel® Corporation, All Rights Reserved.

3. **Select the layer you want to paste above from the Layers palette and choose the Edit > Paste As New Layer menu (Ctrl+L or Ctrl+V).** The new layer will appear and be selected.

4. **Rename and continue.** When I do this, I tend to paste the result and rename it "Merged" (see Figure 2.8) and then duplicate that to start a new working layer. That keeps the merged layers separate from edits, which saves me the time of having to copy and paste over again if I need to delete a working layer (because I don't like the result) and start over.

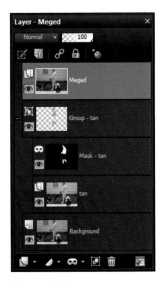

Figure 2.8
Merged layer pasted and ready to move on.

Copy Merged Shortcuts

I often press Ctrl+A to select the entire canvas before I press Ctrl+Shift+C to copy the merged layers together.

You can, however, skip the selection process and go straight to pressing Ctrl+Shift+C (or using the Edit > Copy Special > Copy Merged menu). This automatically selects and copies all visible (even semi-transparent) pixels on the entire canvas, no matter what layer they are on.

There is a catch with the more direct method, however. If you have another selection active (they are sometimes easy to miss) and skip Ctrl+A, you'll create a merged copy of the selected area only when you press Ctrl+Shift+C, not the entire canvas.

Using Clone Layers for Flexibility

FOR THE MOST PART, I do not clone directly on a photo layer unless I have to. I create an empty raster layer above a working layer to clone on (see Figure 2.9) and check the Use All Layers option for the Clone Brush.

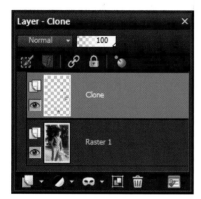

Figure 2.9

Clone layer in action.

© Corel® Corporation, All Rights Reserved. © 2013 Cengage Learning®,
All Rights Reserved.

Later, I'll lock the changes in by selecting the canvas, Copy Merged, and pasting the result as a new layer. I then name the new layer to identify it (see Figure 2.10). This technique (working on a blank layer) doesn't work with tools like the Blemish Remover or Scratch Remover. In those cases, I create a duplicate working layer specifically to use those tools on.

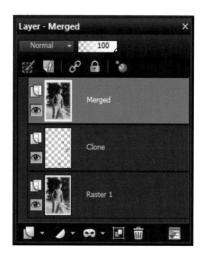

Figure 2.10

Locking in changes.

© Corel® Corporation, All Rights Reserved. © 2013 Cengage Learning®,
All Rights Reserved.

Experimenting with Duplicate Images

WHEN YOU'RE EXPERIMENTING with a solution to a problem and don't want to clutter your Layers palette with a bunch of alternate approaches, use the Window ❯ Duplicate (see Figure 2.11) menu to create a duplicate file, layers and all. The duplicate image will be named something generic (the one in Figure 2.12 is Image4) and need not be saved.

Add new layers to the duplicate file, rename them, and experiment without worrying that you're changing your original past the point where you can undo things. It's also helpful to be able to tab back and forth (or tile the windows, as in Figure 2.12) to compare.

I do this all the time.

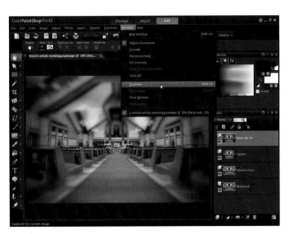

Figure 2.11

Duplicating an image to explore alternate paths.

© Corel® Corporation, All Rights Reserved. © 2013 Cengage Learning®, All Rights Reserved.

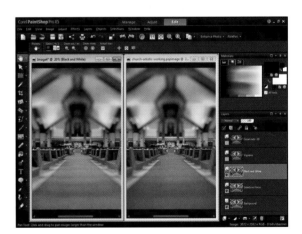

Figure 2.12

Side-by-side comparison of a duplicate image and the original.

© Corel® Corporation, All Rights Reserved. © 2013 Cengage Learning®, All Rights Reserved.

Masking Versus Erasing

JUST ABOUT EVERY TIME I use the eraser in a photo study, I could have used a mask and vice versa. The truth is, though, masks are much better in most cases. Here are some of the reasons I generally prefer to use a mask instead of the Eraser:

▶ You can see the mask in the Layers palette. That makes it more obvious (even to yourself) what you're doing.

▶ You can stack masks inside a layer group to create very complicated behaviors. When you create a mask, you have to have a layer selected. The program takes that layer, then creates a mask layer that goes with it, and then puts them both in a group.

▶ It's easy to create a gradient on a mask layer so you can gradually transition from opaque to transparent or vice versa. You can also experiment with textures or patterns. The creative possibilities are endless, but fairly simple to apply.

▶ You can come back and edit masks later if you see something you missed or accidentally erased.

▶ You can also create complex selections from masks, invert them, stack them, and so forth.

▶ You can select a mask and choose Layers ❯ Invert Mask/Adjustment (Shift+K) or press the Invert mask area button on the Layers palette to instantly mask the opposite portions of the layer.

Despite these things, the Eraser is still very useful—it's easy to understand, simple to use, and doesn't bloat the Layers palette with extra layers and layer groups. You can modify the opacity of the Eraser, as well as other brush parameters such as density and rotation. You can use the default or choose a different brush if you like, and load or change Brush Variance values like Position Jitter. You can also "unerase" material that you've previously erased by right-clicking as you "erase" instead of left-clicking.

Frankly, I have had a hard time getting used to being able to "unerase." I've always considered the Eraser a "use it and lose it" tool. However, I've performed tests on multiple layers in the same file, performed adjustments on them, saved the file, closed PaintShop Pro, and come back to find that "unerase" still works.

There are a few caveats, however. First, you may not be able to "unerase" material from an old PaintShop Pro file. Second, you'll get black in areas where there had never been any material to "unerase." That's one way of knowing it doesn't have the data hidden in the file somewhere to put back on the layer.

Using Adjustment Layers

ADJUSTMENT LAYERS ARE VERY COOL, but you have to know their limitations. The cool stuff first.

▶ **Editable:** You can change an adjustment layer, but you can't change a dialog-based adjustment after it's applied. That alone makes them worth using. Just double-click the layer in the Layers palette to bring up the settings, as shown in Figure 2.13.

▶ **Size:** Adjustment layers don't bloat the size of your document like full-sized photo layers can.

▶ **Built-in mask:** Adjustment layers have a built-in mask. That simplifies the process of making an adjustment to a particular part of your photo because you don't have to go the extra mile and create a mask (which then creates a group). You just mask what you don't want to be affected out of the adjustment layer, as shown in Figure 2.14, where I have brightened Anne's face and masked out the rest of the photo on the Levels 1 adjustment layer.

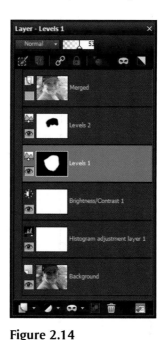

Figure 2.14

Adjustment layers have easy built-in masks.

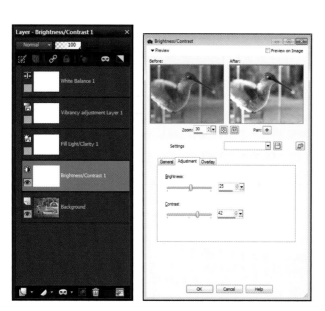

Figure 2.13

Double-click an adjustment layer to alter the settings.

However, it's not all rosy. Adjustment layers have some quirky things about them that you will have to work around.

▶ **Comparison is sometimes harder.** Comparing different effects with different adjustment layers is harder to do on the fly than just toggling different working layers on and off. When I'm looking at two different options, I want to flicker back and forth quickly. What I do, then, is lock the effects of several adjustment layers by copying a merged canvas and pasting that as a new raster layer; then I use a different set of adjustment layers (or a single one) to compare that to. It's not all that fun, but it is workable.

For example, Figure 2.15 shows the Layers palette with several adjustment layers and two merged comparison layers, named Compare 1 and Compare 2. To compare the effects of Fill Light/Clarity 1 and Brightness/Contrast 1 to Levels 1 and Fill Light/Clarity 2, all I have to do is toggle Compare 2 on and off. I've hidden the adjustment layers between it and Compare 1.

▶ **Mask is sometimes too simple.** The problem with a simple mask is that you can't embed more masks into the group like you can with a normal mask group. There are also times when I use a mask I created for one purpose and reuse it for another. To do this, I duplicate the mask layer in the Layers palette and drag it to a new location. I may also use the mask to create a selection from. You can't do this with adjustment layers. The mask is built into the layer.

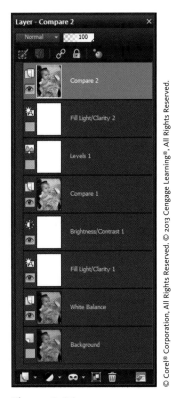

Figure 2.15
Comparing the effects of adjustment layers by showing and hiding copied raster layers.

Using Temporary Adjustment Layers

AT TIMES, I WILL USE a temporary adjustment layer to help me see things in a photo. For example, when I'm looking for damage or need to brighten parts of the photo to see problems, I will create a Levels adjustment layer and temporarily brighten the photo for inspection, as shown in Figure 2.16.

Sometimes, I will use them when cloning, as I have illustrated in a few of the studies.

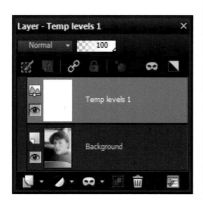
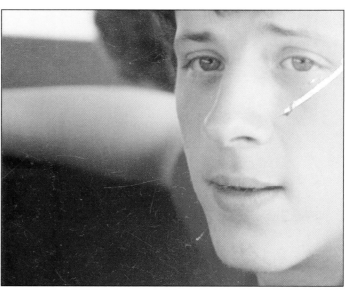

Figure 2.16

Using a temporary adjustment layer to carefully examine the photo.

Finding Out What You Did

IF YOU'RE WORKING ALONG and forgot what settings you applied as you adjusted a photo, you may be able to retrieve them in one of two ways.

First, many dialog boxes preserve the settings from the last operation. As long as you haven't used that command since, and changed the settings, you can re-open the dialog boxes and the settings will be automatically loaded. If the Settings field (seen in Figure 2.17) is blank, call up the Last Used setting by clicking on the list. This works for most adjustments.

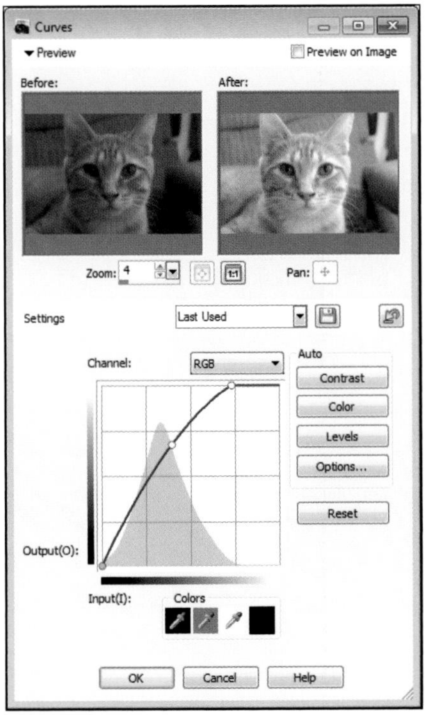

Here's another cool trick. Provided the adjustment is still in the program's History palette, open the palette up (see Figure 2.18) and find the command you're interested in.

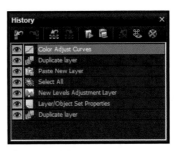

Figure 2.18
Select the setting to copy.

© Corel® Corporation, All Rights Reserved. © 2013 Cengage Learning®, All Rights Reserved.

Right-click the command and choose Copy to clipboard, as shown in Figure 2.19.

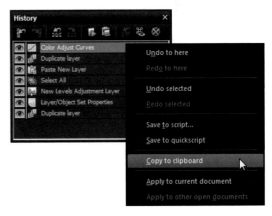

Figure 2.19
Copying the settings to the clipboard.

© Corel® Corporation, All Rights Reserved. © 2013 Cengage Learning®, All Rights Reserved.

Figure 2.17
Recalling the last used settings in a dialog box.

Open up Notepad or another text editor and paste the command into a blank file, as shown in Figure 2.20. Although you may have to look closely to be able to tell what the settings were, they are there.

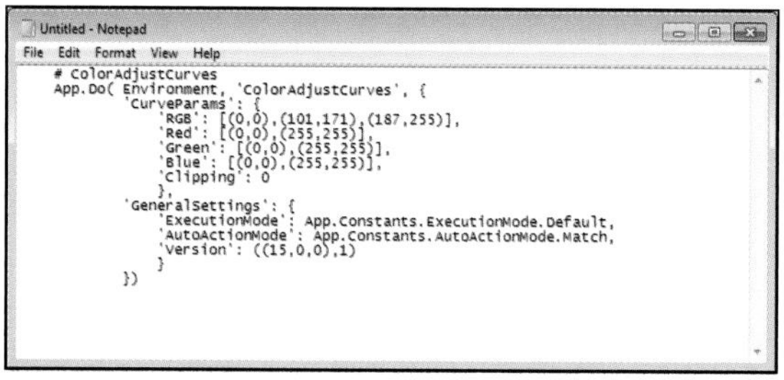

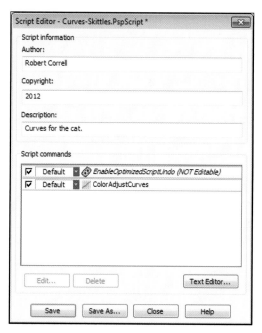

Figure 2.20

Upon close inspection, the settings are there.

© Corel® Corporation, All Rights Reserved.

Alternatively, you can right-click the command in the History palette and choose Save to script, then open the script to view the settings (File ❯ Script ❯ Edit), or choose Save to Quick Script and peek in that. To edit a script, and hence view the settings, choose the File ❯ Script ❯ Edit menu.

Select the command from the Script Editor (see Figure 2.21) and choose Edit. This opens the dialog box of the command in question (which, in this case, is Figure 2.17).

You can also open the command in a text editor from the Script Editor.

Figure 2.21

Accessing the settings via the Script Editor.

© Corel® Corporation, All Rights Reserved.

Saving Settings

DON'T BE AFRAID TO SAVE THE SETTINGS of the tool or command you're using into a preset. For example, I've created a cross processed look in the Curves dialog box in Figure 2.22 that is an artistic preset, which may be suitable for many photos. Instead of having to re-create the effect every time, press the Save Preset icon, give the preset a name, and press OK.

(For some strange reason, the Save Preset icon is an obsolete 1.44MB floppy disc. When was the last time you put something on a floppy? I suppose this icon has become so prevalent, we don't think about it anymore.)

Alternatively, if you prefer using scripts, save what you've done as a repeatable script by using the History palette.

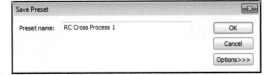

Figure 2.22

Saving a preset.

Blending with Opacity

BLEND! GO AHEAD, BLEND. Don't settle for setting each layer's opacity to 100%, every time, all the time.

Blending is one of the easiest and most effective ways to control the strength of your adjustments and manage their effects. You can blend almost everything:

▶ Normal photo layers (for example, Raster layers)

▶ Adjustment layers

▶ Layer groups (including those containing masks)

▶ Mask layers within a layer group

▶ Photo layers within a layer group that contains masks or other layers

▶ Vector layers

▶ Text

▶ And so forth!

I find it very effective to blend adjustments such as Digital Noise Reduction and Unsharp Mask as well as exposure (brightness and contrast) changes.

Figure 2.23 shows the Layers palette of one of the photo studies you'll see later. There are a number of stacked layers that represent my work. Beside them are the opacity percentages I used. I enhanced the color of my daughter's eyes (you can barely tell, but that's the way I wanted it) and in the process, reduced the opacity of the layer group that contained her "bluer" eyes to 12%. Not only that, I reduced the opacity of the blue eyes layer to 26%.

I reduced the opacity of the Unsharp Mask (USM) layer to 43%, reduced the opacity of the layer where I slightly dodged her eyes to 55%, reduced the opacity of the Digital Noise Reduction (DNR) layer group to 75% and the Texture Preserving Smooth group to 75%.

The whole point is that I was able to apply an adjustment and then pull it back to the exact strength I wanted. I could change my mind easily and either increase or decrease it. Flexibility aside, you will get better pictures if you know you can sharpen a layer and then lower its opacity to control the effect. The same goes for noise reduction, brightening, contrast, and color changes. Well, you name it!

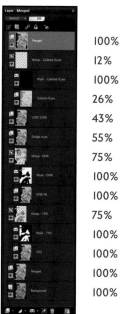

Figure 2.23

Going crazy with opacity blending.

Enlarging Versus Cropping

I HAVE TO ADMIT, I like working with a canvas the same size as the original photo, so I tend to enlarge layers when I want to recompose the photo rather than crop it. Figure 2.24 shows the final layer of a study before it has been scaled. There is a distracting pole on the right that I decided to get rid of.

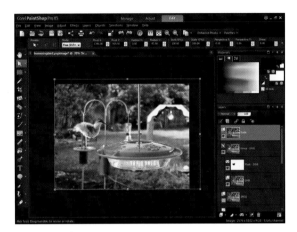

Figure 2.25

Enlarging a layer with the Pick tool instead of cropping the photo.

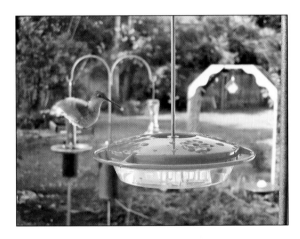

Figure 2.24

The final unscaled layer.

Instead of cropping it out, I used the Pick tool and scaled a duplicate layer upward, as shown in Figure 2.25.

Technically, you may be able to get higher quality results if you crop and either resize the image from the Image ❯ Resize menu, but to be honest, it doesn't bother me, and I would rather keep the contents of my file as a whole intact and unresized. If you want to take the resize route, you can duplicate the image, flatten it, crop it, and then resize it back to the original dimensions (or close) to publish or print without changing the original.

Preserving or Deleting EXIF Data

DIGITAL PHOTOS (see Figure 2.26) have additional information embedded in them, called *EXIF data* (a type of meta data). There are quite a few types of information stored, such as the date and time the photo was taken, the exposure settings of the camera, color profile, style settings, whether the flash went off, the metering mode, and so forth.

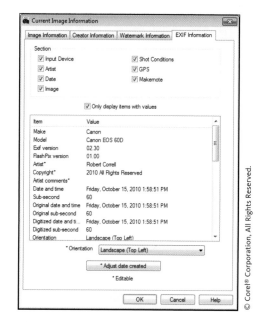

Figure 2.27
EXIF information is very useful.

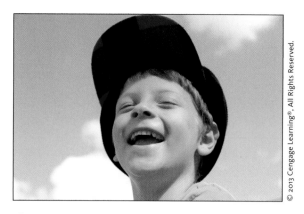

Figure 2.26
Jake having a blast.

You can see this by selecting the Image ❯ Image Information menu. Click the EXIF Information tab, as shown in Figure 2.27, to see the information. As you can see, I shot this photo of my son, Jacob, using a Canon EOS 60D on October 15, 2010.

When you open up a digital photo to retouch it and save your work as a .pspimage, this data is automatically preserved. No problem there.

When you use File ❯ Save As to save a version of your work in a format that supports meta data, such as TIFF, JPEG, or PNG (for printing, archiving, or distribution), the information is normally saved along with the photo.

You have the option when you save a JPEG this way to keep or toss the EXIF information. Click the Options button in the Save As dialog box to access the JPEG options, as shown in Figure 2.28.

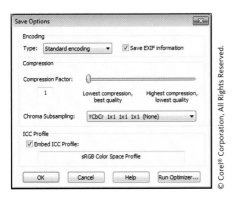

Figure 2.28
*Check Save EXIF information in the JPEG Save
Options dialog box to save it.*

You also have this option when using the File ❯
Export ❯ JPEG Optimizer. Click the Save Exif data
box (see Figure 2.29) if you want to preserve it and
are saving a JPEG in the Standard format.

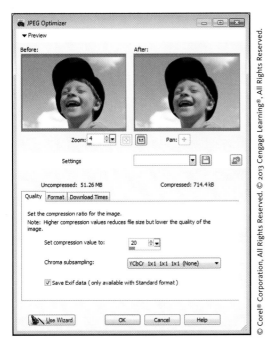

Figure 2.29
Saving EXIF information when exporting a JPEG.

Some formats, such as GIF, store no additional
data, so your EXIF information is always lost in
those cases (see Figure 2.30).

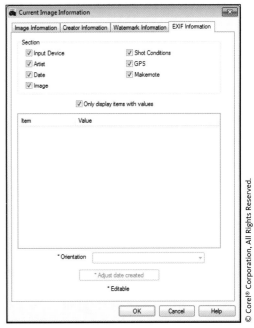

Figure 2.30
Sad little dialog box with no information.

Sometimes it's good to strip out all the information. For example, you may want to preserve your
privacy or hide the specifics of how you took the
photo from people. It's your photo. Sometimes you
want to keep it in there. For example, Figure 2.27
shows my copyright information and name. That
can protect my photos and remind people that it's
my property. In the end, use the approach that
serves your purposes.

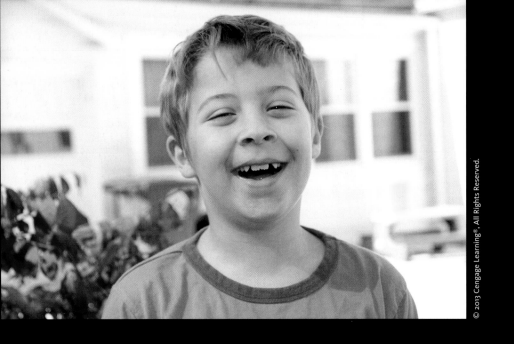

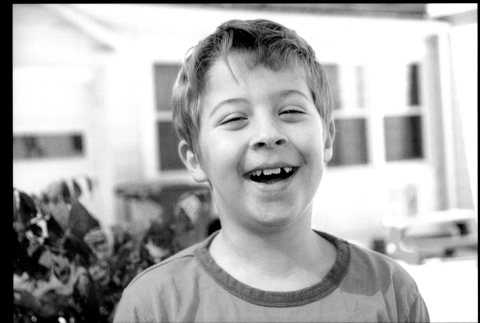

Improving Brightness and Contrast

3

B RIGHTNESS AND CONTRAST PROBLEMS are among the most common. You'll run into them whether you're working with older prints or new digital photos. Much of the time, brightness problems are linked to flash (whether too much or too little), a bright sky (possibly through a window), or a poorly lit interior. Contrast problems make a picture look like there is a gray veil over it.

These photo studies show you how to address both types of problems:

 ▶ **Photo Study 1: Basic Brightness and Contrast**—You'll make brightness and contrast adjustments on almost every photo you retouch, whether the original is old and in need of a complete makeover or is a new digital photo of your spouse, as in this study.

 ▶ **Photo Study 2: Brightening an Older Photo**—Old photos are particularly susceptible to fading. This Polaroid photo of me taken in the early 1980s should be brighter and have more contrast.

 ▶ **Photo Study 3: Brightening Faces**—Faces are particularly important to get right, and they are often photographed in shadow. I'll show you how to brighten someone's face by using a picture of my wife at a local festival as an example.

 ▶ **Photo Study 4: Restoring Detail to Washed Out Areas**—On the other hand, there are times when people's faces reflect too much light and look washed out. This is mostly confined to the forehead, cheeks, and chin. You'll learn a color changing and blending technique that handles this problem very well in this study.

▶ **Photo Study 5: Boosting Contrast**—This photo of flowers is a great example of how boosting contrast can help even good photos look better.

 ▶ **Photo Study 6: Localizing Adjustments**—Learn how to make different adjustments to different areas of a photo using this digital photo of a laughing hyena. Spots, smudges on the glass, and someone's arm in the corner need to be removed. Also, glare needs to be taken out of the grass and sky.

 ▶ **Photo Study 7: Taming Highlights**—This study shows you how to pull back highlights in digital photos taken in the RAW file format.

Photo Study 1: Basic Brightness and Contrast

FIGURE 3.1 IS A PHOTO OF MY WIFE, taken in 2012. We were out testing a new lens and our path led us into a gourmet kitchen store we both like. After introducing ourselves, I explained what we were doing and asked permission to take photos in their store. The friendly sales staff said yes, so we spent some time taking casual shots of her looking at their wares.

I took this shot to see what the background would look like and generally evaluate the lighting. I used an external flash, but by this time of day the batteries were wearing out. The result is that this photo turned out decidedly dark. It's a nice shot of her, though, and I would like to save it.

That makes this photo a great choice to go over PaintShop Pro's basic brightness and contrast options.

Camera RAW Lab

It's easy to adjust brightness using the Camera RAW Lab. In fact, there is only one control for adjusting brightness, and it is called *Brightness*. Raise it to lighten the photo and lower it to darken the photo. Adjusting contrast is just as easy, but the control is named *Shadow*. Raising the Shadow level darkens the dark areas of the photo, which has the effect of increasing the contrast, especially if you raise brightness.

Figure 3.2 shows the settings I chose for this photo. The most important change is that the Brightness has been raised to 1.5. That's quite a bit.

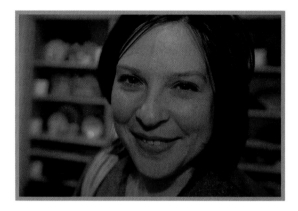

Figure 3.1
Shopping spree in dim light.

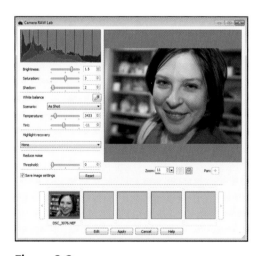

Figure 3.2
Attempting to brighten using the Camera RAW Lab.

The photo looks much brighter as a result. When brightening, consider raising the Shadow setting. This will keep the dark areas from brightening too much, thereby preserving (or increasing) the contrast in the photo.

Using the Adjust Workspace

There are several ways to alter a photo's brightness and contrast from PaintShop Pro's Adjust workspace (whether you are working with a JPEG, or a RAW file, as I am here). Start with the Smart Photo Fix feature and work your way down.

As shown in Figure 3.3, there are four main Smart Photo Fix controls. Brightness controls the overall brightness of the image. Shadows and Highlights can be made darker or lighter. In this case, Brightness and Highlights have been raised while the shadows have been made darker. You can also adjust the values for the brightest and darkest pixels in the photo by dragging the white or black triangle slider controls underneath the Saturation control. Do this to spread the brightness values in the photo over the entire range of the histogram.

(The histogram is a chart that graphs the number of pixels in the photo by their brightness, with shadows on the left and highlights on the right.) That ensures that you're using the entire range of contrast you have available to you.

Further down the list of features in the Adjust workspace is the Brightness/Contrast control. This control works as you would expect. Raise or lower either control to lessen or strengthen the photo's brightness or contrast. Figure 3.4 shows the effect of raising both of them for this photo.

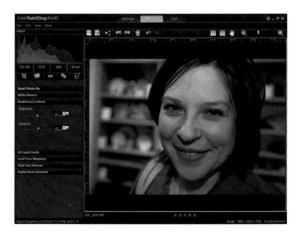

Figure 3.4

Brightness/Contrast is simple, but it works.

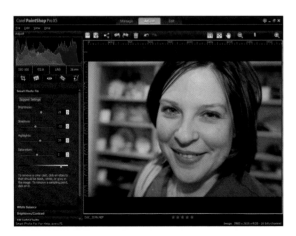

Figure 3.3

Using Smart Photo Fix in the Adjust workspace.

You can also alter brightness and contrast with Fill Light/Clarity. Because it adds light, Fill Light/Clarity works with photos that need to be lightened. Clarity boosts edge contrast. Figure 3.5 shows the effect on this photo of adding light but reducing the Clarity setting to try and soften the photo. It's not the best, but it's not the worst either. Most often, you will make your main brightness and contrast adjustments elsewhere and then tweak them with Fill Light/Clarity.

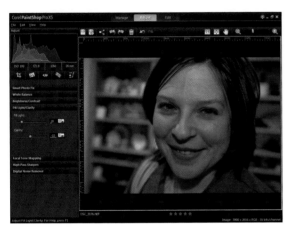

Figure 3.5

Fill Light can be effective, but is not so much here.

© Corel® Corporation, All Rights Reserved. © 2013 Cengage Learning®, All Rights Reserved.

Using the Edit Workspace

You have access to the entire set of brightness and contrast tools in the Edit workspace. I won't repeat those you've already seen in this study (Smart Photo Fix, Brightness/Contrast, and Fill Light/Clarity). The remaining tools are: Levels, Curves, Histogram Adjustment, and Highlight/Midtone/Shadow.

Levels (Adjust ❯ Brightness and Contrast ❯ Levels) is an excellent tool for altering brightness and contrast. Although a bit more complicated than using Brightness/Contrast, it is still relatively straightforward. Press one of the Auto buttons to see what PaintShop Pro suggests; then Adjust the diamond sliders yourself until you're happy. In this case (see Figure 3.6), the high slider was brought well in, which did most of the work of brightening the photo. The low slider was raised a small amount, and the gray slider pulled to the left to finish. The result is a brighter photo with more contrast.

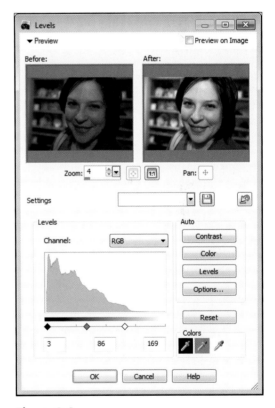

Figure 3.6

Levels can adjust brightness and contrast at the same time.

© Corel® Corporation, All Rights Reserved. © 2013 Cengage Learning®, All Rights Reserved.

Curves (Adjust ❯ Brightness and Contrast ❯ Curves) enables you to remap the brightness of each pixel in the photo. In this case (see Figure 3.7), the photo has been remapped so that the entire brightness spectrum is used and the middle of the curve has been bent outward to brighten up the midtones even more. The bottom and top points act just like the black-and-white diamond sliders in the Levels dialog box.

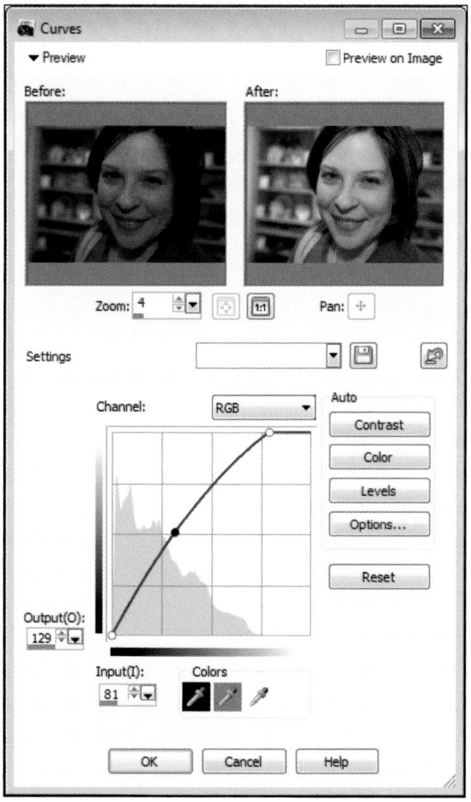

Histogram Adjustment (Adjust ❯ Brightness and Contrast ❯ Histogram Adjustment) is yet another command you can use to alter brightness and contrast. The black-and-white diamonds of the Levels dialog box have been replaced by triangles, but they act the same. In this case, however, the gray triangle slider, or Gamma, acts the opposite. When you slide it up, things lighten as if you were pulling the histogram toward the direction you move Gamma, as shown in Figure 3.8.

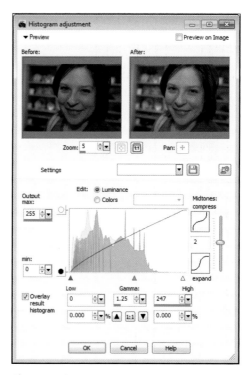

Figure 3.7

Curves also works well.

Figure 3.8

There are more possibilities with Histogram Adjustment.

Another adjustment command that can work in many situations is called Highlight/Midtone/Shadow (Adjust ❯ Brightness and Contrast ❯ Highlight/Midtone/Shadow). It's not the simplest way to bring out brightness and contrast, but it is effective at changing the relative brightness of each tonal region, shown in Figure 3.9.

Finishing the Photo Study

Figure 3.10 shows the final, retouched photo, which has increased brightness and better contrast. I also smoothed Anne a bit and cloned out a few imperfections. This was a good digital photo to begin with, so it didn't need a ton of work. However, even good photos can often be improved, and brightness and contrast are some of the first places you should look.

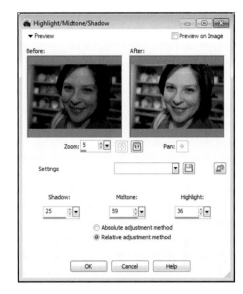

Figure 3.9

Highlight/Midtone/Shadow enables you to selectively brighten and darken areas.

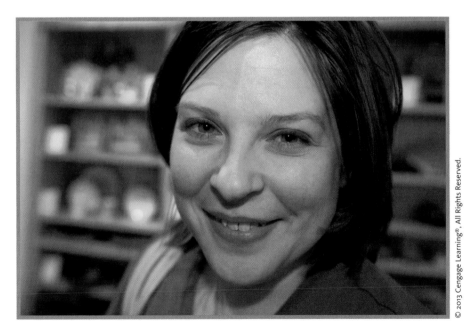

Figure 3.10

This photo springs alive with a basic brightness and contrast adjustment.

Photo Study 2: Brightening an Older Photo

THE PHOTO IN FIGURE 3.11 was taken in the early 1980s by my mom. I played the alto saxophone and was in jazz band throughout junior high and high school. This was a summer jazz ensemble, and we were performing on a downtown sidewalk in Muncie, Indiana. That's me in the front row. I'm the one with the tube socks on.

This photo is an example of a Polaroid print. The film came in large packages that looked like toaster pastries. You put the film package in the camera and pulled each photo out by a tab after you took the picture. The obvious advantage to a Polaroid camera was the film developed "instantly." Our family had a Polaroid camera, and I had fun holding the film under my arm while it developed. When it was time, you peeled the print off the "negative," and you had your photo.

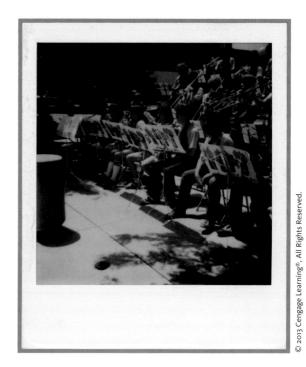

Figure 3.11
Polaroid photo suffering from brightness and contrast issues.

The Death and Rebirth of Polaroid

Due to a number of reasons, not the least of which was having to compete with digital cameras, Polaroid went bankrupt in 2001. The Polaroid brand name survived and, after a number of legal battles, emerged under new ownership in 2009. While they don't manufacture any "original" Polaroid film anymore, Polaroid has reintroduced a smaller instant camera by rebranding an existing Fujifilm instant camera and film to go with it. If you have an old Polaroid camera, Impossible runs the Impossible Project (*www.theimpossibleproject.com*), and currently manufactures new film for old Polaroid cameras.

Using Curves and Levels Together

There are times when using either Curves or Levels to adjust brightness and contrast works well. There are also times when you can get a better result by using them both. The key is to use the different dialogs to focus on what they both do well.

It is easy to set the black-and-white points (the darkest and brightest spots) of a photo with Levels. Do this by dragging the black or white diamond sliders inward. It is also easy to change the brightness of the midtones of a photo by dragging the gray diamond slider left to brighten or right to darken them. As Figure 3.12 shows, dragging the gray diamond slider to the left brightens the photo, while leaving the black-and-white diamond sliders alone leaves the lows and highs intact.

Although it can do more, think of Levels as the tool to use when you need to make adjustments to either end or middle of a photo's brightness spectrum.

Curves, on the other hand, excels at making targeted adjustments to specific tonal regions. For example, you can easily brighten the lower tones of a photo without clipping (turning to featureless black or white, depending on the end of the spectrum you're adjusting) the low end or drastically changing the rest of the photo. Figure 3.13 shows this in action. There is a single point toward the dark end of the spectrum, which remaps input values of 25 to a brightness of 45. The overall shape of the curve helps blend in this adjustment.

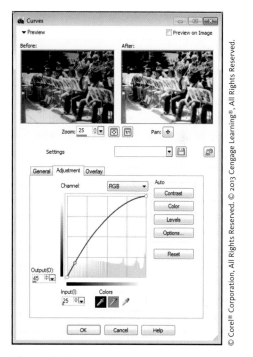

Figure 3.13
Brightening the low end with Curves.

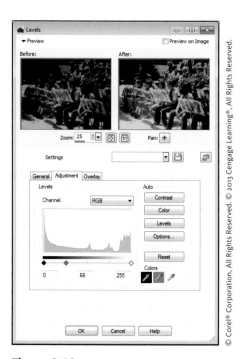

Figure 3.12
Altering midtones with a Levels adjustment layer.

Finishing the Photo Study

Figure 3.14 shows the final, retouched photo, which used a combination of Levels and Curves adjustments to achieve the right balance of brightness and contrast. Aside from these fixes, a lot of small specks and dust were cleaned up using the Clone brush. Edge Preserving Smooth and Salt and Pepper were used to reduce noise and specks slightly. This layer was made semi-opaque (59) to blend in with the brightened layer below.

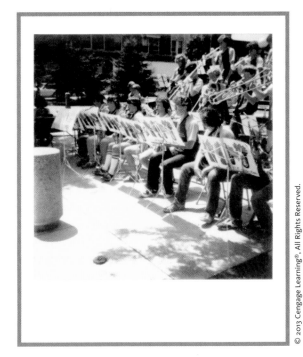

Figure 3.14
Improved brightness and contrast in this Polaroid shot.

Photo Study 3: Brightening Faces

THE PHOTO IN FIGURE 3.15 of my wife was taken in 2006 by my oldest son, Ben. I was away for eight weeks studying audio engineering and music production, and my wife took the kids to the annual Johnny Appleseed Festival. The festival is full of exhibits of what life in the Northwest Frontier of the United States was like back in the early 1800s.

Make a habit of trying to figure out what you want to do before you get too far into the details. The right path may not come to you immediately. Open the photo up in PaintShop Pro and experiment with Smart Photo Fix, Levels, Curves, or Histogram Adjustment. See what looks promising as you try and define the problem. In this case, although the photo isn't unreasonably dark, Anne's face and eyes are in shadow. This happens when you take photos of people in the sunlight without a flash, especially when they're wearing hats.

Correcting the Problem

The challenge here is to lighten her face without making everything else too bright. Figure 3.16 shows the Histogram Adjustment dialog box as I created the Histogram Adjustment layer. The initial graph (in light gray) is weighted toward the bright side of the histogram. In this case, moving the Gamma slider to the right lightens the photo as a whole. When you don't want to reduce the range of brightness, don't touch the low or high sliders.

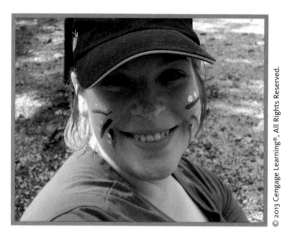

Figure 3.15
The original photo looks great, but is dark.

As you make your adjustments, try and find something in the photo to use as a reference point. I used Anne's ear to make sure I didn't brighten the photo too much. I knew that if her ear got too bright, it would lose detail. That meant I had gone too far and needed to pull back.

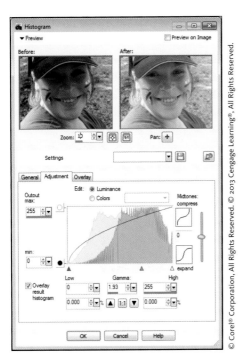

Figure 3.16
Brightening by adjusting midtones.

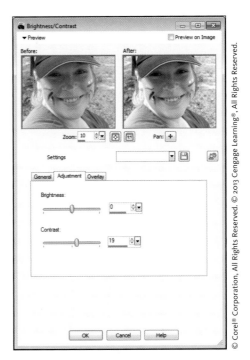

Figure 3.17
Enhancing contrast.

Brightening a photo can sometimes lower the overall contrast. If that happens, the easiest way to address it is to add a Brightness/Contrast adjustment layer to add some contrast back in, as shown in Figure 3.17. You may be wondering why you can't simply use Brightness/Contrast to brighten and add contrast simultaneously. The answer is that you have more control over what you're brightening (shadows, midtones, or brighter areas) if you use the other brightness and contrast tools that PaintShop Pro offers. Brightness brightens everything at the same time.

While the photo is doing much better, Anne's face needed more brightness. Brightening the rest of the photo will make things too bright, so a selective adjustment around her face was necessary. One quick way of accomplishing this is to use an adjustment layer and mask out everything you don't want to change.

For example, Figure 3.18 shows another Levels adjustment layer dialog box. I am focusing on Anne's face and adjusting the middle slider to brighten it even more. I am not worried about what the rest of the photo looks like because I will mask it out later.

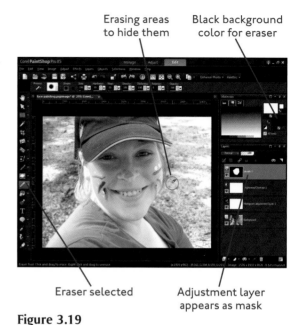

Erasing areas to hide them

Black background color for eraser

Eraser selected

Adjustment layer appears as mask

Figure 3.19
Masking out everything but her face.

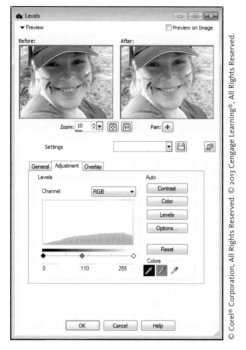

Figure 3.18
Making another brightness adjustment.

When that adjustment layer is created, it is essentially a Show All mask. To keep specific areas of the adjustment layer from altering the layers beneath it, paint the areas you want to hide black on the adjustment layer, as shown in Figure 3.19.

To blend the adjustment even more, lower its opacity from the Layers palette. In this case, I set it to 53, as shown in Figure 3.20. The cool thing about playing with opacity is that you can quickly add in more or less brightness until you find the right level.

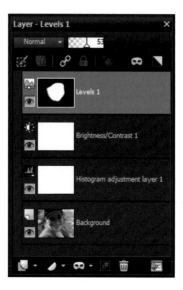

Figure 3.20
Blending an even brighter face.

When you're working on photos, don't be afraid of incremental improvements. You don't have to get it all right in the first step. In fact, you will often not be able to re-create the same result you achieved in five steps by condensing it down to three.

This example is a case in point. At this juncture, the photo looked fine and Anne's face was brighter. Mission accomplished? Not quite. It's apparent that the rest of the photo was a bit too bright. To correct that, everything but her eyes needed to be darkened.

Figure 3.21 shows the Levels adjustment dialog box with the gray diamond slider moved to 145. Nothing else was changed.

Because I didn't want her eyes darkened by this, I painted black onto the adjustment layer to mask her eyes, as shown in 3.22. Afterward, I lowered the opacity of the Levels adjustment layer to 70.

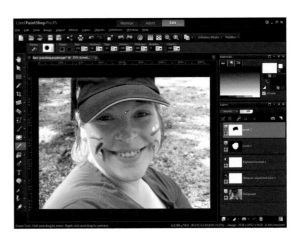

Figure 3.22
Masking out the eyes this time.

Finishing the Photo Study

After I was happy with all the brightness and contrast adjustments, I locked in the effects of the adjustment layers by selecting all, performing a merged copy, and pasting as a new layer. Then I polished her teeth slightly with the Dodge brush and applied the default level of Skin Smoothing to finish the photo.

Does it look like I did some things upside down and backwards? It might. However, when I went back to try and clean things up and make the path from start to finish straighter, I realized how much harder it was to try and mask the background than it was to mask out the area around her eyes.

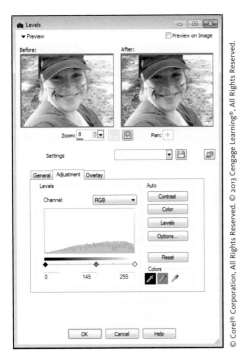

Figure 3.21
Darkening everything slightly.

Here is a recap of the steps I took to complete this study (it can be confusing at times):

1. Created a Histogram Adjustment layer to brighten the entire photo (Figure 3.16).

2. Created a Brightness/Contrast adjustment layer to enhance the contrast (Figure 3.17).

3. Created a Levels adjustment layer to brighten her face (Figure 3.18).

4. Masked out the background of that layer so it would not be brightened (Figure 3.19). It's easy to do this using an adjustment layer. You simply paint black (or erase with black as the background color) onto the adjustment layer.

5. Created another Levels adjustment layer to darken the photo a slight amount (Figure 3.21).

6. Masked out her eyes to preserve their lightness (Figure 3.22).

7. Created a merged copy (Edit > Copy Special > Copy Merged (Ctrl+Shift+C); then Edit > Paste As New Layer (Ctrl+V)) to lock in the effects of the adjustment layers into a single photo (raster) layer.

8. Whitened teeth using the Dodge brush.

9. Performed Skin Smoothing.

Figure 3.23 shows the final result. Anne's face is brighter, and her eyes are more visible in the retouched version. That's what I was after.

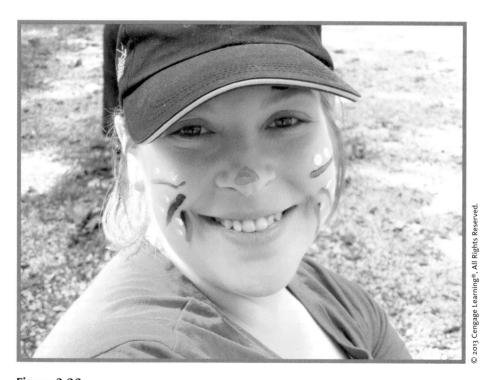

Figure 3.23
A much better, brighter photo.

Photo Study 4:
Restoring Detail to Washed Out Areas

FIGURE 3.24 IS A PHOTO of my wife, Anne, and me on our wedding night. Our wedding day was the first of many "best day evers" (something our kids love saying) to come.

This photo is shortly after the wedding, during our small reception at the resort where we were married. (We had something called a *destination wedding*: one where you fly to an exotic or exciting locale to get married and honeymoon in the same place.) It was a pretty hot evening, and we were sweating. These areas caught the flash and caused bright spots on our faces (see Figure 3.25). Our cheeks stand out the most, but you can also see bright spots on our chins and my forehead.

Reminder

This is a good time to make a point about color sampling. Sample color from one photo and use it for something else in another. The photos can be taken at the same or at different times, places, and occasions.

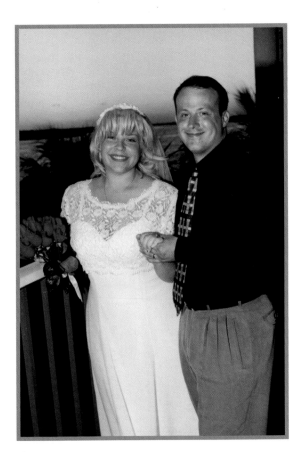

Figure 3.24
Newlyweds posing for the camera.
© 2013 Cengage Learning®, All Rights Reserved.

Bright spots   Bright spots

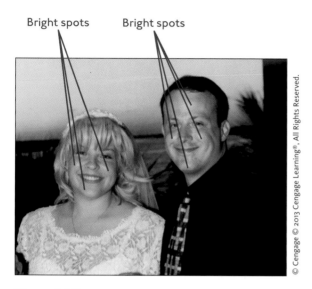

Figure 3.25
Close-up of overly bright areas.

My Magical Miracle Cure

I've tried many different techniques in an effort to solve this problem, ranging from darkening the entire image to using the Burn brush to darken the bright spots. I was never satisfied with the result, so I developed a different approach based around the Color Changer.

I came up with this approach after I tried to use the Color Changer to replace the shiny spots with a better skin tone. The bright spots got better, but it made everything else look horrendous. I decided I could use the Color Changer on the bright spots only and blend them back into the photo on another layer. Here's how you can do it, too:

1. Take care of housekeeping tasks first (clean your scanner). Scan your photo if it is a print or make a working copy if it is digital.

2. Open the photo. Save the file as a .pspimage with an appropriate name.

3. Duplicate the photo layer and name it something clever, like *Darken* or *Blend*. The duplicate layer should be above the Background layer. Leave the Background layer alone. You're going to be working on the layer you just duplicated.

4. Select the top layer.

5. Select the Freehand Selection tool and change the Selection type to Point-to-Point. Doing so enables you to click and draw a straight-edged selection area. It's just like connecting the dots. Click where you want the dots to be, and PaintShop Pro connects them.

   Use this tool to select the general area that needs to be darkened. I am making my selection in Figure 3.26. You don't need to be too picky with this. Get all the areas you need, plus some extra space around them. That will be your blending space. You'll erase everything else or mask it out in the end.

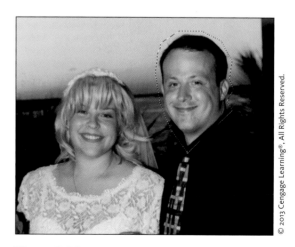

Figure 3.26
Limiting the work area.

6. Select the Color Changer tool, as shown in Figure 3.27. This tool is located with the Flood Fill tool on the Tools toolbar.

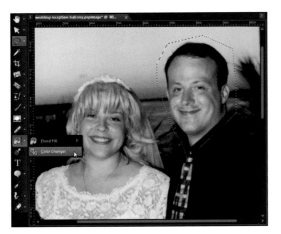

Figure 3.27
Going for the Color Changer.

7. Be patient with this part of the process. You may have to come back and try several times until you get the right color that will blend in perfectly. Press the Control key to change the Color Changer tool temporarily to the Dropper tool and click on a darker skin color to use to replace the bright spots. I can't tell you exactly what the color should be, but it should be in the same color range (like skin tones to replace like skin tones) although somewhat darker than the bright spot.

8. Click a bright spot to replace the color. You may have to click, undo, click, and undo several times until you hit just the right pixel or decide to try another color. It's going to look funny even when it works (see Figure 3.28), but don't worry. You're looking for a blend between the bright spot and the surrounding areas. It took me a few tries and a one-color change to achieve my result.

Alternate Ideas

I've chosen to do all my selecting and color changing on one layer, but you can promote each selection you've made to a new layer every time you want to work with a bright spot. That will make erasing unneeded areas easier when the time comes to start blending, but you'll have to align the layers exactly. You can also use a mask instead of erasing.

If you don't want to use the Color Changer, you can try painting a new skin color on a blank raster layer over the bright areas with the Paint brush or copy and paste patches of skin to a new layer from another photo. Blend them in the same way I have done in this study.

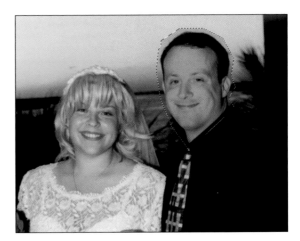

Figure 3.28
Changing the bright spots.

9. Now do the same thing in other areas of the photo that need to be changed. Anne needs her bright spots blended, and since her skin tone is different, I will return to step 5 and repeat the process. I've used the Color Changer on her face in Figure 3.29. It looks like she put on a layer of makeup, which is exactly what I'm after. Don't worry if it looks like thick makeup, because you'll blend it later.

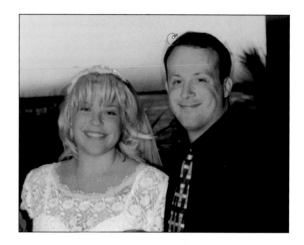

Figure 3.30
Erasing unwanted areas.
© Corel® Corporation, All Rights Reserved. © 2013 Cengage Learning®, All Rights Reserved.

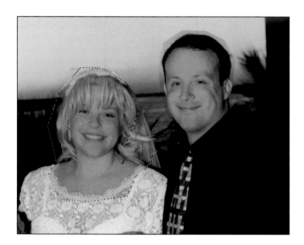

Figure 3.29
Doing the same for Anne.
© Corel® Corporation, All Rights Reserved. © 2013 Cengage Learning®, All Rights Reserved.

10. Next, start erasing the outer area of your selection where the color changed but is obviously not an area where you're going to blend. (You could also use a mask and mask out the areas I erased here.) I'm erasing the area around my hair where I don't want the color blended at all in Figure 3.30. Don't erase too much. You want enough area to blend with what's outside of the bright spots.

11. Now it's time to blend. Double-click the layer thumbnail of the layer you've made the color changes to in the Layers palette to open up the Layer Properties dialog box (see Figure 3.31). Lower the opacity until it blends in nicely with the lower (original photo) layer. Take special care to look at how the bright spots disappear and blend in with the rest of the photo. Experiment to find the right setting. In this case, 50% looks good. You can also lower this layer's opacity directly from the Layers palette.

You can also lower a layer's opacity by using the Opacity slider on the Layers palette. I chose to open the Layer Properties dialog box to illustrate an alternate method of doing the same thing.

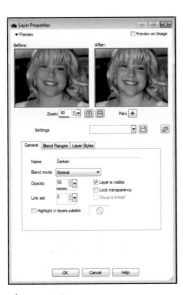

Figure 3.31
Blending with opacity.

12. Finally, it's time to do some small touch-ups. Look for areas of the blend layer that might need to be erased to make the photo better. I've chosen to erase around Anne's teeth and eyes on the blend layer in Figure 3.32. Spend some time on this step to achieve the perfect blend.

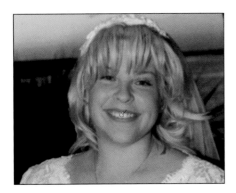

Figure 3.32
Touch-ups.

Finishing the Photo Study

Figure 3.33 shows the fully restored photo of my wife and me at our wedding reception. To complete the study, I erased dust and specks around the photo, brightened the overall photo, desaturated our faces a small amount, and smoothed out skin.

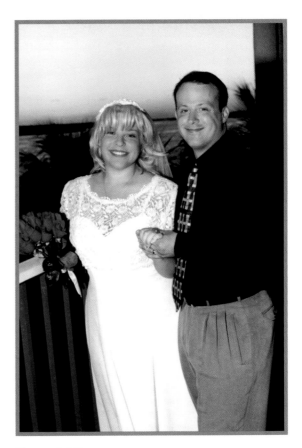

Figure 3.33
Corrected bright spots blended nicely.

Photo Study 5: Boosting Contrast

FIGURE 3.34 IS A PHOTO of some of my mother-in-law's flowers just in front of her garage. I took this shot in 2012 with my Nikon D200 and 50mm f/1.4G lens. I created a very narrow depth of field both by using an aperture of f/3.2 and by being so close to the flowers. I selected an autofocus point on the group of flowers just beyond me. Although the photo looks very good, it could have more contrast. You can tell this because it appears to have a dull, gray sheen. The white siding of the garage is dull, and the dark areas in the foliage are more gray than black.

This study makes use of adjustment layers to initially battle the contrast problem.

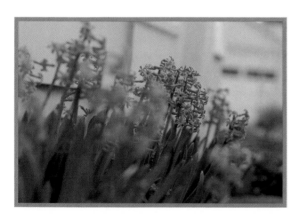

Figure 3.34
Flowers in need of contrast.
© 2013 Cengage Learning®, All Rights Reserved.

Fixing the Contrast Problem with Adjustment Layers

Sometimes the simplest approach to solving a problem is the best. In this case, that means creating a Brightness/Contrast adjustment layer and increasing the Contrast level, as shown in Figure 3.35. To create an adjustment layer, choose the Layers > New Adjustment Layer menu and choose the type of adjustment layer you want to create. You can also click the New Adjustment Layer icon at the bottom of the Layers palette to access the different types of adjustment layers.

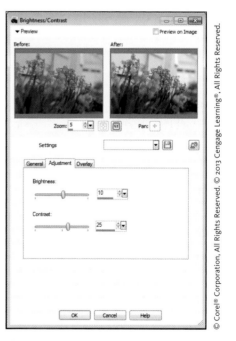

Figure 3.35
Increasing contrast with a Brightness/Contrast adjustment layer.

You can create a Levels adjustment layer (see Figure 3.36) to tweak contrast. Notice the histogram in the dialog box. It is obvious that there aren't enough highlights in the photo, but it also suffers from too few shadows. Bringing both sliders closer to the middle pushes existing levels both brighter and darker.

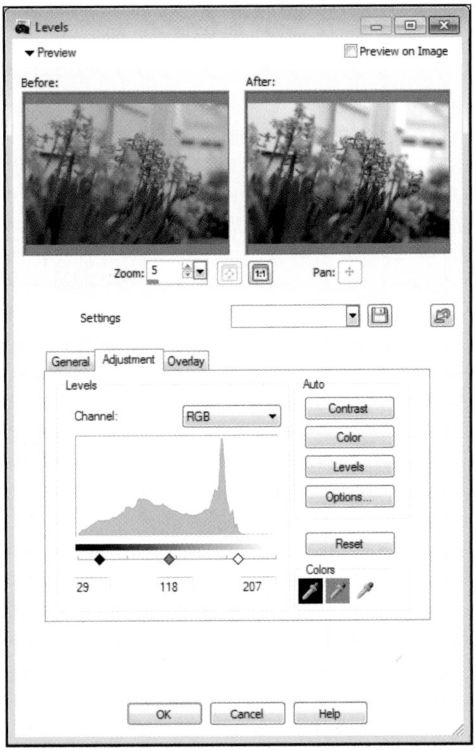

The Curves adjustment layer dialog box (see Figure 3.37) also has a histogram that you can use to figure out what's going on. In this case, however, you move points on the graph. The line created by the two points boosts contrast effectively.

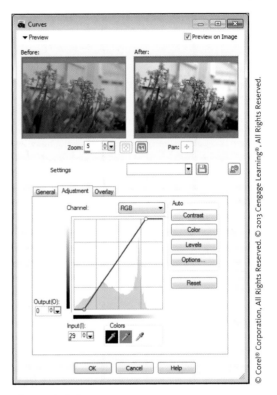

Figure 3.37
Curves is also effective at boosting contrast.

Figure 3.36
Using a Levels adjustment layer to enhance contrast.

Finally, you could create a Histogram Adjustment layer (see Figure 3.38).

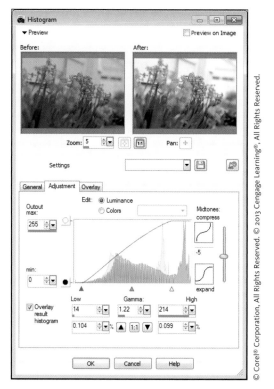

Figure 3.38
Expand midtones after adjusting the sliders to enhance contrast.

Be familiar with all three of these techniques. Any one of them might work best on a given photo.

More Ways to Control Contrast

There are other ways to alter contrast in the Edit workspace. First, there is the tried and true Smart Photo Fix. Figure 3.39 shows the dialog box with the suggested settings. Notice that the shadows have been darkened and the highlights brightened. You've seen this in all the other figures, only using different techniques. Increasing the luminance difference between highlights and shadows is the essence of increasing contrast.

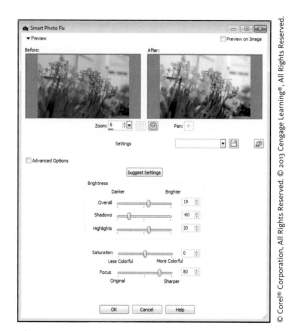

Figure 3.39
Use Smart Photo Fix for helpful ideas.

Another way to push shadows and highlights away from each other is to use Highlight/Midtone/Shadow, shown in Figure 3.40. In this case, the Shadows setting is negative. This makes the shadows darker. At the same time, the Midtone and Highlights settings are positive. This brightens them. The effect of these settings, using the Relative adjustment method, is to push shadows and highlights further apart, thereby increasing the contrast between them. You can see the result in the After window of the dialog box.

If nothing else is working to increase contrast to your liking, try Fade Correction. Although the problem might not be caused by fading due to age, the effect on the photo (lack of contrast) can be similar between an old scanned print and a new digital photo. As shown in Figure 3.41, Fade Correction does a decent job of putting "oomph" back into a photo.

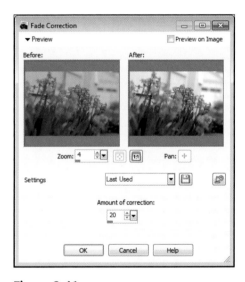

Figure 3.41
Interestingly, Fade Correction boosts contrast even in new digital pictures.

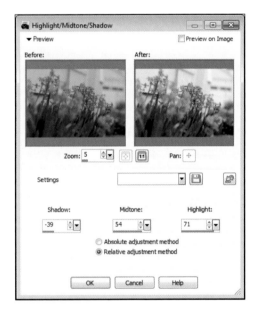

Figure 3.40
Push shadows and highlights apart using Highlight/Midtone/Shadow.

Finally, you can try to improve contrast in your photos by using one or more of the new Instant Effects. If they are not visible, turn the palette on by selecting View ❯ Palettes ❯ Instant Effects. Using Instant Effects is easy. Select the layer you want to apply the effect to in the Layers palette and double-click the Instant Effect from its palette. Figure 3.42 shows the result of applying the Contrast effect.

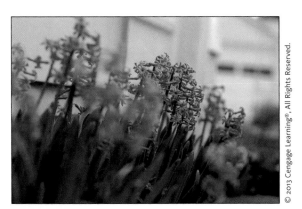

Figure 3.42
Try Instant Effects to increase contrast.

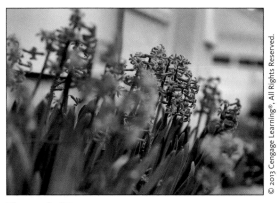

Figure 3.43
You can also create interesting artistic effects with Instant Effects.

Figure 3.43 shows the result of the Tone Map low effect. This effect increases contrast and adds a lot of definition to your photos. You may not like the full effect on many photos. If not, try blending the effect layer with another layer beneath it using opacity or a different Blend mode.

Finishing the Photo Study

The final photo is shown in Figure 3.44. It was good to begin with, but the final result is much better than the original. As you work on your photos, make sure to fix the main problem (in this case, contrast), but be on the lookout for other ways to make things look better. In this case, I boosted the colors a bit and straightened the photo.

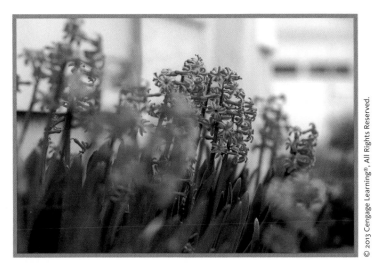

Figure 3.44
Improving contrast is like removing a gray layer from the photo.

Photo Study 6: Localizing Adjustments

ANNE TOOK THIS PHOTO (see Figure 3.45) during a trip to the zoo in 2009. The zoo had just opened a new exhibit called African Journey, and she caught a spotted (aka laughing) hyena at rest. It's quite close, and you can barely tell there is a window separating the hyena from the observers.

Pictures like this are fun to work with, because you can make them look like they were taken in the wild with only a few changes. In this case, that means removing the smudges and reflections from the glass and cloning out the child's arm in the lower-right corner of the picture.

The other element that makes this photo a good study is that it requires different lighting adjustments for different depths. The things you would do to spruce up the hyena are not the same thing you would do to fix the overly bright background. The key is to keep the adjustments separated, or localized. You do this by working with layers and masks.

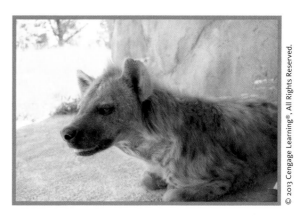

Figure 3.45
Great shot from behind the glass.

Working from Front to Back

For photos like this, it is best to work out all the smudges and other physical imperfections before tackling the lighting. In this case, I erased the arm in the corner of the photo with the Clone brush first (see Chapters 6, "Removing Specks and Dust," and 7, "Repairing Scratches, Tears, Creases, and Holes," for a lot more information on how to use the Clone brush). When working with glass, make sure you don't clone smudges, reflections, or other imperfections. This photo has a small smudge-free area to the left of the arm that makes a good source for the Clone brush (see Figure 3.46).

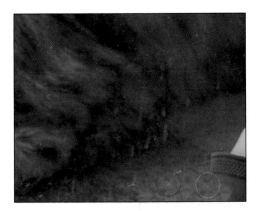

Figure 3.46
Cloning to clean a corner.

The next step was to clean the glass. There are a few ways to remove glass smudges. First, try the Scratch Remover. In this case, it did a pretty good job of removing the linear smudge. I kept the strokes short and the width wide to try and hide the blending (see Figure 3.47).

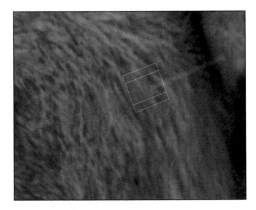

Figure 3.47
Trying Scratch Remover.

If that doesn't work (or you think you can do better manually), switch to the Clone brush. Figure 3.48 shows the difference.

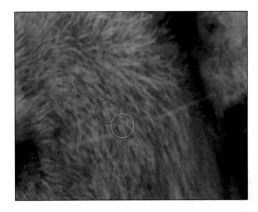

Figure 3.48
Cloning gives you total authority.

You can use the Clone brush on the other smudges or switch to the Blemish Fixer to zap the specks (see Figure 3.49).

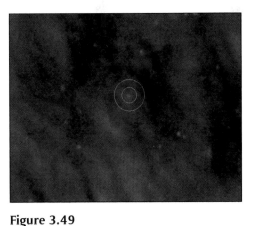

Figure 3.49
I love zapping blemishes.

Fixing the Exposure Problem

What you should have now is a clean photo. It shouldn't have scratches, smudges, specks, reflections, or other distractions. If you didn't want to mess with the light, you could quit here. I do want to mess with it, however, because this photo has a very bright background and a slightly dark foreground. If there is a way to tone the background down to blend in with the rest of the photo while doing the opposite with the foreground, I want to pursue it.

The method I used was to create different adjustments on different layers and use a mask to selectively blend the two together. Doing this allows you to darken the brighter areas on one layer and brighten the darker areas on a separate layer. When you're done, perform a merged copy to combine the two.

The Foreground

To fix the foreground, I created two duplicate working layers and then applied a Levels adjustment, as shown in Figure 3.50, to the bottom layer (after hiding the top layer). My goal here was to make the hyena look as good as possible while ignoring the background. In this case, the contrast and brightness were both improved.

Notice that the histogram doesn't really look out of whack. That makes your analysis of the photo important since the histogram doesn't always give you an easy answer. You can spin your wheels if you spend too much time trying to make the histogram look "right" or miss an important adjustment if you think the graph (as opposed to the photo) looks pretty.

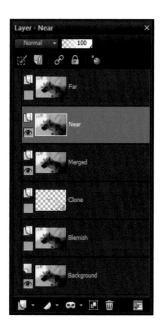

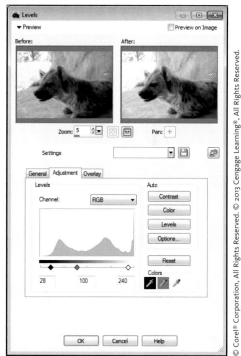

Figure 3.50
Making an initial Levels adjustment.

This adjustment took place on the bottom working layer, reserved for the foreground. The upper working layer will have the background adjustment and will have the foreground masked out.

Now for a twist. This didn't look bad, but it didn't really interest me. That happens sometimes when you're retouching a photo. Don't lock yourself into a specific solution and refuse to change. Remember, this is about making the photo look the way you want it to. That involves a combination of accentuating positives, removing negatives, and boosting or reducing realism or artistry. It doesn't involve using Levels or Curves or any particular adjustment.

I wanted more contrast, so I decided to give Local Tone Mapping a try. I created another foreground working layer called *Near + LTM* and hid the near layer I had just performed the Levels adjustment on, just in case I wanted to go back to it. I then opened up the Local Tone Mapping dialog box, as shown in Figure 3.51, and experimented with the strength to get more contrast.

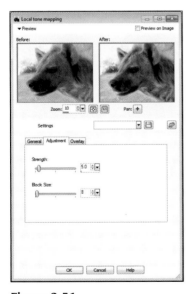

Figure 3.51
Local Tone Mapping adds pizzazz.

The Background

Fixing backgrounds like this is a two-step process. First, create a mask layer grouped with your top working layer and mask out everything but the bright corner (see Figure 3.52).

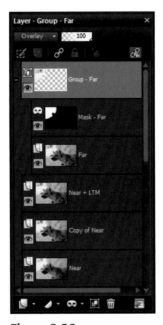

Figure 3.52
The Layers palette showing the mask.

Next, select the photo layer within the group and darken it, as shown in Figure 3.53. This makes the bright corner darker. After this, adjust the strength of the background by lowering the opacity of the layer group it's in.

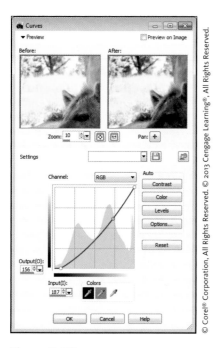

Figure 3.53
Darkening the background.

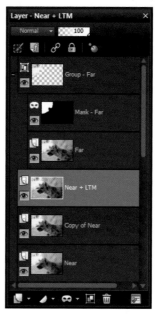

Figure 3.54
*Layer ordering and masking enables
you to make sophisticated adjustments.*

In the end, you're left with a layer (or layer group, as in this case) devoted to improving the background of the photo and a layer (or group) that improves the foreground. Figure 3.54 shows the Layers palette with the foreground layer, called Near + LTM, selected. This layer shows through the mask of the layer group named Group – Far.

Finishing the Photo Study

In the end, I made a slight Vibrancy enhancement to make the color of the hyena stand out. Although I wanted to sharpen the image, doing so exaggerated blemishes from the glass I couldn't quite remove. I would have used noise reduction to smooth them, but that took too much texture away from the hyena and the rock. So, that's it. Figure 3.55 shows the result.

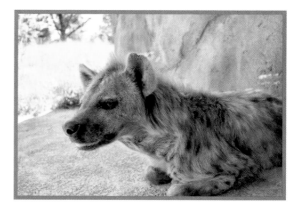

Figure 3.55
Retouched to look au naturale.

Photo Study 7: Taming Highlights

FIGURE 3.56 IS A SHOT from 2010 of my oldest son, Ben, outside playing around as I took his photo. It's a charming shot, but there are some problems with it. Namely, his face is partially in shadow and the house behind him is pretty bright.

The problem is that JPEGs aren't very forgiving when you're working with brightness issues. When you try to darken something that is very bright, you often end up with featureless gray. The details that should have been there aren't. On the other hand, trying to brighten dark pixels in JPEG photos often brings out noise or makes it obvious that someone has been retouching the photo.

You can try your best with JPEG photos, of course. You may have no choice. However, if you have a camera that shoots RAW photos and have set the camera up to use them (I always save both the RAW and JPEG files), you have more options.

Using Highlight Recovery

In this case, I want to use this photo to illustrate how the Highlight recovery routine works in the Camera RAW Lab. It will tone down the bright background and bring out details that are hidden in the JPEG. I don't want to do too much in the Camera RAW Lab, however. In fact, I will use Highlight recovery and nothing else. The photo will be finished in the Edit workspace.

Figure 3.57 shows the RAW photo loaded into the Camera RAW Lab with the default settings. The photo looks good, but the house is too bright. Notice how the yellow bucket sitting on the small picnic table is blown out.

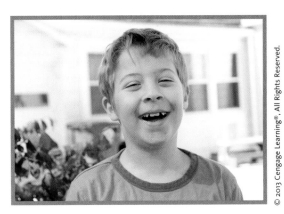

Figure 3.56
The house behind Ben is pretty bright.

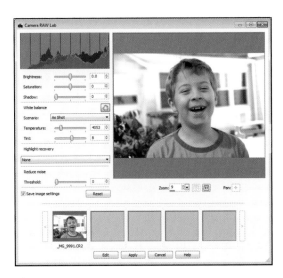

Figure 3.57
The Camera RAW Lab with default settings.

Figure 3.58 shows the Normal setting. The lighting in the background has been toned down quite a bit. The problem with this one is that Ben is too dark. If I were to use this approach, I would have to brighten him up later.

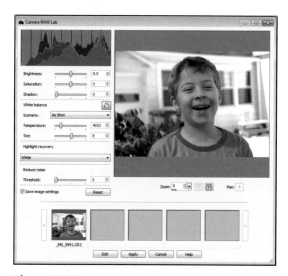

Figure 3.59
Highlight recovery set to White.

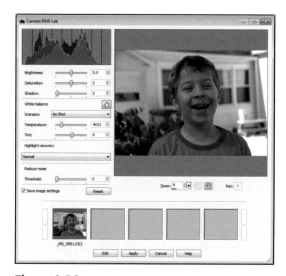

Figure 3.58
Normal Highlight recovery.

Figure 3.59 shows the White setting. This is my favorite for this photo. The background is, on the whole, not too bright, and Ben looks reasonably good. I can fix all these problems without too much hassle.

Figure 3.60 shows the Balanced setting. It is close to Normal, but a bit darker. The picnic table looks good, but remember, it isn't the subject of the photo. Use things like this, though, to measure the effectiveness of different settings.

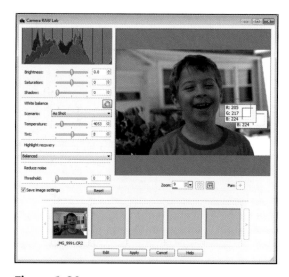

Figure 3.60
Balanced Highlight recovery does well, but is dark.

Figure 3.61 shows the Color setting. It is almost identical to Balanced. The yellow bucket looks best in this version, but Ben and the house are too dark. What you could do is process this version and use it just for the bucket. Make sure to mask everything else out of this layer if you do that.

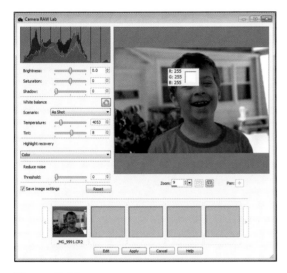

Figure 3.61
Color Highlight recovery protects bright colors best.

You can make other changes to the settings in the Camera RAW Lab, but I found that for this example, using the lab to recover highlights and then fixing the other exposure problems in the Edit workspace gave me the best results. In other words, I was interested in recovering the highlights first and then fixing the other problems, rather than trying to do it all at once.

When finished, press Apply to save the RAW file or Edit to open it in PaintShop Pro. I prefer the latter, which I immediately save as a .pspimage before continuing to work with the photo.

Moving to the Edit Workspace

Once you're in the Edit workspace, treat the photo as a standard retouching job. In this case, I needed to brighten Ben without blowing out the background, improve the contrast, color balance, and throw in the yellow bucket using the Color setting from earlier.

Remember, when combining areas from different photos, or using different settings for different areas, that you can mask what you don't need out of the photo. You don't have to erase. Figure 3.62 shows the mask group. Note that the Group contains a Mask layer and the Photo layer I pasted in from applying the Color Highlight recovery setting. I've masked out everything but the bucket so it is the only thing that shows, and I lowered the Group's opacity to help it blend in better with the layer below. The Group is above the master photo background, which was brought into PaintShop Pro using the Camera RAW Lab.

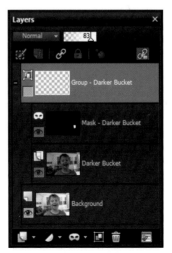

Figure 3.62
Using a different recovery and masking in the bucket.

I used three adjustment layers to fix the exposure problems in the photo. Figure 3.63 shows the Levels layer. I wanted to darken the blacks in the photo and tweak the contrast a small amount with this adjustment, knowing I would continue to brighten Ben next. It may be hard to see it in this figure, but compare the dark red of the bush and the shadows on the window. They are darker in the After window.

When they are lighter, the contrast suffers. Notice also that I used the adjustment layer as a mask. I simply erased on the adjustment layer around Ben (you can also paint with black on the adjustment layer instead) to hide this area of the photo and prevent the adjustment from taking place. In the end, I also decreased the layer's opacity to 75 to blend it in better.

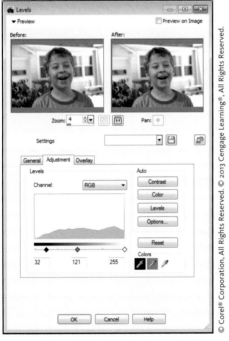

Figure 3.63
Darkening shadows to improve the low end of the spectrum.

Next, I used a Brightness/Contrast adjustment layer to brighten Ben. I also had to increase the contrast, as shown in Figure 3.64. This often happens. When you increase brightness, be prepared to increase contrast. This is due to the fact that you're brightening the dark pixels in the photo.

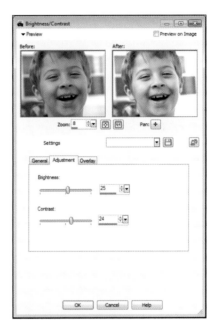

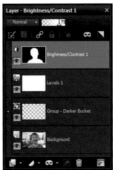

Figure 3.64
Brightening and adding contrast to Ben only.

After this, I corrected a slight color cast in the photo by using a White Balance (formerly Color Balance) adjustment layer. Figure 3.65 shows the dialog box. I have taken some Red and Yellow out of the highlights by adding in Cyan and Blue. Notice that the house in the background looks whiter as a result.

Finishing the Photo Study

When the exposure and color cast were fixed, I whitened Ben's teeth a small amount, sharpened the photo, and then removed a tiny bit of noise. The end result, as shown in Figure 3.66, is vastly improved from the original. Ben is brighter, while the house in the background was kept from blowing out. Using Highlight recovery in the Camera RAW Lab helped tremendously.

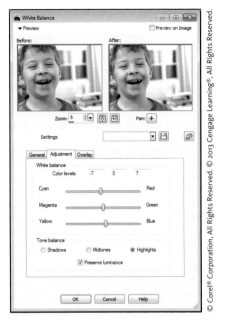

Figure 3.65
Taking some of the reds and yellows out of the photo to balance the color.

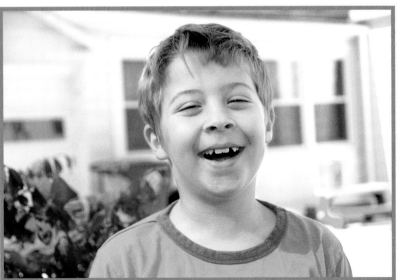

Figure 3.66
The photo almost feels three-dimensional now.

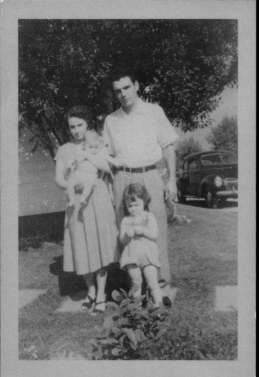

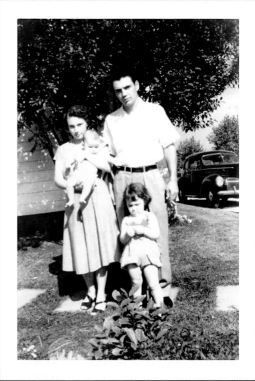

Solving Color Problems

THE SUBJECT AT HAND IS COLOR CORRECTION. That can include older photos (even black-and-white ones) that have aged, yellowed, or were not vibrant to start with. It can also include newer digital photos that have color problems. Digital cameras, in and of themselves, don't guarantee a good photo or good color. This is because the camera has to guess at the color temperature (which is based on the type of lighting) of the scene—and sometimes it gets it wrong. Although color problems may appear to be insurmountable, you can do a lot to correct them—probably more than you realize. Learn how to correct many color problems by following along with these seven photo studies:

▶ **Photo Study 8: Adding Color and Vibrance**—I didn't think there was much wrong with this scanned photo until I opened it in PaintShop Pro and started experimenting with different techniques to remove the minor imperfections. It became apparent, though, that the photo needed a color transfusion.

▶ **Photo Study 9: Improving Muted Colors**—Learn about color saturation and vibrance in this photo study featuring my dad's 1968 Pontiac Firebird.

▶ **Photo Study 10: Dealing with Oversaturated Colors**—In this photo, the colors are too strong (still a saturation problem, but the opposite of too little). So strong they almost hurt your eyes! Learn how to turn down color "brightness" in this study.

▶ **Photo Study 11: Restoring Photos Yellowed with Age**—Yellowing is a very common problem with older photos, even if they have been stored properly. Air and the oil from hands react with prints and cause them to chemically age. Learn how to restore yellow photos and make them look close to new in this study.

▶ **Photo Study 12: Cooling a Warm Photo**—Digital photos aren't immune to color problems. Learn how to subtract specific shades of color out of a photo and enhance what's left.

 ▶ **Photo Study 13: Warming a Cool Photo**—There is too much blue in the photo, resulting in a "cool" appearance. Learn how to warm photos by taking out excess blue.

 ▶ **Photo Study 14: Working with White Balance**—When you work with RAW exposures, you have the option of tackling color temperature (also known as *white balance*) as you process the RAW files in the Camera RAW Lab. Learn how in this photo study of my daughter playing.

Photo Study 8: Adding Color and Vibrance

IF YOU GET A CHANCE TO TAKE a business trip to Hawaii, do it. I was in the U.S. Air Force in the mid-1990s, assigned to the Intelligence Plans office within the Intelligence Directorate of Headquarters, Air Mobility Command.

Planning is a huge function of any military, and in this phase of my career, I was heavily involved in ongoing contingency operation planning and execution (ah yes, the jargon comes back to me). I was attending a planning conference that was held in Hawaii.

Still with me? That's how I came to be standing on the rim of Diamond Head volcano sometime in 1994 or 1995, on the island of Oahu, looking down on Waikiki and Honolulu, taking the photo you see in Figure 4.1.

Enhancing the Photo

Since this photo seemed like it was basically in good shape, I decided to start by cloning out the specks and dust. Even the best photo will have some of these imperfections if you have to scan it in.

Start at a pretty high magnification (200%) and slowly work your way around the photo in a search pattern, diligently looking for dust and scratches to clone out. Figure 4.2 illustrates my progress. There were quite a few light specks in the darker hills that needed to be removed.

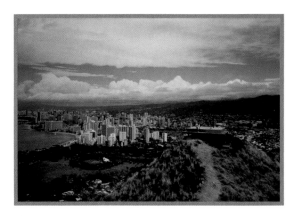

Figure 4.1
Sightseeing on the island of Oahu.
© 2013 Cengage Learning®, All Rights Reserved.

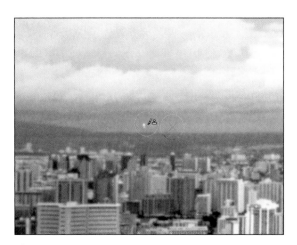

Figure 4.2
Cloning away specks.
© Corel® Corporation, All Rights Reserved. © 2013 Cengage Learning®, All Rights Reserved.

Next, I decided to correct the color problem. This photo is too warm. It needs more blue to correct the overly yellow cast on the buildings in the background and sky. One way to correct this is to open the White Balance command (Adjust ❯ White Balance). Select Advanced Options if you want more control over the color than simply "Cooler" or "Warmer." I prefer this route when there's something I want to click on in the photo to establish a white point (a point that you identify in the photo that should be white). That something, in this case, was a building in Waikiki. Notice in Figure 4.3 that the buildings in the After preview window are whiter.

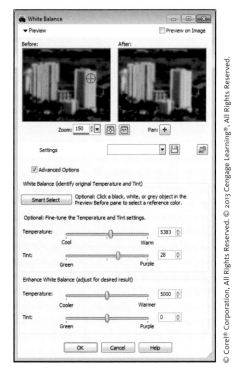

Figure 4.3
Selecting a building to turn white.

Following this, the photo appeared to need more definition (detail and focus). One way of enhancing how objects stand out is to increase Clarity. In this case, I created a Fill Light/Clarity adjustment layer and increased both controls. This had the desired effect, as shown in Figure 4.4.

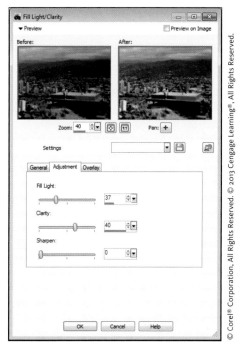

Figure 4.4
Clarifying the photo.

Despite adding Fill Light, the photo still needed brightening. Therefore, I created a Levels adjustment layer (see Figure 4.5) and pulled down the white diamond slider to brighten the photo. The effect is subtle, but helpful. Pay particular attention to clouds whenever you have the chance. Normal clouds (not the dark, threatening kind) are good indicators of color and brightness.

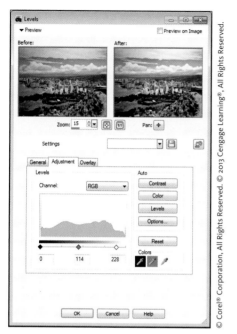

Figure 4.5
Brightening slightly.

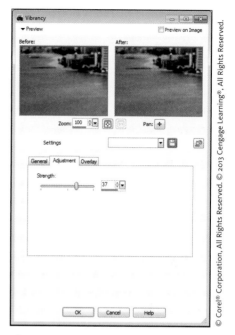

Figure 4.6
Strengthening color.

After this, the colors looked a bit muted. I created a Vibrancy adjustment layer to increase the photo's color saturation, as shown in Figure 4.6. Notice that the water looks very nice and blue now.

Next, I was struck by the fact that the photo looked grainy. I spent some time investigating different techniques. After going back and forth, I settled on One Step Noise Removal. The result looked great from a distance and produced the best sky. I did lose some details in the buildings, however.

There are a few ways to decide how much noise to remove. First, you can accept more noise in the photo than you want. Sometimes, photo restoration is like that. Second, you can apply different levels of noise reduction to different parts of the photo.

For instance, I could duplicate the working layer and apply heavy noise reduction to the duplicate layer and less noise reduction to the working layer and then selectively blend areas of the two together using masks or the Eraser. That way, I could smooth the clouds and sea and keep the foreground and buildings relatively well defined. Third, you can make the artistic decision to smooth away the noise and not worry about losing the details.

In this case, I chose the latter approach: a good deal of noise reduction to make the photo appear smoother, as shown in Figure 4.7. It made me feel like I was looking at a nice picture postcard.

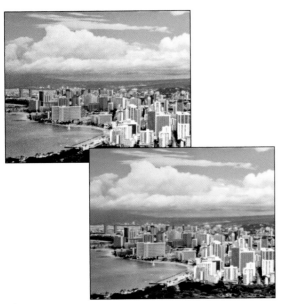

Finishing the Photo Study

Figure 4.8 shows the final result (after adding a bit of detail back in with Unsharp Mask). This photo had more problems than I realized at first, which happens a good percentage of the time. You'll look at a photo, think there's nothing wrong with it, load it into PaintShop Pro, and after fixing or adjusting five or six things, realize how much better it is now. Not bad for a 15-year-old photo taken from a disposable film camera.

That's the point of this chapter. Exactly!

Figure 4.7
Before versus After noise reduction.

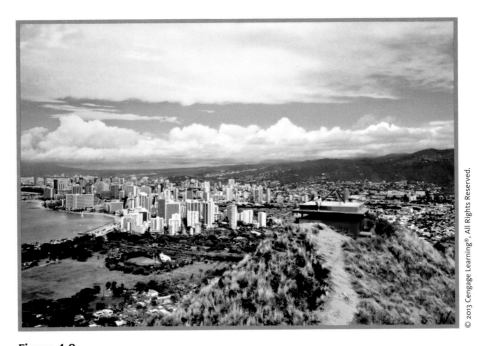

Figure 4.8
The final version is much better.

Photo Study 9: Improving Muted Colors

MY DAD BOUGHT THIS 1968 FIREBIRD (see Figure 4.9) when I was very young, and this is one of the few pictures I have of it. The energy crunch of the early 70s made it impractical to have, so he got rid of it in favor of something that had better gas mileage. I've always loved the red stripe on the tires and the car's green color.

This picture looks pretty good in person (scanning has a way of bringing out a photo's flaws), but it needs some sprucing up. The years have taken away some of the original luster, and it is a little out of focus. Being a physical print taken from a film camera and scanned into the computer, there are also specks and physical imperfections that need to be cleaned up.

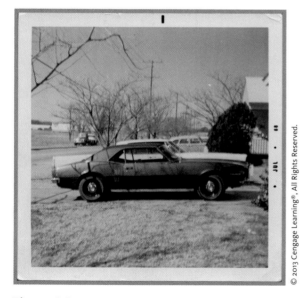

Figure 4.9
Muted muscle car.

Examining the Options

In this photo study, you have a photo whose colors are basically correct (for example, the blues are blue, and the greens are green), but they aren't strong enough. As with many aspects of photo retouching, you have several different options to choose from when trying to decide how to make the photo more vibrant.

One Step Photo Fix

Here we go. One Step Photo Fix. Figure 4.10 shows the result.

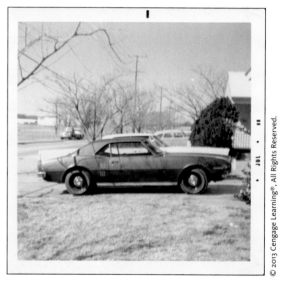

Figure 4.10
Fast One Step Photo Fix.

If this were all I had time to do, I would be pretty happy. It lightened things up and helped with the contrast.

Smart Photo Fix

Figure 4.11 reveals the trusty Smart Photo Fix in action. I've taken care to select objects in the left-hand panel that are black, white, and gray in order to get the right color balance, and in this case it worked well. The colors are brighter and closer to what they should be (although the green is a bit too bright). I'm going to keep looking for a better solution than this, though. If you have to, you can always come back to this and lower the saturation a bit.

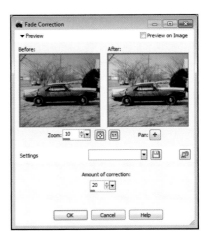

Figure 4.12
Fade Correction works very well here.

The thing I like most about how Fade Correction worked in this instance is that it removed the fade without compromising the colors. They still look natural, and their hue wasn't changed. However, I would like to see them more vibrant.

Vibrancy Versus Saturation

Here's the point of the whole study: boosting the color intensity. Saturation is the traditional setting. Boost it when you want stronger colors. Figure 4.13 shows a moderate increase in saturation. The car, sky, and grass all look more colorful, but, there is still a color cast to the photo. It's best to correct that before boosting existing colors.

Since X3, there is another setting that boosts color intensity: Vibrancy (see Figure 4.14). Choose Adjust ❯ Hue and Saturation ❯ Vibrancy to see the effect. There's only one setting: Strength. More is more and less is less. It doesn't get much easier than that. Whereas Saturation increases the color intensity of the entire image (or select hues), Vibrancy is supposed to boost only the least saturated areas. In other words, it turns up the colors that are weak while leaving the ones that are strong alone.

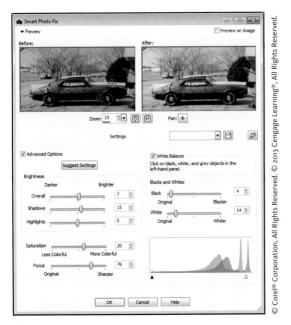

Figure 4.11
Smart Photo is normally very dependable.

Fade Correction

Figure 4.12 shows what a Fade Correction of 20 would look like. The fade, seemingly imperceptible until you remove it, is gone, and the colors look brighter. They aren't so bright that they look artificial either, as compared to the last figure.

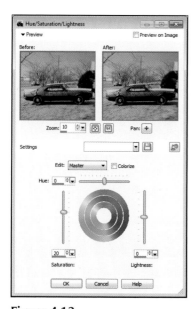

Figure 4.13

Saturation boosts all color intensities.

In this case, there isn't much difference. You could probably adjust either Saturation *or* Vibrancy and be fine with an image like this. (Despite how it performs here, Vibrancy is still a cool feature.)

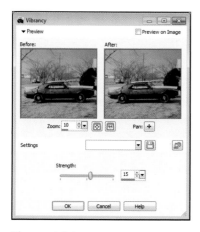

Figure 4.14

Vibrancy boosts muted colors.

Finishing the Photo Study

When all is said and done, I used Fade Correction, then Vibrancy, reduced some noise, and finished with a round of sharpening using Unsharp Mask. Figure 4.15 shows the final image. As you look at it, you realize, of course, that I based my evaluation on a before/after paradigm rather than a "Is it perfect in every way?" matrix. It looks better—quite a bit better, even though there are still flaws. That's what I'm after.

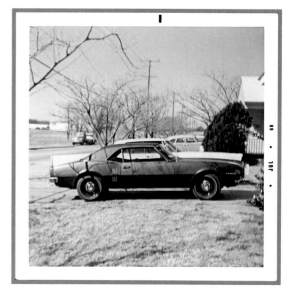

Figure 4.15

This was a great car.

Photo Study 10: Dealing with Oversaturated Colors

FIGURE 4.16 CAPTURES one of my wife's happiest childhood moments. It was Christmas of 1982 at her Grandma Jo's house, and she had just opened her last present. It was a Cabbage Patch doll.

They could hear her screams of glee in the next county. You see, everyone wanted a Cabbage Patch doll that year, and you had to be on a waiting list to even get one. There were fights in stores over these dolls because they were such a hot commodity. In fact, Anne didn't even ask for a Cabbage Patch doll because she knew they were expensive and she didn't think there was a chance of getting it. But miracles do happen.

Her Grandma Jo (she's in several of the photo studies in this book) was able to buy one through a friend who had some extras. Thus, Lyndon Jock came into the family. He had a weird name (part of the appeal, Anne tells me), a birth certificate, and adoption papers. Anne called him Josh, and said he was quite popular. She was the only one in her circle of friends to have a boy Cabbage Patch doll, so Josh got to be the "boyfriend" to all of her friends' dolls. Josh later got a "sister" Cabbage Patch doll named Emmy Aggy.

The photo that immortalizes this event is overly saturated with color. Although extreme oversaturation can irretrievably damage parts of the photo, there are ways to tone these problems down.

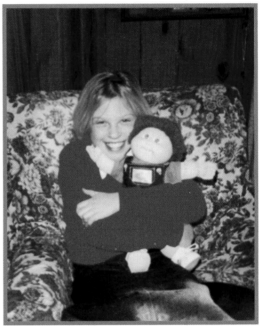

Figure 4.16
Anne with her doll, glowing with color.

Desaturation Options

There are some tough calls to make with this photo. Anne's sweater, for example, is a meltdown of saturation. There's not a lot of detail in it. Lowering its saturation will lessen the pain, but won't make the photo as a whole look much better.

In cases like this, focus on something in the photo that is recognizable so that you can tell if it's better or worse. In this photo, there are several areas that qualify: Anne's face, the couch, the doll, and the wall. When these four elements are in harmony and not overly saturated, the photo will be better.

Using the Histogram Adjustment

Figure 4.17 shows the first step in adjusting the photo's histogram. There's a lot of bright red in the photo, with a couple of prominent peaks. I've brought the Low and High sliders in to match the range of the red in this photo and darkened it a bit by sliding the Gamma downward.

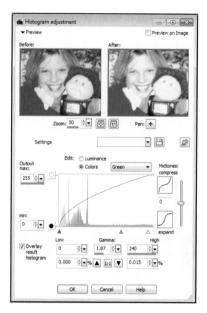

Figure 4.18
A little green.

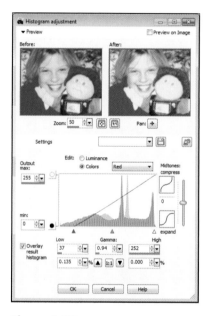

Figure 4.17
Too much red.

There's not much I can do with green, as Figure 4.18 shows. I can bring the High slider down and brighten the green by raising the Gamma slider. Blue has the same problem as green in this photo, as seen in Figure 4.19. It's pretty nonexistent! The same solution applies here.

The overall result of adjusting each color channel in the Histogram Adjustment dialog box is mixed. The couch and Anne looked marginally better, but I wasn't happy with the wall or the contrast.

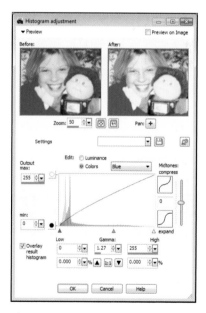

Figure 4.19
Some blue.

Vibrancy

Vibrancy is another color desaturation option. I have entered a setting of -45 in Figure 4.20, which does a good job. Compare that to the next figure, where I lower the overall Saturation by almost the same amount. Vibrancy appears to desaturate this photo more than Saturation (in Figure 4.21). The difference can best be seen in her sweater.

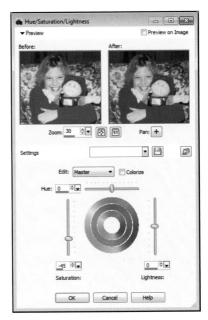

Figure 4.21
Desaturating all channels equally.

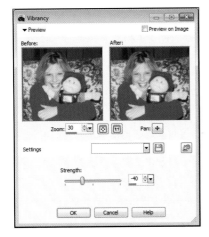

Figure 4.20
Reducing the photo's Vibrancy.

Adjusting Hue/Saturation/Lightness

Next, I tried altering the saturation via the Hue/Saturation/Lightness dialog box. I've desaturated by 45 (which is to say, the Saturation setting is at -45) in Figure 4.21. At first, I thought this took too much life out of the photo, but grew to like it.

I want to try one more thing.

I made the adjustment shown in Figure 4.21 on all the channels. You can tell because the Edit drop-down light is set to Master. However, you can select different colors to edit from this list: Reds, Yellows, Greens, Cyans, Blues, and Magentas. What happens if you select the most offending colors from this list and turn them down? Figure 4.22 shows the answer.

The final settings were Reds: –45 (the main problem), Yellows: –20 (brings down the couch a bit), Greens: 0, Cyans: –20 (keeps Josh's shirt under control), Blues: 0, and Magentas: –10 (to make Anne's denim skirt bluer).

Finishing the Photo Study

To finish the study, I used Curves to push the tonality of Anne's skirt toward truer denim, and then I applied a very light amount of noise reduction, followed by light sharpening using Unsharp Mask. I cloned away the blemishes and called it a day.

Figure 4.23 shows the final product. Oversaturated photos often lose details that can never be recovered. Anne's sweater is devoid of detail in the original. With the exception of the shadow of her lower arm and the cuff of her upper wrist, it looked like a red blob of color. Although the saturation has been improved dramatically, the lost details are still lost. Despite this, the restored photo looks far better and was well worth the effort. You can see the details of Anne's face without being blinded by red, and the overall photo looks much more natural. Mission accomplished.

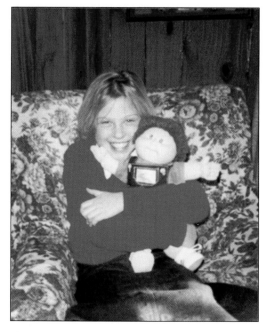

Figure 4.22

Selective desaturation is a winner here.

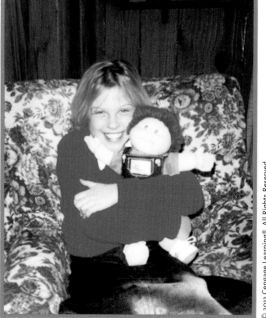

Figure 4.23

Now that's much better.

Photo Study 11: Restoring Photos Yellowed with Age

THIS IS A CLASSIC POST-WAR (World War II) photo taken sometime in July or August of 1949. It's of my mother-in-law's (Mary Anne) family. Her mother is holding her in this photo. Her dad, Bud, was a tenant farmer at the time. He had fought in World War II as an artilleryman and had come home afterward, gotten married, and started a family.

There's an odd twist to this picture (Figure 4.24). It's somewhat rare to have a casual family photo in color from this time period. It took me a while to realize this was 1949 because most of the family photos we have from this time and well into the 1950s are in black and white. Mary Anne says that the camera probably belonged to her grandmother and grandfather (the parents of the woman, Louise, in the photo).

This picture presents us with a classic case of aging and yellowing.

Deciding How

Remember, you should try several techniques on troublesome photos to find the right solution. Which one looks best will depend on each photo, your skill at using the tools, and what day of the week it is. (On Saturdays, don't even try Fade Correction.)

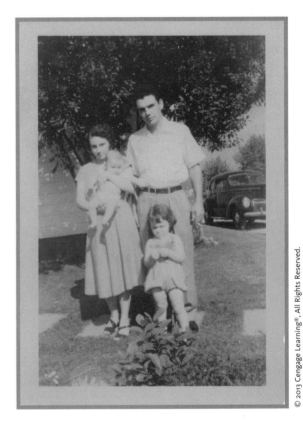

Figure 4.24
Classic Americana, but can it be rescued?

Smart Photo Fix

Figure 4.25 shows the Smart Photo Fix dialog box. It's a pretty good technique to use here. The aged yellow tint is gone, and the photo looks nice. I've chosen spot colors, but you can't see them in the Preview window. Clicking on them (and trying different points in the photo) is crucial to getting the right color balance out of Smart Photo Fix.

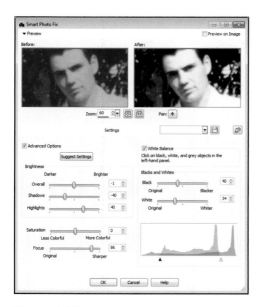

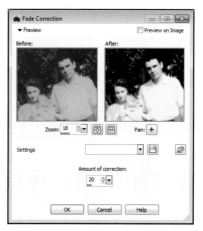

Figure 4.26

Fade Correction results in a greenish cast.

Figure 4.25

Choose spot colors for best results.

I'm not going to use this solution, even though it's pretty good. It looks too washed out. I could lower some of the settings in this dialog box to try and correct that, but then again, those settings are part of why it looks as good as it does.

Fade Correction

Fade Correction is shown in Figure 4.26. The yellow is gone, only to be replaced by green. To be fair, I didn't have to apply a ton of correction to this photo to take the yellow out. Thankfully so, because the green problem got worse the more Fade Correction I applied.

This may be something I can work with. To see, I'm going to use the results of Fade Correction and continue to alter the RGB percentages to see if I can get rid of the green. Figure 4.27 shows the Red/Green/Blue dialog box in action.

I left the Red percentage alone, cut Green, and added Blue. I'm happy with the result of this two-stage process. Notice Bud's shirt and Louise's dress. Bud's shirt is now bright and white, and Louise's dress is blue.

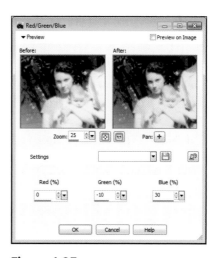

Figure 4.27

Taking the green out.

Histogram Adjustment

Finally, there is Histogram Adjustment. Make sure to press the Colors radio button and switch between the three channels if you want to work with color. I am working on the Green channel in Figure 4.28.

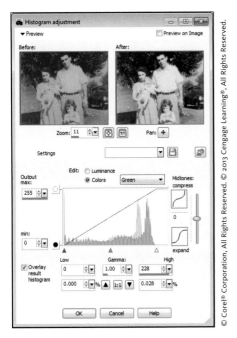

Figure 4.28
Adjusting each Histogram Color channel.

The final result for this technique is very good. It's better than the combination of Fade Correction and RGB and causes no other problems. The Red channel had most of the reds in the upper-mid range.

I simply dragged the Low and High sliders to match the range and tweaked the gamma to make it look good. The Green channel didn't have many highs, having mostly mid-range and dark tones. I performed the same operation on it as I did the reds. I lowered the High slider on the Blue channel and raised the gamma to bring up the midtones.

However, the overall appearance was still too green. I decided to correct that with a White Balance adjustment layer. I took out green and yellow in all three tonal regions (see Figure 4.29). Notice that the car and grass on the right side of the photo have a definite green tint to them in the Before window but it is gone in the After window.

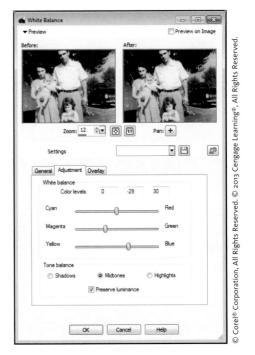

Figure 4.29
Final color tweak.

Finishing the Photo Study

The final, finished restoration for this photo is shown in Figure 4.30. The color problems are (mostly) gone, and I spruced up the rest of the photo.

In this case, fully restoring the photo took a lot of work. The color problem was actually the easiest, least time-consuming part of the restoration. (I used the Histogram Adjustment.) Afterward, I improved the contrast and then did a lot of cloning to remove specks and scratches. I took some noise out and improved contrast; then I cloned some more as a final touch-up (to catch problems not fixed or revealed by my prior efforts). The last things I did were to brighten and sharpen the photo and then clean up the border.

Before moving on, I would like to discuss the "before" and "after" comparison briefly. I sometimes get caught up in wanting to restore the photo so that it looks "perfect." Well, that isn't possible most of the time. You could spend a year working on some of these photos and when you are finished, they still wouldn't be perfect. A lot of that has to do with the original photo. Was it in focus? Was there a lot of noise? Was it developed correctly? Did it have the right exposure?

Always compare the "after" shot to the "before" shot, and if it's better, you've done your job. If it's worse, or you can tell there's been an excessive amount of retouching, then you should go back to the drawing board.

For this particular study, the end result looks a lot better, but it's not perfect. There is an odd color cast to it, the right side of the photo (a vertical swath that is aligned with the grille of the car) had some problems when it was developed, and it's just not quite in focus. But it's better than it was, and that's saying a lot.

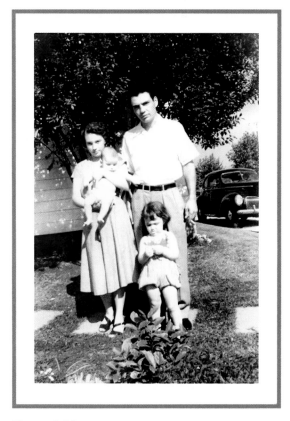

Figure 4.30
Aging process successfully reversed.

Photo Study 12: Cooling a Warm Photo

FIGURE 4.31 IS A PHOTO of my daughter Grace being held by her grandmother. This photo is marred by the fact that it is really yellow. The scene is dominated by yellows and browns, which were picked up by the camera. It makes everything look too yellow. Another way of describing it is to say that this photo is too "warm" and that it has a color balance problem.

Thankfully, here are several ways to alter the color balance of a photo in PaintShop Pro.

Technique Smorgasbord

For our purposes, color has three components, and I want to talk about each one briefly:

▶ **Hue**: The perceived color, which for computer graphics (including digital photos), is traditionally a mixture of red, green, and blue values. The strength of each RGB component (from none, or 0, to full, or 255) determines the overall color. In the context of an RGB triplet, pure red would be written as 255,0,0. Hue also exists in different color spaces, such as HSL, which stands for hue, saturation, and lightness. In this context, hue is a continuous wheel of color ranging from red to yellow, through green and blue, to purple, and then back to red. Think of hue as the color, with different ways to measure and change it.

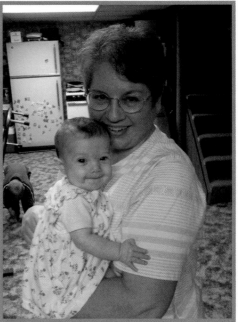

Figure 4.31
Grace and her grandmother.

▶ **Saturation**: The balance between the color itself and gray. A totally saturated color would be pure, such as pure blue, with no gray in it. Think "vibrancy." Blue with a lot of gray in it is muted by comparison. We can saturate (take gray out) or desaturate (put gray in) photos. Saturation is also related to contrast. The more gray a photo has, the less contrast it will appear to have. Ever go driving on a foggy day?

▶ **Lightness**: The balance of the color with white or black. This is pretty intuitive. Dark green has more black in it than light green.

As you look at the different photo studies, think in terms of RGB or HSL in order to come to a conclusion on how to fix the problem. Too little vibrancy? That's a saturation problem. Too dark? That's a lightness problem. Too blue? That's an RGB issue. Are the greens red and the blues yellow? There's something wrong with the hue.

There are several ways to turn colors up and down in PaintShop Pro, and there are a lot of ways to push colors from one hue toward another and add or subtract the amount of gray present. I will show you several techniques as I restore this photo.

Camera RAW Lab

You have the option of opening RAW-format digital photos in the Camera RAW Lab. (Check the General tab in File Format Preferences to make sure it's turned on.) The problem with this photo is that it was shot with an old, compact digital camera that didn't support RAW, so it's a JPEG file.

One Step Photo Fix

There's little to say here. I often give One Step Photo Fix a try, and sometimes it works. Figure 4.32 shows the result for this photo. It didn't correctly identify the hue problem.

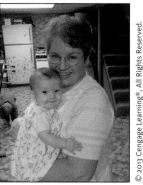

Figure 4.32
One Step Photo Fix doesn't fix this photo.

Smart Photo Fix

Smart Photo Fix, shown in Figure 4.33, is much better. The key with using Smart Photo Fix when you're addressing a color problem is to enable the White Balance check box (formerly known as Color Balance in earlier editions of PaintShop Pro) on the right side of the dialog box and then do what it says. Zoom in on areas in the left preview window and pick out good examples of objects that *should be* black, white, and gray and click on them to give PaintShop Pro good reference points.

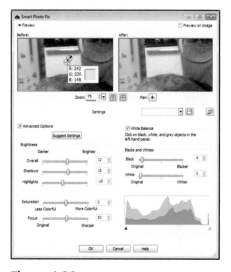

Figure 4.33
Smart Photo Fix is much better—note my color spot.

I was able to find good color spots in this photo. The gas range in the background had black trim around the temperature controls, and the door should be bright white. Manually selecting these points adds your "smarts" to the equation. The "white" spot I am in the process of choosing has a little color swatch come up for us to see, and it reads out the measured RGB value. Nice touch! You can also see that what should be white is very yellow. That's the problem, right there in a nutshell.

White Balance

If you want a faster, easier fix, try White Balance (also formerly known as Color Balance) from the Adjust menu. Figure 4.34 shows the dialog box, which is decidedly simpler than the Smart Photo Fix dialog box. The easiest approach is to leave the Smart White Balance option enabled and drag the Temperature slider back and forth from cooler to warmer until you find the right balance in the preview window or on your image.

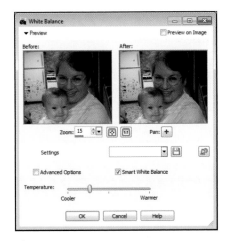

Figure 4.34
Cooling down a photo with White Balance.

This photo has far too much yellowish orange in it, which makes it too "warm." I've drug the Temperature slider toward the Cooler side. It's not bad. You don't get as many options as you do with Smart Photo, but this is often a good place to start. If you're feeling adventurous, select Advanced Options (as in Figure 4.35) and continue to experiment by clicking objects in the Before preview window and fine-tuning the color temperatures and tints yourself.

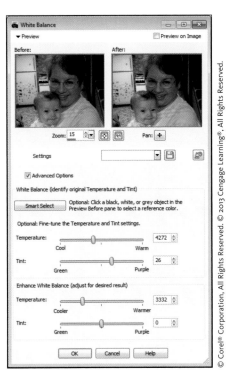

Figure 4.35
Taking advantage of the Advanced Options to fine-tune.

Channel Mixer

Figure 4.36 shows the Channel Mixer. You can open the Channel Mixer from the Adjust > Color menu. This command gives you control over the mixture of color information that goes into each of the three output channels. Normally, each source and destination channel is paired (red to red, green to green, and blue to blue) and operates independently of the others. The Channel Mixer lets you pull color intensity from any of the three source channels and mix it with a different output channel.

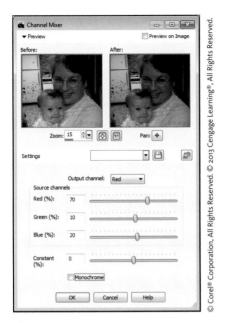

Figure 4.36
Channel Mixer is not for the timid.

Uncheck monochrome for a color photo and then choose an output channel from the top list box. Figure 4.36 shows the Red channel. The main part of the dialog box shows how much the source channel is contributing to the output channel. The default is for each matching source channel to contribute 100 percent to its own output channel. If you work with the matching pairs (and do not add in other source channels), think in terms of saturation. Adding in information from the other color channels mixes up the overall relationship.

The values range from negative 200 percent to positive 200 percent. To maintain the overall brightness of the image, make sure the sum of the values for the three source channels (per output channel) is 100. If not, adjust the Constant setting up or down to compensate for the resulting change in brightness levels. Don't forget to switch to the other channels and adjust them as well.

Fade Correction

Fade Correction, from the Adjust ❯ Color menu, works to restore the proper color balance to a scanned photo print that has aged or faded. Fade Correction often produces good results with digital photos, as shown here. Figure 4.37 shows the dialog box with a preview.

Fade Correction looks good when strongly applied to this photo. You should understand why at this point. (Hint: Old photos often yellow with age.) Increase or decrease the amount of correction to strengthen or weaken the effect.

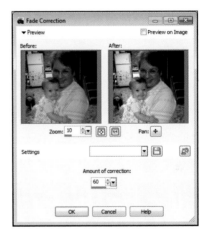

Figure 4.37
Try Fade Correction to reduce yellow.
© Corel® Corporation, All Rights Reserved. © 2013 Cengage Learning®, All Rights Reserved.

Adjusting Red/Green/Blue

Want to adjust the strength of the red, green, and blue component colors? Simply go to the Adjust ❯ Color menu and choose Red/Green/Blue. The Red/Green/Blue dialog box is shown in Figure 4.38.

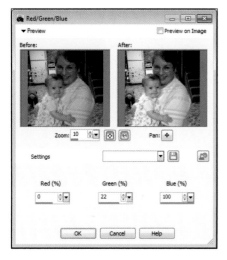

Figure 4.38
Red/Green/Blue is easy and effective.
© Corel® Corporation, All Rights Reserved. © 2013 Cengage Learning®, All Rights Reserved.

Go to the Red, Green, and Blue colors and change them until you get a good balance. You can add or subtract up to 100 percent either way for each color. To use this method, it helps to know a little about color and where specific colors sit on the spectrum. For example, there's no option to turn down yellowish orange, which is what I need to do. Click on the foreground color in your Materials palette and look at the color wheel. Yellow and orange sit between red and green, with orange close to red. That's why I turned up blue a lot and green a little. I was able to counteract the excessive yellowish orange by turning those colors up. I love it when art and science come together!

Making Histogram Adjustments

Histogram Adjustment is back in action here, because it's a useful command with powerful color options. Figure 4.39 shows the Histogram Adjustment dialog box, with the Edit radio button set to Colors and the Red channel displayed. You can use the Histogram Adjustment settings to adjust the histogram of each color component of your photo by selecting the color (red, green, or blue) from the drop-down menu. Look carefully and compare the graphs for each color. You can use Histogram Adjustment to diagnose or repair.

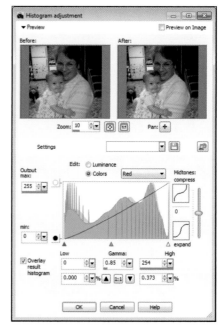

Figure 4.39
Adjusting individual colors can be powerful.
© Corel® Corporation, All Rights Reserved. © 2013 Cengage Learning®, All Rights Reserved.

Red doesn't actually look too bad. I've adjusted the gamma (which is related to brightness and contrast) downward. This has the effect of darkening the red colors.

Figure 4.40 shows the Green channel. This one looks reasonable, so I have not changed it.

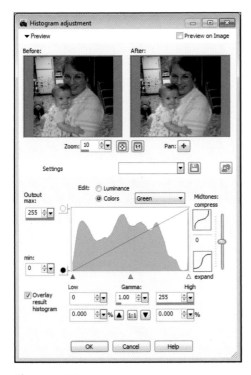

Figure 4.40

Green looks fine in this photo.

Figure 4.41 shows the last channel, Blue. Where is it? It's not really there. There is very little blue in this photo. which is why it looks so "warm" and very yellowish orange. Drag the High slider down to lighten the blues in the photo.

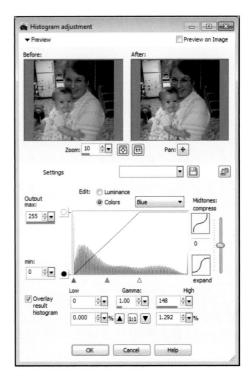

Figure 4.41

An overly warm photo lacks blue.

Finishing the Photo Study

Figure 4.42 shows the final photo. It's amazing what a little bit of color correction can do. The winning technique? Fade Correction.

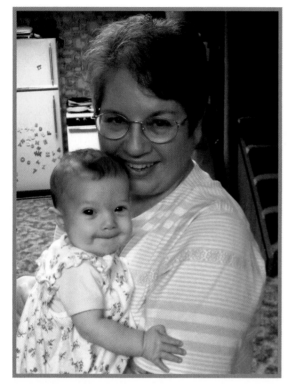

Figure 4.42
Touching photo rescued from yellow fever.
© 2013 Cengage Learning®, All Rights Reserved.

Remember, the finished photo in each study in the book is the result of *more* than what I've been showing you how to do. This is so I can show you the main teaching point but not leave you with a half-finished photo.

To illustrate this fact, consider that I took the following steps to finish this photo:

1. Applied a Fade Correction adjustment from the Adjust menu. This was the main teaching point for this study and did the job of correcting the color imbalance. I wasn't done, though. When working on your photos, you will apply a number of the different techniques, too, ranging from noise reduction to color balancing to contrast adjusting or fixing physical damage, all on one photo.

2. Reduced noise with Digital Noise Removal (30 percent).

3. Followed that up with Skin Smoothing (20 percent).

4. Tried to reduce JPEG artifacts with JPEG Artifact Removal (High).

5. Gently used a Dodge brush to brighten their faces a bit (40 percent opacity, limited to highlights).

6. I tried using a bit of Perspective Correction (look at the lines of the refrigerator), but that made the subjects look wrong. So I straightened the photo a bit and then cropped it to recompose the scene.

7. Sharpened the photo very gently with High Pass Sharpen, which was blended in by lowering that layer's opacity.

In the end, this isn't the sort of photo you could print out poster-sized and get away with it. It wasn't to begin with, though. After being restored, it looks fantastic at normal sizes, which is what I call "mission accomplished."

Photo Study 13: Warming a Cool Photo

FIGURE 4.43 SHOWS THREE of my four children (this was taken two days before Sam, our fourth, was born) sitting on the front porch posing for a group portrait. This digital photo was taken late one afternoon in the winter. It was cold, but it wasn't to the point where they needed their Arctic gear that day. We had Ben and Jake in their fleece jackets, cool sunglasses, and light-up shoes. Gracie was decked out in her pink coat, pink pants, pink boots, and, of course, pink sunglasses. (She has since branched out to master other colors of the rainbow.)

This is probably the sort of photo you have. It's a casual shot of everyday life that's off. The problem is that it's incredibly blue. The kids are cute, but the blue has got to go.

Photo-wise, blue is the opposite of the reddish-yellow colors in the previous photo study. Reds, browns, and yellows (think skin tones) make a photo look warm. Blue makes a photo look cool.

I'm going to run through several different ways to warm this photo up and then decide on a winner.

Technique Trials

I won't go over the color theory again, but I will say this photo has the opposite problem than the previous photo study. There is too much blue instead of too little. The result is a photo dominated by the "cool" hue of light blue.

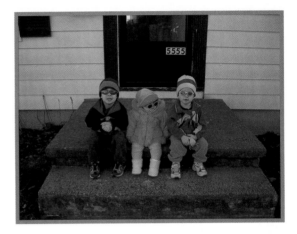

Figure 4.43
Brrrski-brrr.

Color Temperatures

I keep putting the terms "cool" and "warm" in quotes because we use them to describe how we perceive the photo. Unfortunately, these descriptions are backward when compared to the scientific description of color temperature. This is because scientists and engineers got involved and decided to frame the temperature of light in terms of the temperature it would take an idealized body to glow that color. It takes a lot of heat to make that something glow blue, and less to make it glow red, which is the opposite of how we describe the color of the light with our eyes.

Smart Photo Fix

The Smart Photo Fix dialog box is shown in Figure 4.44. This opens up when you choose the Adjust > Smart Photo Fix menu. I've pressed the Suggest Settings button, as I traditionally do, to see where PaintShop Pro leads me. Then I tweak and adjust. I've selected three color balance points in areas of the Preview window you can't see. I've chosen the black of the screen door, the white of the house siding, and the gray of the concrete porch as the color samples Smart Photo Fix will rely on to adjust the white balance. The result is good.

White Balance

Trying to fix the overly blue cast using the White Balance technique, as shown in Figure 4.45, doesn't work too well for this photo. It takes out the blues when I drag the Temperature slider toward the Warmer region, but the result seems lifeless.

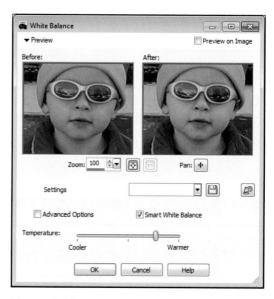

Figure 4.45

A little lifeless.

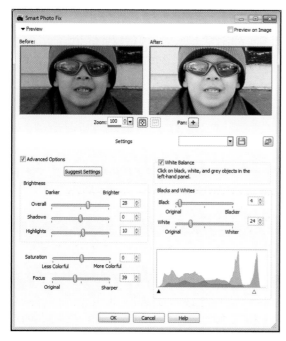

Figure 4.44

Smart Photo Fix rocks.

Channel Mixer

Here again is the Channel Mixer. This time I'm showing (see Figure 4.46) the Blue Output channel. I've increased the Red source a tiny bit, the Green source by a fair amount, and the Blue source a little. I tweaked the other output channels as well. All in all, I wasn't able to get very close to what I wanted.

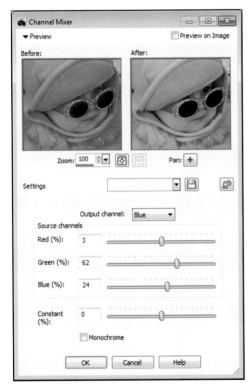

Figure 4.46
Channel Mixer doesn't work well for this photo.

Fade Correction

In the last photo, I showed you that Fade Correction could restore a yellow, faded photo. Figure 4.47 reveals that it has a certain degree of effectiveness here, too. Remember to keep trying alternative methods. If it doesn't work well for one photo, it might work for the next.

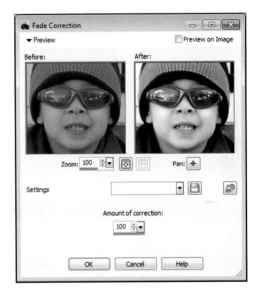

Figure 4.47
A little too much contrast.

I like what Fade Correction has done, but the result has a little too much contrast in it. I want to enhance the contrast in the final photo, but I will use a method to boost contrast that will give me greater control than this.

Adjusting Red/Green/Blue

Adjusting each component channel is the forte of Red/Green/Blue. You would think this might be the perfect solution for this problem. Too much blue? Just turn it down. I've added a lot of red (remember, adding the other components can be as effective as turning the offending one down), some green, and taken some blue out in Figure 4.48.

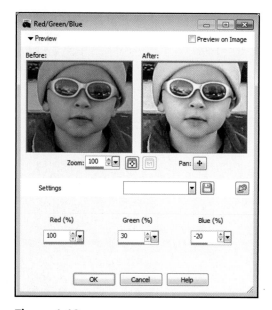

Figure 4.48

Good, but not vibrant enough.

It's not bad, but this too lacks a degree of vibrancy, which indicates a saturation problem. Can you tell what I'm doing as I go along? I'm trying to fix the problem, yes, but I'm also investigating. Contrast and saturation are on my list of things to look into after color.

Adjusting Curves

I'm going to throw you a curve ball in this study and bring back Curves. The Curves dialog box with the Red channel active is shown in Figure 4.49. The great thing about Curves, much like Histogram Adjustment, is that you can switch to each channel and therefore change the color balance. We can see from the plot that the red is too dark in this photo. There isn't enough of it because the blue has squeezed it all out. As you make these changes, look for matching colors in the photo to help you find your way. Jake's shirt is blue, and he has a nice yellow stripe on his jacket. (You can see the stripe in Figure 4.49). Those are good signposts. Whatever I do, that shirt should be blue and the stripe yellow. By the same token, Ben has a red shirt, and Jake has a plush bug with green ears. All of these are good reference points for me to look at.

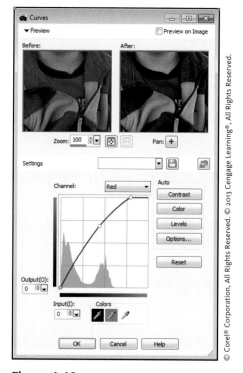

Figure 4.49

Not enough red.

Figure 4.50 shows that there is green, but it's a little squished down. I can help that by adding a few dots at the correct places. I've snuck the top down and the bottom up a bit, and bowed the curve some to lessen the intensity of the green. In the Curves dialog box, a convex shaped curve (think "outy") intensifies that component color, and a concave shape (like an "inny" belly button) turns the color component down for each pixel.

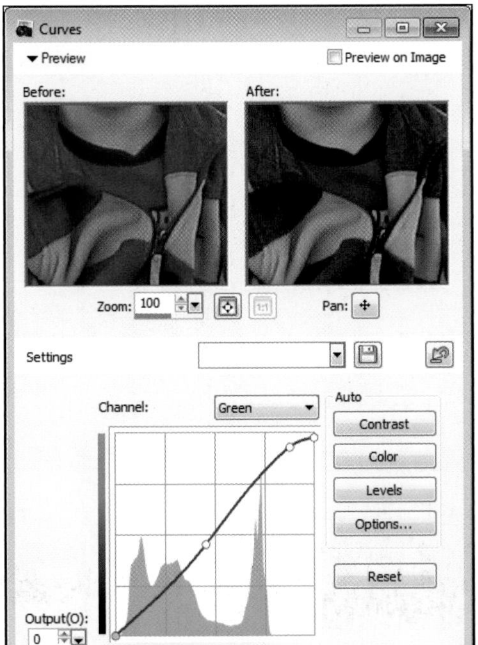

The Blue channel in the Curves dialog box is shown in Figure 4.51. There's a pretty even distribution of blue from dark to light. That figures. There's a lot of blue in this photo!

The solution? Bow the curve inward and bring the right side of the plot down to mix some blue out of the photo.

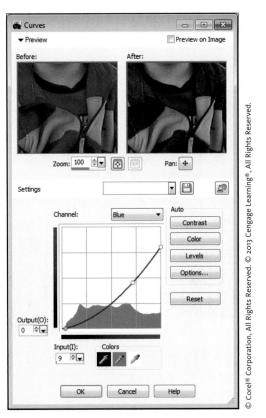

Figure 4.50
Enhancing the greens.

Figure 4.51
Removing too much blue.

Finishing the Photo Study

This fully restored photo, shown in Figure 4.52, is one of those "miracle" restorations. It's one that you can pull out of your portfolio and show people, and they'll all go "Wow, how did you *do that*?"

Here are the steps I took to restore this photo completely. First, I used the Smart Photo Fix as a baseline to start from. (In retrospect, I could easily have used Curves instead.) Then I fixed contrast with a Histogram Adjustment. Next, I bumped up the saturation to make it a bit more vibrant (subtly, but you can tell if you look at Grace's pink coat). I then removed some noise, but after I did, the concrete looked funny. No matter how I tried to take out the noise, the concrete suffered. My solution? I duplicated the working photo layer and then applied Digital Noise Removal to the top layer. I wanted my kids' faces to look better, so I erased everything on that layer but their faces. I blended the two layers together by lowering the opacity of the layer with the kids' faces (the one on top, which had the noise removed). When I was satisfied, I did a Select All, Copy Merged, Paste as New Layer. Finis!

Setting White Balance

Improve your photography by experimenting with the white balance setting in your camera. Even compact cameras have this capability. For example, I can adjust the white balance on my Canon A480 (a very inexpensive starter camera) from AWB (Auto) to Day Light, Cloudy, Tungsten, Fluorescent, Fluorescent H, or Custom. By all means, experiment. Take and review test photos to make sure they have the tone and color you're after.

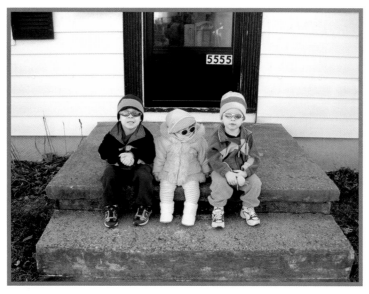

Figure 4.52
The kids are all right.

Photo Study 14: Working with White Balance

FIGURE 4.53 IS A PHOTO of my daughter, Grace, bowling. Well, almost. It's mostly a photo of the pins. I positioned myself behind them to be able to catch the action from an unusual angle. I took this frame a fraction of a second after she released the ball. This shot does a good job of showing the natural lighting and color problems.

Natural lighting can fool digital cameras quite easily when you take photos inside without a flash. We were in a large gymnasium that relied on windows at either end to provide most of the light. It was a bright day, and the lights were on in the gym, but it was still too dim to take great action shots with a fast shutter speed. Unfortunately, I left my external flash at home, so I couldn't take advantage of the high speed sync that it provides to get the shutter speeds I wanted. When using the pop-up flash on my digital SLR, I was restricted to 1/250 second or slower. In the end, I opened the lens up to f/1.8 and increased the ISO to 1600 to be able to set the shutter seed to 1/640 second. It's a bit warm, as her face has picked up orange and red. Now, this isn't the end of the world. You could print this out (Figure 4.53 is the JPEG that the camera saved), and most people would ooh and aah over it. No big deal.

Once you know the background to this photo you can understand why, in part, it looks the way it does (a bit dim and yellowish; those foam bowling pins should be bright white). Had I been able to use the flash, the light would have been white. The camera would have set the photo's white balance based on a known quantity. As it was, it was forced to guess, and the lighting in the gym was complicated enough for it to guess wrong.

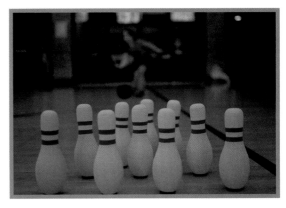

Figure 4.53
An interesting photo that could look a lot better.
© 2013 Cengage Learning®, All Rights Reserved.

However, if you have a digital SLR or compact digital camera that supports the RAW file format, you might be surprised by how much you can improve your photos by shooting RAW and correcting color casts in the Camera RAW Lab.

The Camera RAW Lab

Within the context of the Camera RAW Lab, color issues are resolved in the White Balance section. Cameras aren't as smart as we are—they have no way to tell what should be white in a scene and are more affected than we are by the light's color. You can help the situation by indicating what type of light the shot was taken in or by manually setting the color Temperature and Tint so that white actually appears white.

First, make sure that PaintShop Pro is set up to use the Camera RAW Lab. Open File Format Preferences (File ❯ Preferences ❯ File Format Preferences) and check the Open RAW images with Camera RAW Lab option.

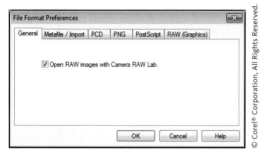

Figure 4.54
If this isn't checked, PaintShop Pro will open RAW photos in the Adjust workspace.

Once that is settled, you're good to go. To launch the Camera RAW Lab, drop a RAW image onto the PaintShop Pro interface or use File ❯ Open. Figure 4.55 shows the photo as it appears in the lab.

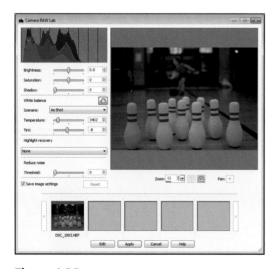

Figure 4.55
The initial RAW exposure.

You'll see in the rest of the Camera RAW Lab figures that I have tweaked the other settings so the photo looks better. Namely, I brightened the photo a bit and applied noise reduction. The point here, however, is white balance.

Select from one of the following Scenario options to see if it fixes the color, or try to find the right Temperature and Tint settings on your own.

▶ **As Shot (Figure 4.56):** Data provided by the camera is used to set the white balance.

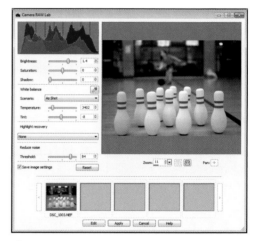

Figure 4.56
As Shot is pretty good, but yellow.

▶ **Auto (Figure 4.57):** Similar to telling the camera to figure the white balance based on its own internal algorithms (most people shoot with Auto White Balance), but in this case you're asking PaintShop Pro to do it.

If you want a good comparison between how your camera and PaintShop Pro differ in their estimation of the white balance, switch back and forth between As Shot and Auto, noting the changes in the photo as the Temperature and Tint change.

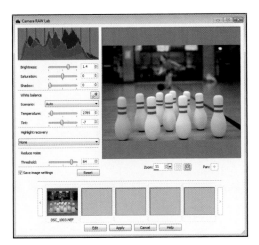

Figure 4.57

Auto works really well here.

▶ **Daylight (Figure 4.58):** Assumes the lighting conditions were daylight. Temperature is set accordingly. Tint is not. It stays on the setting provided from the As Shot setting or Auto, whichever you last previewed from the list.

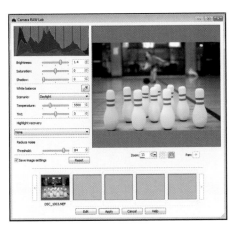

Figure 4.58

Daylight is too warm.

There is no point in repeating all this for each type of lighting, so here are the rest of the settings:

▶ **Cloudy (Figure 4.59)**

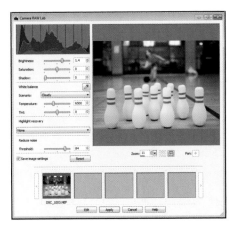

Figure 4.59

Cloudy is even warmer.

▶ **Shade (Figure 4.60)**

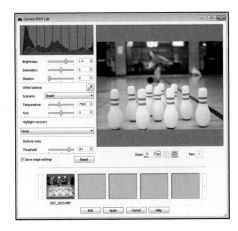

Figure 4.60

Shade is warmer still, to compensate for blue in shadows.

▶ **Tungsten (Figure 4.61)**

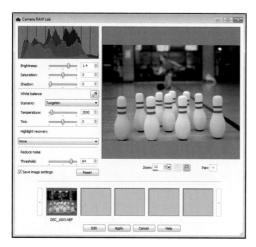

Figure 4.61
This looks very nice, but a hint too blue.

▶ **Fluorescent (Figure 4.62)**

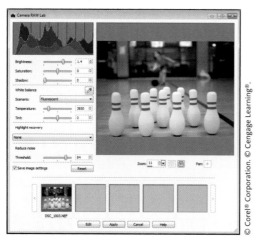

Figure 4.62
A bit warm, but not bad.

▶ **Flash (Figure 4.63)**

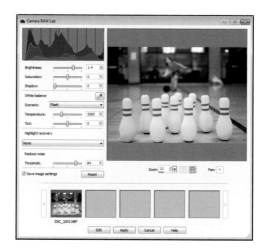

Figure 4.63
Nope.

▶ **Custom:** As soon as you grab the Temperature or Tint controls yourself, the setting changes to Custom. The Temperature is the actual temperature of certain types of light. Some are hotter than others, and being hotter changes whether it comes across as blue or red. Tint applies either a green (more) or purple (less) tint to the photo. That seems odd, but you can use it to counter the opposite shade. If your photo has a purple tint, increase Tint, which adds green to the equation.

You may also use the dropper to click something that should be white or black in the preview window.

Remember, the effect that the Scenario setting has on the color is to compensate for the lighting named in the scenario. When previewing the result, it might look the opposite of what you think it should. For example, setting the Scenario to Flash strengthened the yellow color in this photo.

The reason is that, if the photo were taken with a flash, it would need no color correction to remove a yellow tint. In fact, it might need to add some warmth to keep it from looking too blue. That's why Flash looks so bad in this situation. It adds in the very colors you want to remove.

Finishing the Photo Study

Once the photo was processed by the Camera RAW Lab using the above settings and the Auto White Balance scenario, I only had to straighten the photo and enhance the brightness and contrast slightly with a Curves adjustment layer. The final result is shown in Figure 4.64.

Retouching this photo was fantastically easy, and it helps show you the power of shooting RAW photos instead of JPEGs. The white balance adjustment was applied by PaintShop Pro as it converted the RAW data into a format suitable to view and edit. Nothing was lost or compromised. It's the high-quality solution, and if you're willing to process your RAW photos in PaintShop Pro, you'll reap a number of benefits.

I shoot RAW+JPEG so I have the best of both worlds. If the JPEG looks right, I don't have to mess with RAW. If I need to use it, I have the flexibility.

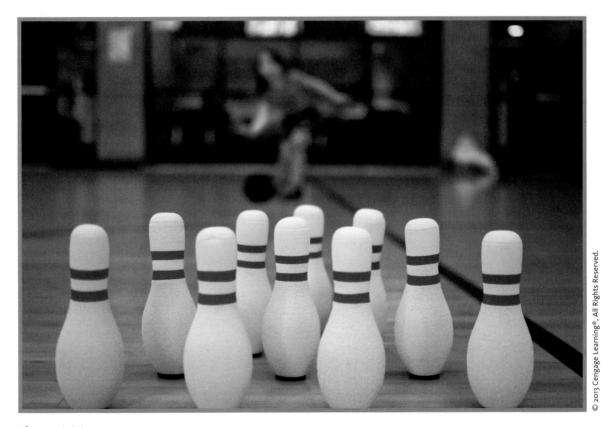

Figure 4.64
Fun times at the gym, ready for framing.

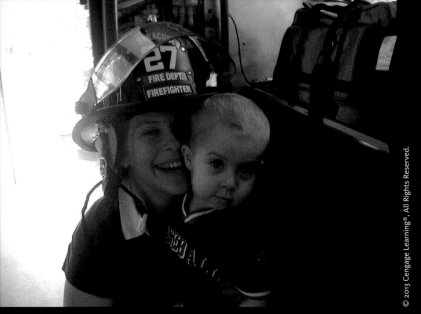

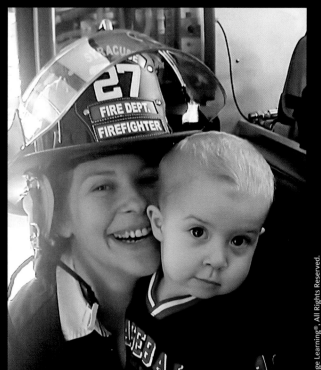

Sharpness, Noise, and Distortion

5

THIS CHAPTER SHOWS YOU HOW TO TACKLE problems with photos that need a bit of sharpness, have too much noise, or are plagued with lens distortion or a poor perspective. You'll find all these problems in both digital photos and scanned photo prints.

As you address these problems, try not to overdo it. Oversharpening introduces artifacts and noise into a photo and makes the whole thing look terribly unrealistic. Overaggressive noise reduction removes sharpness and makes a photo look too soft. Likewise, if you try too hard to stamp out distortion, you can make the photo look less realistic.

Having said all that, these studies will give you an idea of how to handle these problems and choose the best approach to remove them.

▶ **Photo Study 15: Sharpening Photos**—Almost all photos suffer from softness caused by the lens not focusing the light of the scene perfectly on the film or digital camera sensor. Using professional caliber lenses can help. Another solution is to sharpen your photos after you take or scan them. Learn how to use PaintShop Pro's sharpening tools in this digital photo study.

▶ **Photo Study 16: Selective Sharpening**—Learn how to use the Sharpen brush to sharpen select areas of a photo when just a little dab will do it.

▶ **Photo Study 17: Tackling Digital Noise**—When you increase a digital camera's sensitivity to light by cranking up the ISO, it also magnifies random electronic "noise," which is picked up by the sensor and recorded in the photo. Learn how to remove or reduce digital noise in this photo study.

▶ **Photo Study 18: Reducing Noise and Removing JPEG Artifacts—** This photo study combines brightness and contrast trouble with digital noise and JPEG artifacts. Sounds like the perfect recipe for a photo study.

▶ **Photo Study 19: Removing Lens Distortion—**All lenses have a certain amount of distortion to them. Learn how to correct lens distortion and correct the overall perspective in this photo of a commemorative plaque.

▶ **Photo Study 20: Manual Perspective Correction—**Sometimes, as in this shot of a lamppost overlooking our downtown area, photos suffer from perspective problems. They can quickly be corrected manually, using the Pick tool.

Photo Study 15: Sharpening Photos

OUR KIDS PLAY BASEBALL IN THE LOCAL Wildcat League. This year, Ben and Jake moved up to the age division where kids are allowed to start pitching. Needless to say, they were both very excited about throwing "fireballs" like they do in the majors.

I took this photo on the last day of the 2012 season as Jake and Ben played in their park's Showcase game (a type of all-star game for kids who had perfect attendance). I used my Nikon D200 dSLR and 300mm super telephoto lens.

This particular photo is a bit on the soft side. The background is and should be out of focus due to the limited depth of field. That's not the problem. Jake needs to be sharpened for the photo to look better.

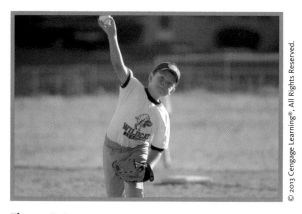

Figure 5.1
Jacob in action.

Sharpening Techniques

Sharpening a photo is all about edges. No matter what happens "under the hood," every sharpening technique detects and increases contrast along the edges. We perceive the increase in contrast as an increase in sharpness. On the other hand, things that don't have well-defined, contrasted edges look out of focus and fuzzy.

With noise reduction, you're always fighting a battle against losing too much detail. With sharpening, the struggle is against adding too much detail or detail where you don't want it. For example, if your photo is noisy or has a lot of grain or surface texture, when you sharpen, you run the risk of making the noise stand out even more.

Figure 5.2 illustrates this danger. Shown is a small area from another photo. It's a scanned printed photo at high resolution that has a lot of specks and surface detail to it. I applied Unsharp Mask, and it increased the visibility of the noise dramatically as it sharpened.

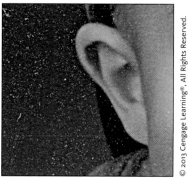

Figure 5.2
Sharpening specks.

Another danger of sharpening is trying to sharpen something that purposely isn't sharp. By this, I am referring to photos that have a limited depth of field, which is the depth of the area that can be in focus. Depth of field is controlled by the size of the lens's aperture when you take the photo. Larger apertures (small f/numbers) used at close range limit the depth of field, sometimes to only a few millimeters. Smaller apertures (larger f/numbers) increase the depth of field, from a few feet to infinity.

By contrast, the area that isn't in focus is called *bokeh.* (I'm not talking about an out-of-focus photo here, but the out-of-focus area that isn't in the depth of field.) The characteristics of the bokeh depend on the lens. Some aren't as pleasing as others. People spend a lot of money on lenses that create the most aesthetically pleasing bokehs.

Figure 5.3 is a close-up of the background of the photo in this study, beside Jake's face for comparison. The background is out of focus by design. Sharpening this area won't do anything up to a point, but if you oversharpen it, it will start looking noisy and will develop overcontrasted halos around some of the objects.

Don't be afraid to sharpen photos with nice bokehs, but realize that you can't sharpen areas that are extremely out of focus (like the fence line in this photo study). If you push it too hard, you'll ruin the photo. If you need to, mask out the background and selectively sharpen the subject of the photo.

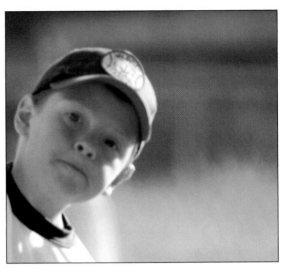

Figure 5.3
Pay attention to the background when sharpening.

With these preliminary warnings out of the way, I want to run through the main techniques quickly so that you can use them to sharpen photos. Each has its pros and cons, of course. At one time or another, I've used all of them, so don't be afraid to experiment and test which techniques work best on your photos.

Smart Photo Fix

Smart Photo Fix (Adjust ❯ Smart Photo Fix) is a quick and easy way to sharpen a photo. I often apply sharpening when I am using Smart Photo Fix to retouch a photo. There is only one setting: Focus. Raise it, as shown in Figure 5.4, to increase sharpness. I don't normally use this for problematic photos. In other words, if I need to really work on sharpness or if I need to use a mask, I'll use a different technique. Don't be afraid to zero out Focus and use your own sharpening technique later.

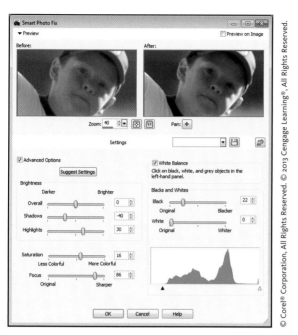

Figure 5.4
Sharpening with Smart Photo Fix.

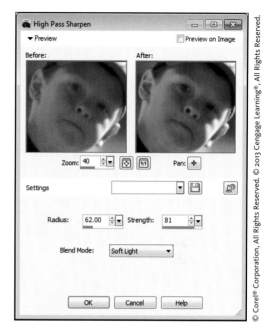

Figure 5.5
High Pass Sharpen.

High Pass Sharpen

High Pass Sharpen (Adjust ❯ Sharpness ❯ High Pass Sharpen) is a very good sharpening routine that gives you plenty of control over the process. There are three settings, as shown in Figure 5.5: Radius, Strength, and Blend mode. Strength is pretty intuitive, but the other two deserve some explanation.

Think "range" when you see Radius. In other words, each pixel of the photo is evaluated, and if pixels within a certain range (this is the Radius) are different enough from that center pixel, they are sharpened (their differences are increased). Use a small Radius to limit the area in which dissimilar pixels are evaluated to be sharpened and use larger values to increase this area.

Use Blend mode to control how the sharpened pixels are blended back in with the original. There are three options: Overlay (increases edge detail), Hard Light (emphasizes contrast), and Soft Light (softens things so it doesn't look too sharp).

Sharpen

Sharpen (Adjust ❯ Sharpening ❯ Sharpen) is the ultimate in easy, but you pay for it by having no control. Select the menu, and the adjustment is applied. This works great when you just want a touch of sharpening and don't want to fuss with it.

Sharpen More

Sharpen More (Adjust ❯ Sharpening ❯ Sharpen More) is just like Sharpen, only more. There is a definite increase in sharpness with Sharpen More when compared to Sharpen. Use this when you want a little more sharpness all at once.

Radius Versus Strength

Be careful not to confuse Radius with Strength. It's easy to do, and I catch myself doing the same thing sometimes. *Radius* refers to *area. Strength* refers to how much the pixels are sharpened over this area. It's possible to sharpen very little (low Strength) over a wide area (large Radius) or vice versa.

Given a certain Strength, increasing Radius may appear to increase the effect, but what is happening is that there is simply more of it—not that it's stronger. At high Strengths, Radius can have interesting effects, large or small. For example, setting the Radius to between 80 and 100 and the Strength to 40–60, lets you produce an effect much like Local Tone Mapping.

Unsharp Mask

Unsharp Mask (Adjust ❯ Sharpness ❯ Unsharp Mask) is the sharpening routine that gives you the most power and control. Figure 5.6 shows the dialog box.

Don't be afraid of Unsharp Mask, even if the name seems odd. It's your friend, and it can make the difference between a so-so photo and one that brings out detail perfectly. There are four settings:

- ▶ **Radius:** The same as Radius in High Pass Sharpen. I normally keep this very small for what I call "focus sharpening" (tightening the focus), but raise it if I have to.

- ▶ **Strength:** Also the same. I raise this more than you might think. My normal settings are between 100 and 250.

- ▶ **Clipping:** This is a setting that ranges from 0 to 100 and allows you to control when the onset of sharpening occurs. At 0, everything is sharpened. At 100, most edges are not sharpened; only those with extreme differences in lightness are. Use Clipping to protect more delicate edges in the photo and keep them from being sharpened, even as you sharpen the rest of the image.

  If you are basically happy with the other settings but see areas where sharpening looks too strong, try raising Clipping and see if that softens the effect.

- ▶ **Luminance only:** Check this to apply the sharpening to the Lightness channel only. This is great when you want to sharpen the Lightness channel without messing with the color channels. Be careful, though, because sharpening only the Lightness channel can increase the noise level in your photo. If you need a high degree of sharpening, leave this unchecked.

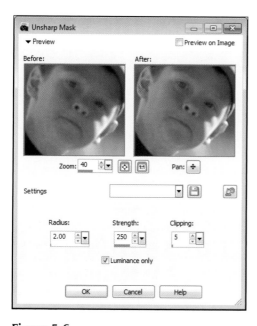

Figure 5.6

Unsharp Mask.

Multiple Passes

Experiment with applying multiple passes of Unsharp Mask with different or the same settings. Make a light first pass and then reapply. Compare that to one pass with moderate or stronger settings.

Sharpen Brush

Finally, you can use the Sharpen brush to selectively sharpen areas of the photo. I use this in the next study, so I won't go into depth here. If I need to be selective over large areas, I'll use a mask and one of the other techniques. However, the Sharpen brush is a great way to sharpen single lines or areas of the face without having to go to the trouble of masking.

Finishing the Photo Study

This photo was not so terribly blurry that it needed extensive sharpening. That's on purpose. I chose it to show you how limited sharpening can make a positive difference in a photo. In fact, I use some form of sharpen on virtually all the photos I work on, even the best ones. The challenge here was to sharpen Jacob's face and body without damaging the smooth background.

For this photo, I applied Unsharp Mask, reduced the noise gently, and then applied High Pass Sharpen to finish it. On top of all this, I corrected the lighting and contrast with Curves adjustment layer, then rotated the photo and cropped out all the extra space. Figure 5.7 shows the final result.

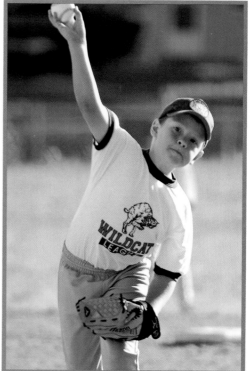

Figure 5.7

Sharper and brighter equals better.

Photo Study 16: Selective Sharpening

FIGURE 5.8 IS AN OLD PHOTO of my father-in-law, Don, as a young boy. He is standing with his Aunt Jo (the family calls her Grandma Jo because she raised Don after his mother died) and her husband's son from a previous marriage, Leonard, in front of their car, a Dodge. From markings on the back of the picture, we know that the photo was developed on May 26, 1944.

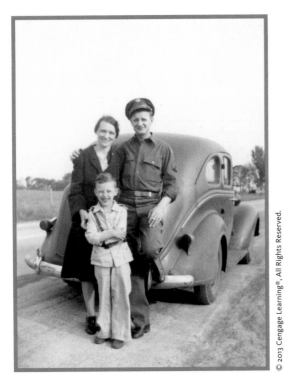

Figure 5.8
Lighthearted moment, 1944.

Cleanup

When you're faced with a photo that needs sharpening, first test to see what routines and strengths look the best. Then go back to the beginning and clean up the photo. There's no sense in sharpening noise, dirt, specks, or fibers in or on the photo. This photo has a lot of little things that I cleaned up, and I used the usual tools: the Clone brush and Blemish Fixer. No need to show that here, but you should know not to skip over this important step yourself. If you do skip this step, you'll end up with a wonderfully sharp but messy photo that you'll have to redo.

Sharpen, Smooth, Sharpen

Figure 5.9 is a close-up of Leonard's uniform. It looks a tad noisy. I want to use Edge Preserving Smooth, which is in the Adjust menu under Add/Remove Noise to smooth some of the noise out, but I know it's going to remove some detail from the edges. That's not what I want to do at this stage of the process.

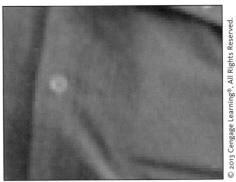

Figure 5.9
Noise or scan artifacts at close range.

What I want to do is sharpen, smooth, and then sharpen again. I used to get a queasy feeling when I sharpened a photo and then applied noise reduction or smoothing. It felt backward, not to mention a waste of time, when I had to sharpen the photo again. I got over it and get good results. Think of it this way. Some photos need an edge detail boost to undergo the rigors of smoothing successfully without losing too much crispness. At the end of smoothing, there's enough left to resharpen without adding too much noise back in. Not all photos, of course, but some—especially those that are a bit soft to begin with, like this one.

Therefore, I applied a subtle Unsharp Mask to this photo first, as shown in Figure 5.10. Notice that Leonard's face is pleasantly sharper, but not to the extreme. I did this to add crispness to the edges so they weren't removed completely by the next step.

Always Look at Faces and Eyes

When you are smoothing a photo or reducing noise, always look at people's eyes. From this vantage point, you can see drops in clarity and decide whether the noise reduction or smoothing is worth it or not.

Next, I smoothed the photo. I experimented with two different types: One Step Noise Reduction and Edge Preserving Smooth. Figure 5.11 shows the latter, very lightly applied. This technique does a good job of preserving edges, but even so, I had to lower the strength quite a bit. Thankfully, it did a good job smoothing Leonard's uniform.

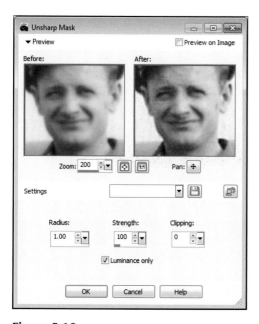

Figure 5.10

First round of sharpening.

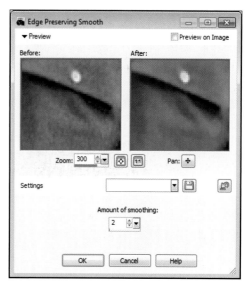

Figure 5.11

Using Edge Preserving Smooth to smooth.

Finally, you can apply another round of Unsharp Mask at a different strength or use the Sharpen brush to touch up any edges that look like they need it. I used the latter approach. Figure 5.12 shows where I am gently sharpening the features of Leonard's face with the brush. I have the brush hardness at 0 and the opacity (which translates to how strong you're sharpening) at 4.

Although it doesn't look so hot when you zoom in this close, further back it adds a certain "legibility" to a photo because the lines are well defined.

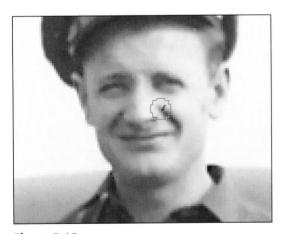

Figure 5.12

Sharpening select features.

Masks and Sharpening

To selectively sharpen parts of a photo, you can also first mask out what you don't want sharpened. Then, apply a filter such as Unsharp Mask to the photo layer in the layer group that includes the mask. This way you can have original (unsharpened) areas from the lower layers show through and keep the parts you want sharpened visible by not masking them out.

There's no need to go over everything this way. Concentrate on important features and lines. In this case, that meant everyone's faces, the cut of their clothes, and the car.

Finishing the Photo Study

One of the lessons from this chapter is that some techniques work for some photos and not for others. Sometimes, you have to sharpen and then smooth and then sharpen again. Don't be afraid to experiment and find what is best for each individual photo. Your persistence will pay off, and you will soon be able to judge which techniques to try first. You'll still be surprised at times, but that's part of the fun of restoring photos.

Figure 5.13 shows the final photo. After sharpening, I corrected the yellow color with Fade Correction and then made brightness and contrast adjustments with Curves.

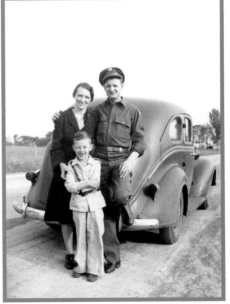

Figure 5.13

Fully restored photo with selective sharpening.

Photo Study 17: Tackling Digital Noise

FIGURE 5.14 IS AN ACTION SHOT of my daughter, Grace, taken in 2007. She is running back and forth in the basement, playing with her brothers. (She just turned 6 and is playing baseball with the boys this summer.)

Pardon the mess. I didn't realize I would be putting such candid photos of my life into a book like this. It's real, though; the type of photo you might take in your basement. That's an important ingredient to my approach for this book. I want it to include photos that everyone can relate to and learn from, not just photos a professional photographer would take.

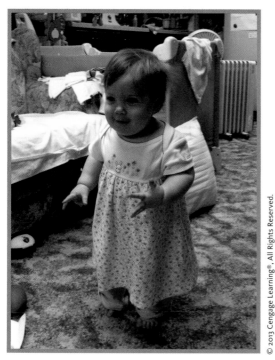

Figure 5.14
Great action shot marred by digital camera noise.

Trial and Error

With so many different ways to remove noise, it's helpful to come up with a method to keep your evaluations straight: something that enables you to evaluate different strategies and decide on the best method without going crazy. I've found that I can make sense of the process when I create duplicate layers and apply different techniques to them; then I toggle them on and off to compare. Here's how I do it:

1. Open the digital photo in PaintShop Pro.

2. Duplicate the Background layer several times.

3. Rename the duplicated layers according to the techniques you want to try (see Figure 5.15).

4. Apply the techniques. I will illustrate several different techniques in the following subsections.

5. Show and hide the layers for a direct comparison.

When you've decided on the best way to solve the problem, hide or delete the other layers. If you want to avoid "image bloat," delete the extra layers—they can add significantly to the file size of your photo.

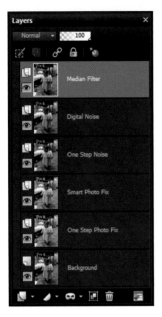

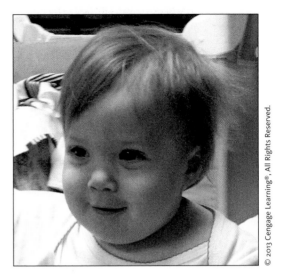

Figure 5.16
Better, but still noisy.

Figure 5.15
*Create duplicate layers to experiment
with possible solutions.*

One Step Photo Fix

It always pays to try this first. Select the Adjust
menu and choose One Step Photo Fix. You never
know when you'll hit the jackpot and not have to
do anything else. Figure 5.16 shows the result.

As you can see, One Step Photo Fix is not particularly suited to removing noise. It works best on
photos that have brightness, contrast, or color
problems.

Enhance Photo

There is a button on the Standard toolbar
called *Enhance Photo*. It's located right in
the middle, beside the Palettes button.
Don't forget to check there for commonly
used photo enhancement tools like this
one.

Smart Photo Fix

Smart Photo Fix is a little harder to use than the
One Step Photo Fix, but not by much. Give it a try
by selecting the Adjust menu and choosing Smart
Photo Fix. You'll be given the option of changing
brightness, saturation, or sharpness sliders to see if
those work for your photo, or you can ask PaintShop
Pro for suggested values. I've accepted the suggested
values for this photo in Figure 5.17.

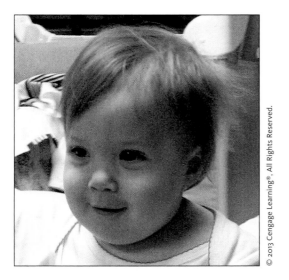

Figure 5.17
Smart Photo Fix isn't the answer here.

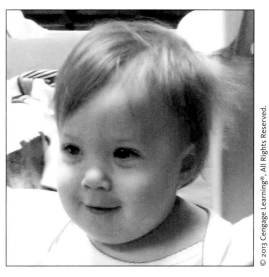

Figure 5.18
Good noise reduction, but I can do better.

As you can see, it's about the same as the One Step Photo Fix, without the one step. Smart Photo Fix is best left for fixing brightness, contrast, and color problems, rather than removing noise. Again, you never know when this will work so it always pays to try it before you discard it.

One Step Noise Reduction

One Step Noise Reduction is available from the Adjust menu. Simply select it and let 'er rip. Figure 5.18 shows the result. (From here on out, the detailed figures are a bit brighter than the working image so you can see the noise better.)

Don't let the fact that there's another noise reduction tool named Digital Noise Removal fool you. Try this on digital photos, too.

Median Filter

Although the Median filter can do a pretty good job at times, it doesn't really help here (see Figure 5.19).

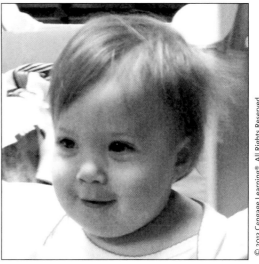

Figure 5.19
Median filter doesn't work as well with this photo.

It obviously has had an effect, but in this case, has caused other problems. I don't particularly like the blotchiness, and because this is a color photo, I think it stands out more.

Digital Noise Removal

I could have jumped right here to this section and told you this was the effect I would use and ignored the rest, but that would have been a disservice to you and not accurately portrayed how I work. I often go through all the above options to see if they work or not. Yes, when I'm removing digital noise from a digital photo I tend to end up here, but I check out other options and examine their effectiveness if Digital Noise Removal doesn't seem to be cutting the mustard.

One of the strengths of Digital Noise Removal is noise sampling areas. The routine selects three areas automatically (one in dark, one in medium, and one in light areas) that you can remove or change in the Preview window. When you draw them, don't make them too large or include areas of detail you want to keep. Otherwise, you'll lose valuable details.

Select Adjust ❯ Digital Noise Removal to open up the Digital Noise Removal dialog box (see Figures 5.20 through 5.24).

Figure 5.20 shows the effects of too much smoothing. I've lost a lot of detail in the photo. Again, you are confronted with the trade-off of detail versus smoothness. Always experiment with the settings.

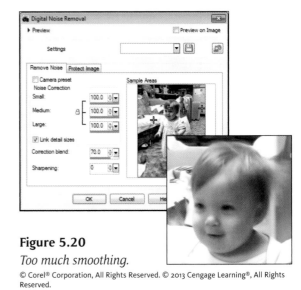

Figure 5.20

Too much smoothing.

The next example (Figure 5.21) shows a moderate noise reduction with 100% blend (which is how much noise reduction gets blended in with the original photo). It's not too bad, but it is still smoothing out too much detail. At high magnification, you can see artifacts around Grace's forehead and the side of her face.

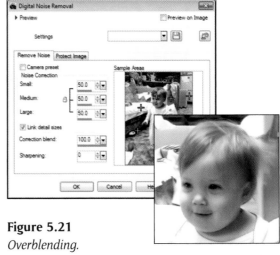

Figure 5.21

Overblending.

The effects of no sharpening, moderate noise reduction, and a good deal of blending are shown in Figure 5.22. It's not too bad. In the end, however, I want something a bit sharper.

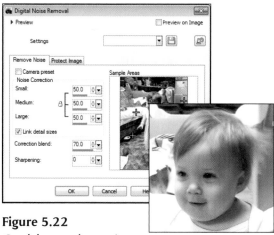

Figure 5.22

Good, but no sharpening.

The next example (Figure 5.23) shows the effects of total sharpening, which are readily apparent. It looks like chicken tracks have been placed on her face. Avoid these artifacts, as they are a pain to remove.

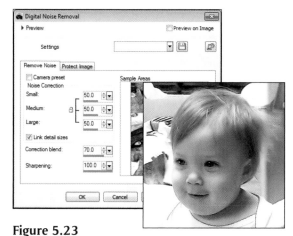

Figure 5.23

Oversharpening in action.

Having seen the extremes of smoothing, blending, and sharpening, I can come up with a pretty good middle ground for this photo (see Figure 5.24).

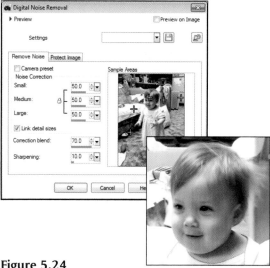

Figure 5.24

Working those settings to our maximum advantage.

I have chosen settings in the middle ground that, to be honest, aren't perfect. However, the result is a good balance between smoothing away the digital noise and preserving important details. By the time the image is finished and printed at a normal size, it will look much better. If you're going for a wall-sized poster (something on the order of 24 by 36 inches—the kind you can't print on your desktop printer), an image with this much noise is either going to show the noise or your attempts to remove it.

Finishing the Photo Study

After deciding what level of digital noise reduction to apply, I went back and corrected the brightness, contrast, and white balance and then applied Digital Noise Removal. After that, I used the JPEG Artifact Removal tool to eliminate some of the odd artifacts around the photo. I then sharpened the photo, smoothed her skin, and finally, scaled the working layer upward to recompose the shot. The last step eliminated the distraction of the basement and put the emphasis on Grace. Figure 5.25 shows the completed photo.

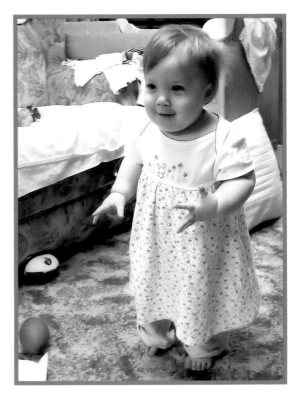

Figure 5.25

Grace, saved from the evils of darkness, clutter, and digital camera noise.

Photo Study 18:
Reducing Noise and Removing JPEG Artifacts

OUR LITTLE FAMILY (when this was taken in 2004, we only had two kids) took a trip with my best friend and his family to his parents' lake house one summer weekend, and Figure 5.26 is a photo of Anne and Ben getting a tour inside a fire truck. It was the weekend before the Fourth of July, so the atmosphere was festive, and the local Fire Department had their trucks on display.

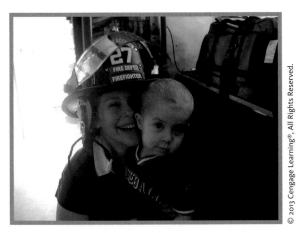

Figure 5.26
Getting the grand tour inside a fire truck.

Brightness and Contrast

When you're working with a dark photo that you know you're going to have to brighten, don't reduce the noise right away. You can't see the noise well enough to remove it effectively. Rather, address brightness and contrast issues first, as I am with a Curves adjustment layer in Figure 5.27.

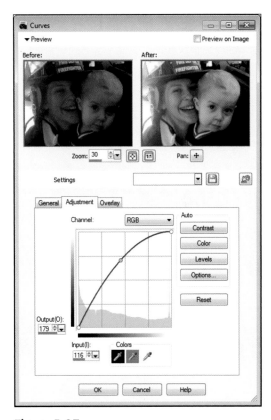

Figure 5.27
Starting with Curves.

With the photo brighter, the noise is more obvious. I've opened the Digital Noise Removal dialog box in Figure 5.28 and have chosen a few extra sampling regions. This helps point the program to the areas we definitely want smoothed.

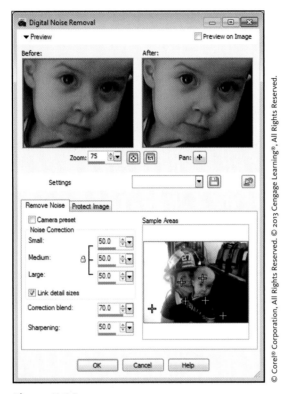

Figure 5.28
Reducing noise.

Notice that I have kept the strength of the noise correction to 50. That's a moderate amount, but I have also increased the Sharpening setting to 50, which is much more than normal. This combination of settings has removed noise and protected the details of the photo. That's the trade-off, and finding settings that gives you the best of both worlds is fantastic.

There is one problem, however. The noise is gone, but JPEG artifacts are more visible than before. They look like pixelated areas, as shown in 5.29. To remove them, select the Adjust ❯ Add/Remove Noise ❯ JPEG Artifact Removal menu. That launches the dialog box, also seen in Figure 5.29. I have increased the Strength to High and lowered the Crispness to 0. That handles the artifacts well and keeps the photo smooth. You can see the after-effect in Figure 5.29 as well.

Blinded by Content

If you're restoring or retouching your own photos, don't fall in love with the content so much that you forget to look critically at the color, contrast, brightness, focus, and composition. That's why you're here.

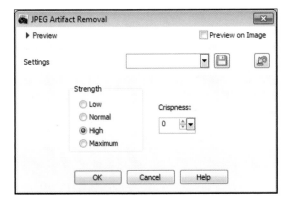

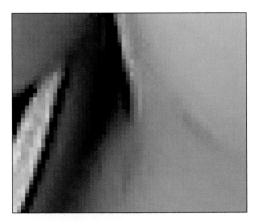

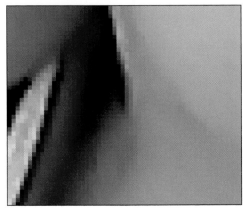

Figure 5.29
Reducing JPEG artifacts.
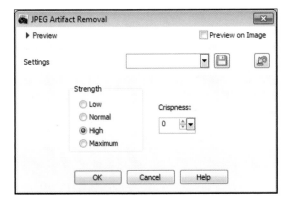

Finishing the Photo Study

With the brightness, noise, and JPEG artifacts handled, this photo only needed a few other tweaks. I brightened Anne's teeth, added a bit of Clarity to strengthen the edges in the photo, and recomposed the photo to take most of the overblown area to the left out of the picture.

Figure 5.30 shows the final result.

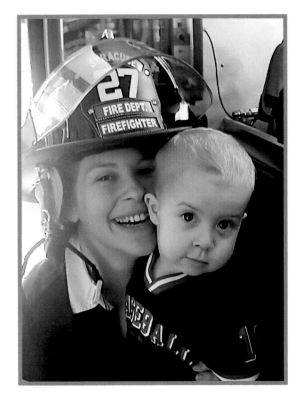

Figure 5.30
Now we can see them better.

Photo Study 19: Removing Lens Distortion

I TOOK THIS PHOTO (see Figure 5.31) of this commemorative plaque in 2006. It dedicates a portion of an elevated rail running through our downtown and is a memorial to the mayor at that time, Harry Baals.

This photo shows off two types of distortion that I want to correct: lens and perspective. I took this with a compact digital camera, but even much more expensive cameras and lenses distort scenes, wide-angle lenses in particular. In this case, the plaque looks like it's bulging out (that's the lens distortion) and the sides aren't vertical (that's where perspective comes in, a combination of horizontal and vertical distortion).

The goals here are pretty straightforward: fix the bulge (aka barrel distortion) and correct the odd perspective.

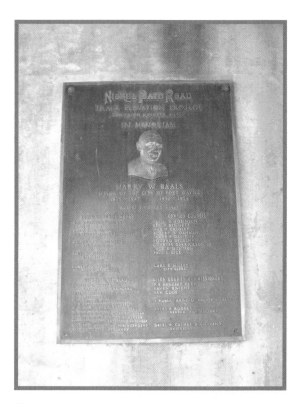

Figure 5.31
Unique dedication plaque.

Types of Distortion

I want to quickly describe the main types of distortion before moving on to remove the distortion in this study's photo.

▶ **Barrel:** Barrel distortion looks like it has a bulge in the middle of the photo. Imagine a sailing ship coming toward you with its sails full of wind. They bulge, which is what barrel distortion looks like. Lines that should be straight in the photo aren't straight, especially around the corners. They bend toward the edges of the photo. It is the most common type and is generally simple to fix. This photo study suffers from barrel distortion.

Remove it with Adjust ❯ Barrel Distortion Correction.

▶ **Pincushion:** Pincushion is the opposite of barrel distortion. It looks like someone has punched the photo in. Imagine a sailing ship moving away from you with its sails full of the wind. The sails are bulging in the opposite direction—away from you. As with barrel distortion, lines that should be straight aren't, but with pincushion they bend toward the center of the photo.

Remove it with Adjust ❯ Pincushion Distortion Correction. The options are the same as Barrel Distortion Correction (shown in more detail below), only they work in reverse.

▶ **Fisheye:** This is a specialized type of distortion created by shooting with a fisheye lens.

Circular fisheye is the ultimate in fisheye distortion. These photos have a complete semi-circular field of view. The photo looks like a sphere in the middle of a dark frame.

Fisheye lenses that don't offer a full 180-degree horizontal and vertical field of view result in less extreme fisheye distortion. The limited field of view results in a photo that fills the frame. Think of it as a crop of circular fisheye distortion. Fisheye lenses that don't say "circular" take these photos, and their specifications should say something about having a "full frame diagonal field of view," as opposed to a "circular field of view."

Remove it with Adjust ❯ Fisheye Distortion Correction. Rather than set a Strength, you set the Field of view.

▶ **Mustache:** This is a combination of barrel-and-pincushion distortion. Lines generally bulge out in the middle and then either level off or go so far as to bend away at the corners.

This type of distortion is not easily fixed, and it is not an option using the Lens Distortion dialog in PaintShop Pro.

Distortion and Workflow

Fix distortion before you crop, resize, reposition, offset, or otherwise change the physical characteristics of the photo or your working layer. The distortion correction routines are mathematical models that translate pixel positions from where they are to where they should be, based on different distortion characteristics and the fundamental assumption that you haven't messed with the photo yet in that way. Feel free to sharpen, brighten, reduce noise, and so forth, before or after you correct distortion. Your call.

Fixing Barrel Distortion

Fixing barrel distortion is straightforward and fast. I like working with duplicate layers, so I always duplicate the Background layer and fix the distortion on its own working layer. Once you're ready, select the Adjust ❯ Barrel Distortion Correction menu. That opens the dialog, as shown in Figure 5.32.

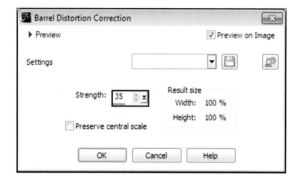

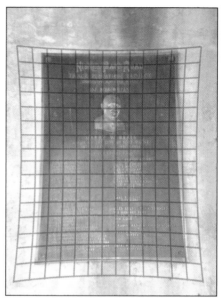

After 100%

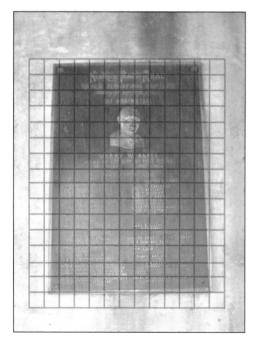

Before

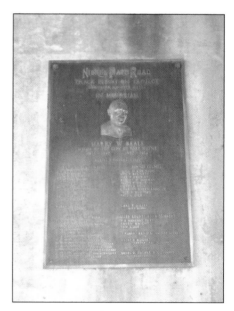

After 35%

Figure 5.32

Removing barrel distortion.

As you can see, there are two options:

▶ **Strength:** From 0 to 100, the strength of the correction to apply. It's simple. Increase Strength to the amount necessary to remove the distortion. If 100 is too little, apply and come back for another round. (Then go get another camera or lens that doesn't distort this badly.)

You can see the effects of strength from the images with the blue grid overlaid on the photo. In the first, the grid is square and the photo is distorted. In the second, the Strength was set to 100 and applied. This bent the heretofore square blue grid inward, which is what happens when you remove barrel distortion. The final image in the sequence shows the result of applying a Strength of 35.

▶ **Preserve central scale:** This setting changes how the correction is applied. It preserves the center and enlarges the photo to flatten the sides. In other words, the scale of the center stays the same and the image gets larger. You can see a readout of how much larger the image will get as a percentage of the original. Without this option, the scale of material in the center shrinks in order to push the offending bulge back in.

Conversely, if you are applying Pincushion Distortion Correction, the photo shrinks to keep the central scale constant, or if not checked, the center grows to flatten the dip.

For this photo, a Strength of 35–40 was adequate to remove the barrel distortion. If you are unsure, apply what you think looks good and then use the Straighten tool and put the end points on a line in the photo. Then see if it's straight. This photo makes that easy, as shown in Figure 5.33. I applied a Barrel Distortion Correction of 100 to show you what too much looks like for this figure.

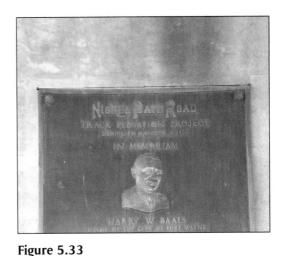

Figure 5.33
Checking for straightness.

Your photos may not have such features, so you'll have to go by "feel." Apply the strength that looks good on your working layer and then toggle that layer on and off to see the original below. If it looks like too much was taken out, create a new working layer and reduce the Strength. If there is still a bulge, create a new working layer and increase the Strength.

Correcting Perspective

Even though the distortion has been corrected, this photo still has a perspective problem. You can tell because it appears to tilt away from you. In this case, the fix is easy. Here's how to do it:

1. **Select the Perspective Correction tool from the Toolbar.** This places a box on the photo, as shown in Figure 5.34.

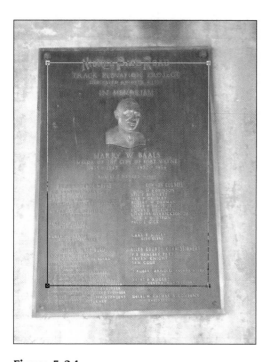

Figure 5.34

Initiating Perspective Correction.

2. **Set the tool options from the Tool Options palette.** The only two you really need to worry about are Crop image and Grid lines. If you check the former, the image is cropped after you correct the perspective. This prevents areas that are added to the canvas to keep it rectangular, but are not part of the original, from appearing (see Figure 5.35). You would have to crop these out at some point anyway. The trade-off here is that you decide when, where, and how to crop if you leave this option unchecked, versus the convenience of having it done for you now.

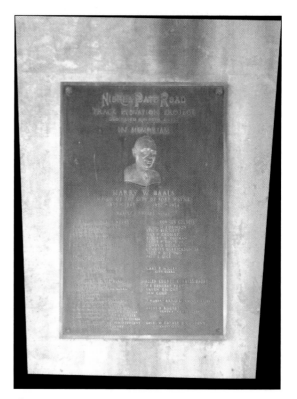

Figure 5.35

Extra material is added to keep the photo rectangular.

Add grid lines if you need the help (see Figure 5.36).

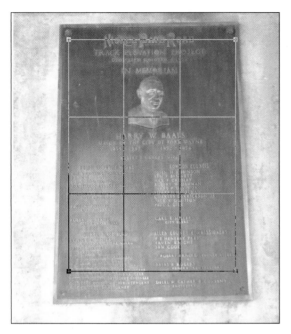

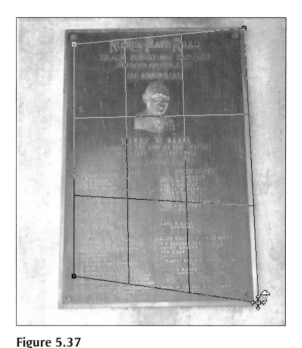

Figure 5.37

Placing corners.

Figure 5.36

Grid lines assist alignment.

3. **Drag each corner handle to a rectangle that should be on the same plane.** I've positioned two of the four corners on the plaque in Figure 5.37. You'll want to zoom in much more than I have, in order to be able to match precisely the corners of the object in the photo with the tool.

4. **Continue until you've positioned all corners.** Then press Apply to finish.

I don't like tools that automatically crop my photos, so I hardly ever let the Perspective Correction tool crop the image for me. I know I will have to go back later and either enlarge my working layer to fill the canvas (generally recompose the shot) or crop the image when I'm done. That extra work is fine with me because I want to control it. Choose whatever solution works for you.

Finishing the Photo Study

This photo shines up nicely once the lens distortion and perspective problems have been corrected (see Figure 5.38). I made standard changes to improve the brightness and contrast with Levels, sharpened the photo with Unsharp Mask, increased the Vibrancy, and then used Local Tone Mapping to bring out some details and textures.

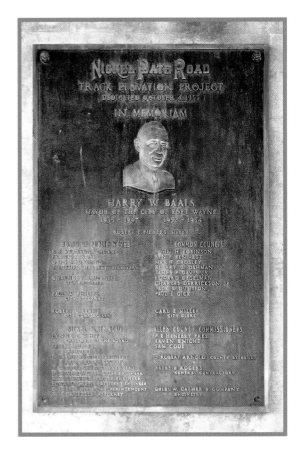

Figure 5.38
That looks a lot better.

Photo Study 20:
Manual Perspective Correction

FIGURE 5.39 SHOWS A HIGH dynamic range image I took in 2012. I was putting the Canon 5D Mark III through its paces and returned to one of the rivers that flows through our downtown area. I took three bracketed exposures of this scene (hand-held) and used them to create and tone map an HDR image.

You're seeing the result, which suffers from a bit of vertical perspective distortion. The lamppost is leaning to the left and away from your perspective. This type of problem is either caused by the camera not being level (vertical problems) or not being aligned straight at the scene (horizontal problems).

If I can correct this a bit, I'll be much happier with the image.

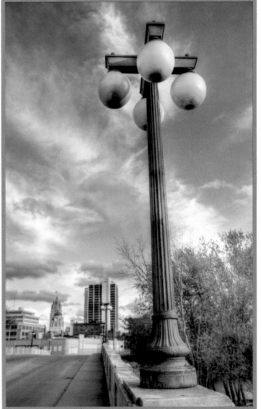

Figure 5.39
Cool HDR lamppost, but leaning.

Using the Pick Tool

This type of distortion can often be fixed best with the Pick tool and your eyes. Here's how:

1. Duplicate the Background layer to give yourself a working layer that you can fix without affecting the original photo.

2. Select the new layer and rename it to something that makes sense, like "Perspective."

3. Turn on the rulers (View ❯ Rulers).

4. Click in the ruler and drag some guides out onto the photo to use for alignment. I've dragged three out in Figure 5.40 and changed their color to purple (View ❯ Change Grid, Guide & Snap Properties) so you can see them in the figure better. If you can't see them in your files, make sure View ❯ Guides is checked.

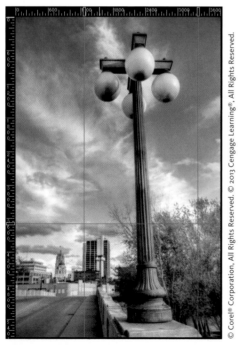

Figure 5.40
Using guides for alignment.

5. You can perform the next step a few ways.

   If you like working with windows, zoom out so the document window shrinks, but not so small that you can't make things out. Then drag the window border to enlarge it, as shown in Figure 5.41. You want to be able to see the gray space outside of the photo. You'll need to see it to work with the Pick tool.

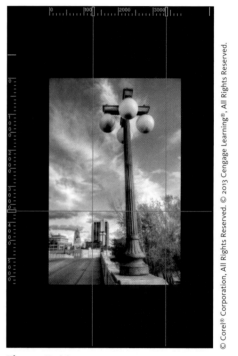

Figure 5.41
Making space to work in.

   Alternatively, maximize the document window or use the Window ❯ Tabbed Documents menu (see Figure 5.42) to maximize the document's window. Zoom out so you can see the gray space around the photo.

6. Select the Pick tool. You'll see the drag handles at the photo layer's corners and midpoints appear.

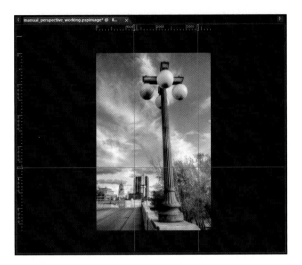

Figure 5.42

Using tabs and zooming out.

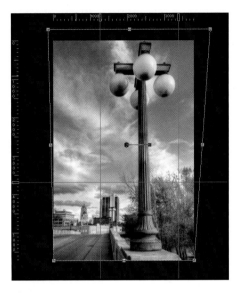

Figure 5.43

Dragging the top corners to begin correcting perspective.

7. Select Free mode from the Tool Options toolbar. This is important!

8. Drag the corner handles around to correct the perspective. This is easier said than done.

Fundamentally, you must recognize which direction the perspective is skewed in order to know what direction to move the corners to correct it, all the while looking at the scene to make sure that the correction doesn't get out of hand and look unrealistic.

Correct vertical problems by widening or narrowing the top or bottom sides. This either enlarges or shrinks that side of the photo, making it appear to turn in your direction. If something is leaning away from you, the top side needs to be lengthened. Therefore, I have dragged the top corners out in Figure 5.43.

You can also reduce the size of the opposite side and produce a similar effect, as shown in Figure 5.44.

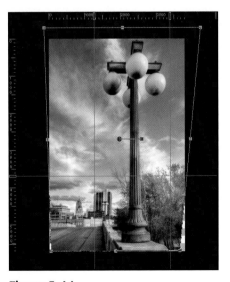

Figure 5.44

Correcting the opposite corners.

I tend to use a combination of shrinking and growing, watching out that I'm not dragging anything off-screen that I want to see. If I need to, I scale the layer down by switching temporarily to Scale mode and reducing the size.

Correct horizontal problems the same way, only grow or shrink the length of the sides. If need be, rotate the layer from a corner, as shown in Figure 5.45 or from the center point (see Figure 5.46). Notice how the cursor changes in each instance.

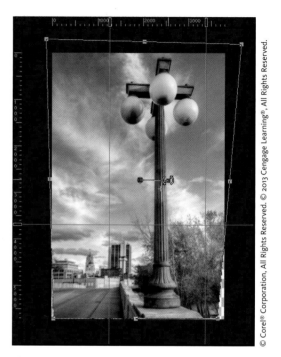

Figure 5.46
You can also rotate from the center.

9. Finally, try to position the layer and scale it so that it covers the entire canvas. This may not always be possible, but if it is, it prevents you from having to crop later. If you would rather crop it yourself, correct the perspective problems now and use the Crop tool at your convenience.

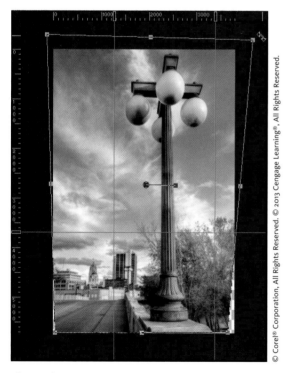

Figure 5.45
Rotate using the corner, if desired.

Finishing the Photo Study

This image didn't need any brightness, contrast, or color corrections. Those issues were already taken care of. Remember, you don't always have to start with photos or images that are completely untouched. I can think of many times where you might be given a graphic or photo by someone else or be using different, specialized software to create images that you want to touch up or finish off in PaintShop Pro.

Figure 5.47 shows my final result. Try your best to make the result look natural. That may mean leaving some perspective problems in your photos. You don't want your "cure" to be worse than the original problem.

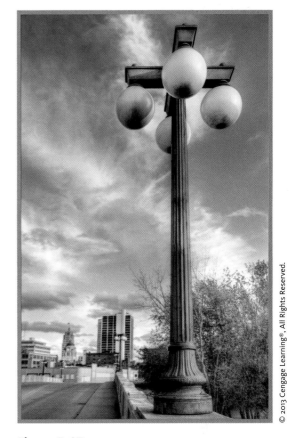

Figure 5.47
Standing straight and tall.

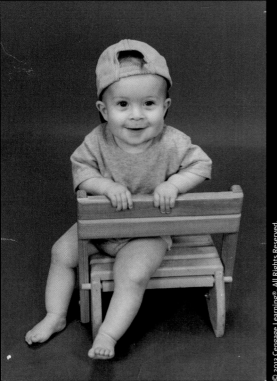

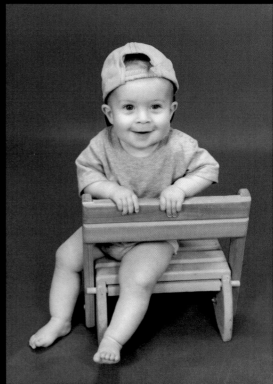

Removing Speteps
and Dust

6

THIS CHAPTER'S FOCUS IS ON COMMON PROBLEMS you'll often
have to deal with if you scan printed photos to retouch or restore them:
dust, specks, and tiny scratches or other imperfections. Dust, oddly enough,
also shows up in some digital photos. Dusty film isn't the problem there, but
rather dust on what you've photographed becomes part of the picture. Here,
then, are the photo studies for this chapter:

▶ **Photo Study 21: Basic Speck and Dust Removal**—Specks are a common
problem with scanned photos, especially at higher resolutions. The effect
of a number of small specks (even tiny ones you can't see with the unaided
eye) is to take away clarity and color from a photo. You'll learn about one
of the most helpful photo retouching tools in this study: the Clone brush.

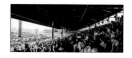

▶ **Photo Study 22: Working in Hard-to-See Areas**—In this study, you'll
learn one approach to tackling dust and other problems in dark, hard-to-
see areas of photos. The photo is of the grandstand and front straightaway of the Indianapolis Motor Speedway. The crowd and bottom of the
upper deck are very dark and contain lots of little imperfections.

▶ **Photo Study 23: Dusting Off Digital Shots for eBay**—The problem
with dust and digital photos is that dust settles on your subject (despite
your best efforts to clean it). When you zoom in, rather than seeing a
nice, clear photo of something, you see dust bunnies! If you're going to
take shots of things to sell on eBay, then pay attention to this photo
study.

▶ **Photo Study 24: Dealing with Background Texture**—If you need to
scan in a studio portrait for digital archival or retouching purposes, then
this study is for you. You'll learn how to get rid of the dust and scratches
while working around the surface texture these prints often have.

Photo Study 21:
Basic Speck and Dust Removal

FIGURE 6.1 IS A PHOTO OF MY father-in-law's late brother, Jim. Jim was a retired veteran of the United States Army and a real firecracker. He had a great sense of humor. He married a German woman named Liz whom he met while he was stationed in Germany in the mid-1950s. When I met them, many years later, Jim had retired, and they lived several states away. They would drive across the country in their large, red Lincoln Town Car for Thanksgiving.

After Jim died, Liz asked me to retouch a special photograph of Jim for her. I was honored, and a little intimidated, because no one had ever asked me to retouch a photo for them. This is going to happen to you after people hear you've been retouching photos. Relax, do the best you can, and learn from each experience.

The photo, which Liz took as they were driving, is not a noteworthy photo, as you can see. It's an everyday snapshot of Jim in the car, driving. These types of photos often become highly valued as time goes by because of the memories they evoke.

Getting Started

Follow these steps to review the scanning, straightening, and cropping steps you would first go through to begin retouching a photo print like this.

1. **Turn on your scanner and clean the glass with glass cleaner and a lint-free cloth, newspaper, or coffee filter.** Make sure the glass is dry before continuing. You might find that a few blasts of "canned air" will help remove dust from the glass or photo.

2. **Place the photo on the glass as straight as you can.** I use a clear ruler lined up against the edge of the scanner to help me position the print. (If you're a woodworker, the ruler is acting as a fence.) You should avoid placing the photo so close to the sides of the scanner bed that you cut off the edges.

3. **Launch your scanner software.** Turn off all automatic color and sharpness features in your scanner software. You want to scan the photo without any automatic adjustments.

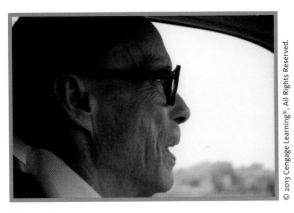

Figure 6.1
This photo looks nice, but a closer look reveals problems.

4. **Choose a resolution, color depth, and file type to save the scan.** For most scans, I choose 300dpi, RGB color, and .tif, but I used 1200dpi here to prove the point that using higher resolution almost always increases the amount of work you have to do.

Save the file as a .jpg only if your scanner doesn't allow you to use any other type. (Then go out and buy a better scanner.) Otherwise, you risk losing some detail. You see, JPEGs use a "lossy" compression scheme that sacrifices data for size. Consider higher resolutions for archiving or if the photo is very small. The larger the print and the higher resolution you scan at, the more memory and processing power you will need to open it up and work on it in PaintShop Pro.

Measure Twice, Crop Once

Scan an area larger than the photo and crop it in PaintShop Pro if you want that warm, fuzzy feeling that says you've got the entire thing. You can get a much more precise crop in PaintShop Pro after you straighten the photo anyway.

5. **When the scan is finished, close your scanner software and open the scanned photo in Corel PaintShop Pro.** (See Figure 6.2.)

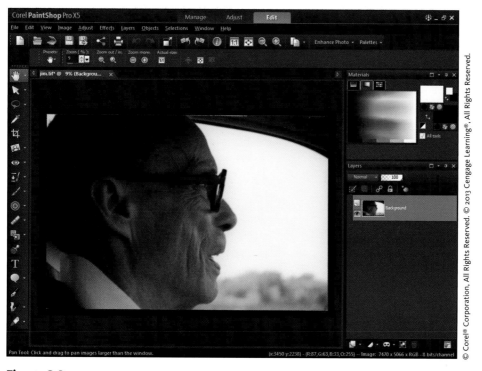

Figure 6.2
The initial scan in PaintShop Pro X5.

6. **Next, make sure that the photo is straight.** Select the Straighten tool and drag one of its ends to a corner of your photo. Zoom in really closely so that you can place the tool precisely (see Figure 6.3).

7. **Zoom out and drag the other end of the Straighten tool to an opposite corner (not diagonally, however).** Then accept the changes. For borderless photos, use the edge of the photo itself as a guide to straighten. For photos with borders, align the Straighten tool with the photo edge rather than the border.

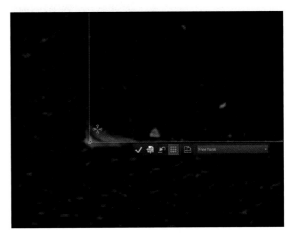

Figure 6.4
Setting the initial crop box to the corners.

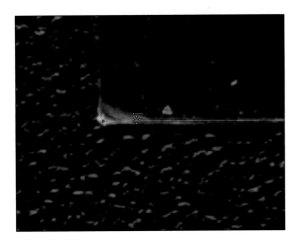

Figure 6.3
Using the Straighten tool.

9. **Zoom out and check the crop area against the sides of your photo.** Adjust the crop area inward to catch areas that aren't straight. You'll often lose a few rows of pixels along one or more of the edges, as photos aren't always perfectly square or rectangular (see Figure 6.5).

8. **Next, crop out the extra area (the scanner bed) you scanned.** Select the Crop tool from the Tools toolbar and uncheck the Maintain Aspect Ratio option. Drag the crop area to one corner of your photo. Expand the crop area toward each of the other corners, either one corner at a time (see Figure 6.4) or diagonally to the opposite corner.

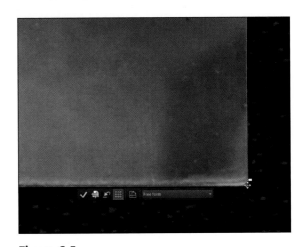

Figure 6.5
Fine-tuning the crop area.

10. **Finish the crop by clicking Apply.**

11. **Finally, save your straightened and cropped photo as a .pspimage file.**
    This preserves your original, unmodified scan as a .tif image and your working copy as the PaintShop Pro file.

Naming Advice

By never modifying the Background layer of your PaintShop Pro file, you can revert to the original photo that has been straightened and cropped by deleting the other working layers or copying and pasting the Background layer to a new image. Leave the original scan untouched. It's your ultimate backup.

Zooming In

After you scan the photo and straighten, crop, and save it as a .pspimage, you're ready to start working, right? Almost. First, look around and see what needs to be done. I chose this photo to illustrate how to remove specks and dust, which are plentiful. In this case, I scanned the photo at a very high resolution: 1200dpi. That almost always results in more tiny specks, dust, and damage that you have to fix. If you have the patience, and the photo isn't too bad to start with, it's worth it. If the photo has too much dust or damage, however, you'll never be able to fix all of it.

Figure 6.6 shows a close-up area of some of the specks and microscopic scratches on the surface of the photo. Notice how they appear to sit "on top" of the photo?

At very high scan resolutions, the damage to the surface of the photo looks like, well, like it's on the surface and not part of the image itself. This makes it easy to distinguish between surface problems and photo content.

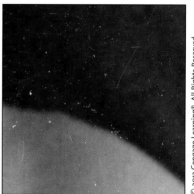

Figure 6.6
Specks galore.

Figure 6.7 shows another area of the image. These are small scratches that were probably caused by sliding the photo on a surface, perhaps into and out of an envelope. How can I tell? The scratches are aligned to the same direction.

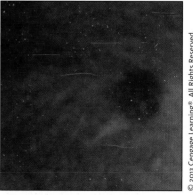

Figure 6.7
Nice scratches, too.

Take a look at the texture of the photo in Figures 6.6 and 6.7. It's pretty complex. This is an example where you won't be able to zoom out and broadly paint with the Clone brush. This calls for very close-in work. For photos of this size and resolution (the original scan is comparable to a 37-megapixel digital photo), in fact, you may need to be at 200% or more to get at all the tiny imperfections.

As always, I recommend creating a new, blank raster layer to clone on. (I call it the clone destination layer, or destination layer.) This preserves the original photo layer underneath. Rename the new layer to something practical, as shown in Figure 6.8, and select the Clone brush from the Toolbox. Enable the Use All Layers option in the Tool Options palette and then select your empty (at first) destination layer in the Layers palette.

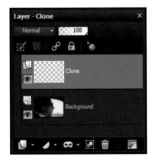

Figure 6.8
Using a destination layer to clone on.

Layers and the Blemish Fixer

I don't often use the Blemish Fixer in cases like this because it can't be used on an empty layer. I like creating a new layer to clone on. That layer makes it possible to undo or erase things later if I see that I've made a mistake. There are examples of using the Blemish Fixer elsewhere in this book (see Chapters 3, 8, and 9).

Developing a Good Cloning Technique

At first, cloning seems incredibly easy. Hit the tool, right-click to select a source area, and lay down the new material over the bad area. Presto, you're done. It looks great, and everyone will applaud your magnificent skills. Not so fast. There are times when cloning *is* that easy. This isn't one of them. The examples from this photo should help you see the difficulties you'll have to overcome. Bad technique will make your work obvious and not improve the photo.

Figure 6.9 illustrates the importance of making sure that you get the right color match between the source and the destination. Notice that I chose a source area (the circle with the *X* in it) that was pretty close to the speck I wanted to cover up. The problem is that I got a little too far into the dark area, and you can see that it doesn't match. If that happens, undo and start over immediately.

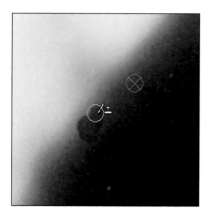

Figure 6.9
Poor color match from source to destination.

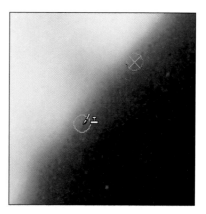

Figure 6.10
Good color match from source to destination.

I am using a better technique in Figure 6.10. I've chosen a source location that matches the tone and brightness of the destination area, and I am brushing with the "grain" of the color gradient. The results are completely invisible.

For Clarity's Sake

Most of the figures in this section are lighter than the image so you can see what's going on. I've also chosen to zoom in and crop very tightly to the action. After all, you don't need to see what's happening on the other side of the photo.

Figure 6.11 shows a different problem. Here, I am trying to cover up a scratch that runs across this small section of the photo. See the problem? I've brushed horizontally across the image, focusing on the shape of the blemish and not the result.

Don't become so focused on the shape of a scratch that you lose track of matching the source and destination material along its length. In this case, the source location was too far from the destination. Although close, it is an obvious mismatch. The other problem is that I used a single, long stroke. That makes matching color and brightness from source to destination very hard. Shorter strokes are often easier to hide.

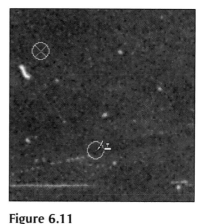

Figure 6.11
Obvious linear cloning.

I am using a better technique in Figure 6.12. I've selected a source area that matches the scratch area, and I am not simply dragging the brush along the scratch. I used a variety of fairly short strokes that didn't all go in one direction. Blending short strokes is much easier than trying to hide a single long one.

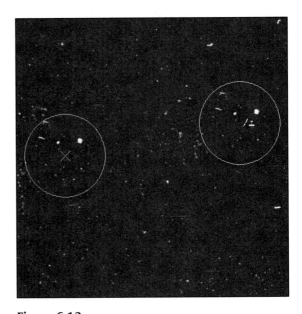

Figure 6.13
Cloning specks.

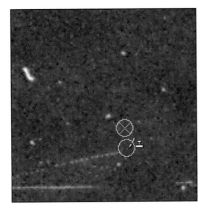

Figure 6.12
Hiding a scratch without it being obvious.

Figure 6.13 illustrates another common problem, the dreaded "speck transplant." I've gotten specks and blemishes in the source circle of the Clone brush and then transplanted them to another area of the photo. Definitely bad. Even if you do this on a small scale, people will notice the repeating pattern of specks, dust, or other features. You want to avoid this.

I am demonstrating the correct technique in Figure 6.14. I've chosen a smaller brush and taken special care to keep any blemished areas out of the source circle of the Clone brush.

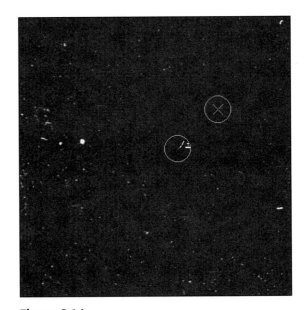

Figure 6.14
Avoiding "speck transplant."

Figure 6.15 illustrates the results of not matching the proper color, even though the source area I've chosen looks like a pretty close match. Always beware of subtle gradients that change colors gradually. Zooming in even more often helps you get the precision you need to select the right colors.

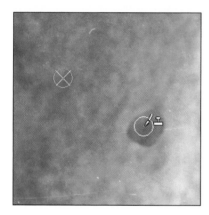

Figure 6.15
Tough color match shows I'm not zoomed in enough.

Therefore, I zoomed in to 200% in Figure 6.16. Notice that each little crease stands out very well, which gave me a fighting chance of getting all the little specks isolated and fixed. Take care to notice and then follow the "lay of the land." In other words, put your source location in dark areas to fix dark areas and likewise for light areas. This almost looks like a contour map. Clone hills to hills and valleys to valleys.

Figure 6.17 shows the results of careful cloning on this small patch of skin. If you didn't have Figure 6.16 to compare this to, you wouldn't know there had ever been a problem.

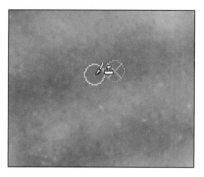

Figure 6.16
Good color match at 200%.

Figure 6.17
Completed section of hard-to-match skin.

Working a Pattern

Completely removing the specks, dust, and very small scratches in this photo study required successfully using the Clone brush what seemed like 10,000 times. As you work on your photos, take lots of breaks, don't be in too much of a hurry, and if your eyes get too tired, stop. I usually work in a grid pattern to ensure that I don't miss any areas of the photo, starting in a top corner and moving down. I work each vertical strip and then move slightly right or left to the next one. In this case, there were so many physical speck and dust problems that 200% was the best resolution to work at.

A representative section of one of the grids (cropped and enlarged for you to see better) is shown in Figure 6.18. There are a lot of problems to fix.

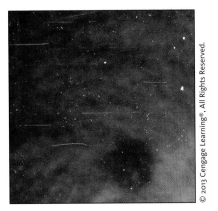

Figure 6.18
Grid number one, before.

Figure 6.19 illustrates the payoff. This is one little area of the photo cleaned up and without problems. This photo required me to fix the problems in 299 more squares. Yes, that is a tremendous amount of work. Don't lose hope and don't get too bogged down. Start. Make progress. Every little bit helps, and before you know it, you'll be done.

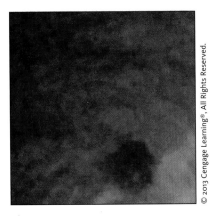

Figure 6.19
Grid number one, after.

Finishing the Photo Study

The completed restoration of Jim driving his car is shown in Figure 6.20. I finished removing all the specks, dust, and other surface imperfections of the photo using the Clone brush. I also worked with the brightness, contrast, and color saturation of the photo. In the end, I also made a color temperature adjustment, as Jim looked a little too yellow. In this case, I used the Adjust > White Balance dialog, and with Advanced Options checked, changed the Temperature to 7388 and Tint to −23 in the Enhance Color Balance section.

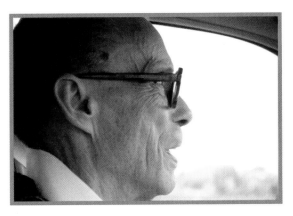

Figure 6.20
A treasured photo restored and now without specks and scratches.

Photo Study 22: Working in Hard-to-See Areas

FIGURE 6.21 IS A PHOTO, taken in 1998, of the grandstand on the front straightaway of the Indianapolis Motor Speedway. Home to the "Greatest Spectacle in Racing," the Speedway is truly an awesome place. Imagine as many people in one place at the same time as you've ever seen in one place at the same time before—and then imagine more. It's astounding, really, and that's before a single car starts its engine and roars by. When that happens, it literally takes your breath away.

Anne and I were engaged at the time, and on this trip to the 500, we had fantastic seats. We were literally within yards of the Start-Finish line. I took this shot looking south down the grandstand toward turn one, and you can see the famed scoring pylon rising up to the left.

Behind the Scenes

It literally took me about an hour to find the name of the scoring pylon. I didn't want to call it "that black tower thingy with all the numbers on it," so I researched different sites on the Web, including the official Indianapolis Motor Speedway site and Wikipedia to find out what to call it.

I took one of those "disposable" panoramic cameras to the race that year. At various times, I try to take photos of different things or events with panoramic cameras. (I shoot digital panoramas and HDR a lot now—and take my old Nikon FE2 along if I want to shoot film.) I really like them for special purposes.

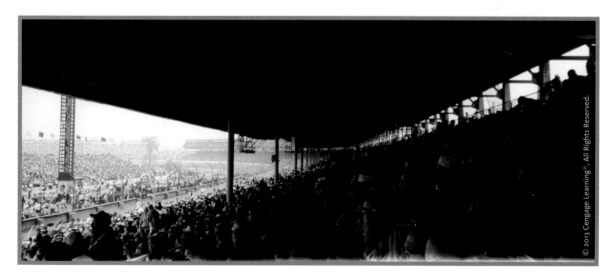

Figure 6.21
A great day at the Indianapolis 500, except for the dust on this dark photo.

This camera wasn't any good for action shots of the cars whizzing by, but it was ideal for sweeping panoramas of the grandstand and crowd. This was shortly before the cars were given the command to start their engines. The front straightaway was filled with the pit crews and their cars awaiting the order.

Obvious and Not-So-Obvious Problems

Looking at the scan of the original photo, you can see dust all over the image when magnified. It's in the crowd and in the rafters. There are other problems as well, but I want to focus on the dust in this photo study. You would think the dark rafters would be an easy fix, but it's hard to fix things you can't see very well.

In cases like this, use an adjustment layer to show the hidden details of a photo; then use the Clone brush to remove the dust, specks, and scratches. After you're done cloning, the adjustment layer can be discarded. Here's how to do it:

1. **Create a Levels adjustment layer in the Layers palette, as shown in Figure 6.22.** Make sure it's on top of the photo layer.

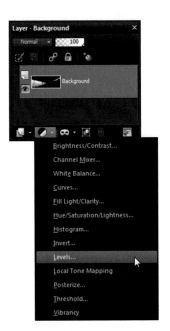

Figure 6.22
Create an adjustment layer to bring out hidden details.

2. **Alter the levels, as shown in Figure 6.23, in order to bring out hidden details in the photo.** To lighten shadows, lower the white diamond slider toward the left side of the dialog box. As you do so, the gray diamond will be "squished" proportionately. Fine-tune the gray diamond to see if you can bring out more details. The point here is not necessarily to make the photo look good, but to make the problems stand out.

The Cool Thing About Adjustment Layers

Adjustment layers are pretty convenient, depending on how you work. You can make dramatic changes without altering the photo and then go back and change the settings or create different adjustment layers to compare effects. I use them mostly to experiment with different settings (usually Levels and Curves) before I lock those in and move on.

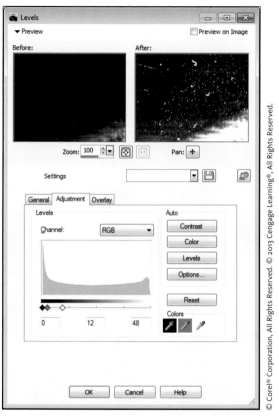

Figure 6.23
Alter levels to lighten dark areas of the photo.

3. **Next, create a new raster layer to serve as your clone destination.** I've named mine "Clone" (see Figure 6.24). Put it between the photo and adjustment layers (named Levels 1 in the figure).

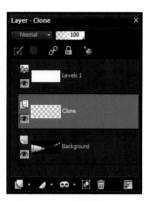

Figure 6.24
Sandwiching the Clone destination layer.

4. **Select the Clone brush tool.**

5. **Uncheck the Use All Layers option.** You don't want to pick up material from the adjustment layer. You'll know if you do because it will look very weird.

Happy Little Accident

I discovered this technique by accident. I was altering the levels toward the end of restoring this photo (the first time), and realized there was much more detail in the rafters than I could originally see. I went back and used an adjustment layer so I could see where to clone, and then started over.

Very Important

These next few steps are critical. Pay attention to which layer is active when you select a source area and which layer is active when you use the Clone brush. Remember, these layers are purposefully very different. Keep practicing until it becomes second nature to switch layers between each operation.

6. **Select the photo layer (in this case, it's called Background) in the Layers palette (see Figure 6.25).** Right-click in the photo to establish a source area on that source layer. It's very important that the photo layer is the source and the Use All Layers option is turned off for this to work.

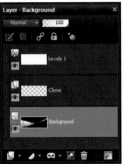
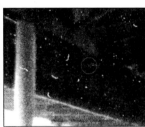

Figure 6.25
Selecting a source patch from the photo layer.

7. **Next, select the layer you want to clone onto (this is the destination layer, which I've named Clone) in the Layers palette (see Figure 6.26) and brush accordingly.** Your cloning should blend right in. If it doesn't, then you've selected the wrong layers.

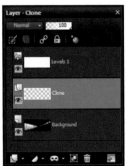
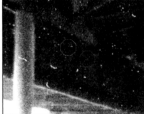

Figure 6.26
Applying the brush on the working layer, named Clone.

8. **Continue alternating back and forth between selecting a source from the photo layer and then applying the Clone brush to the working clone layer (again, the one I named Clone).** Figure 6.27 shows what this region of the photo looked like before and after I cloned out the specks.

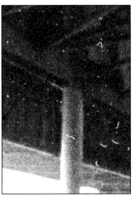
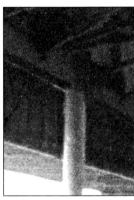

Figure 6.27
Before-and-after cloning, with the adjustment layer active.

If you turn off the adjustment layer now, it would be too dark to see the effects of your cloning. When (or possibly if) you adjust the overall lightness of the photo, you'll be secure in knowing the cloning you completed in the shadows won't show up as a big obvious messy patch in the middle of your photo.

You can apply this technique to the entire photo if you need to. In this case, there are parts of the crowd where it will make a difference. In fact, Figure 6.28 shows two shots of the same area. The first area is prior to cloning, and the second is after (both have the adjustment layer active). It's not perfect in every way, of course, but when this photo is brightened, it will look really good.

Home Study

Try to cause this problem on purpose so that you can see firsthand what it looks like. In other words, find a dark photo that has dust or blemishes and then fix them without the aid of an adjustment layer. After you're done, use a Levels adjustment layer to brighten the photo and see if you can tell where you cloned. Compare your success with this technique.

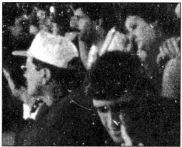

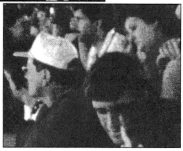

Figure 6.28
Showing the effects of this technique in the crowd.

Finishing the Photo Study

Once I had the cloning technique down, all I had to do was to finish removing the dust, specks, and other imperfections and then do some other touch-ups, including the overall brightness, contrast, and color of the photo. In the end, I also made an additional Levels adjustment, applied a small amount of Local Tone Mapping, and warmed areas of the crowd and sky (they were too blue).

Remember to delete or hide the adjustment layer. After you finish cloning in the hard-to-see areas, you'll no longer need it. Figure 6.29 shows the finished result.

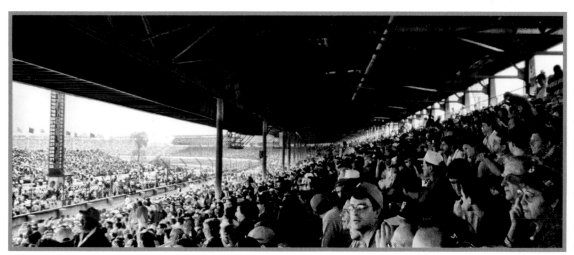

Figure 6.29
Celebrating a dust-free Indianapolis 500.

Photo Study 23:
Dusting Off Digital Shots for eBay

FIGURE 6.30 IS AN UNRETOUCHED photo of a brand new camera I worked with in 2012. It's a Canon EOS 5D Mark III digital SLR, shown here with the 18–105mm kit lens. The 5D Mark III is the newest and most affordable full-frame (that means the sensor is the same size as a frame of 35mm film) dSLR that Canon sells at this time.

This is the type of home studio shot that isn't too hard to put together and can look really great when finished. It's the kind of thing you might use to sell something on eBay. After all, everyone loves a good product shot. All you need to do is clean the camera up a bit and save the result.

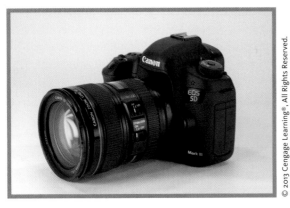

© 2013 Cengage Learning®, All Rights Reserved.

Figure 6.30
Basic shot of a Canon EOS 5D Mark III.

Picking Your Process

As you probably realized by now, when working with digital photos that you've shot yourself, you can choose to follow one of three photo retouching routes. They are the following:

▶ **The Camera RAW Lab:** This is a specialized aspect of PaintShop Pro that gives you some control over the RAW file conversion process. The Camera RAW Lab has minimal, but functional controls. If your camera doesn't support RAW files, or you choose not to use them, the Camera RAW Lab is not an option.

▶ **The Adjust workspace:** The Adjust workspace is a powerful aspect of PaintShop Pro. The Adjust workspace gathers and organizes several photo retouching controls and tools into one seamless interface. You have access to the photo's histogram, can view its parameters, and can fix things such as an incorrect color balance, poor brightness, contrast, sharpness, and reduce the noise level. The Adjust workspace is perfect for single-layer images and a reasonably simple edit.

▶ **The Edit workspace:** The Edit workspace is where you unlock all the powers of PaintShop Pro, and it's where you have the most options and the most control. Menu items that aren't available in the Adjust workspace are available here. You can also work with multiple palettes and create and manage multiple layers.

This is a perfect photo to see what sorts of results are possible using only the Adjust workspace. The photo is basically clean and clear. It needs few adjustments, and since the Clone brush is accessible in Adjust, the dust can be fixed here as well.

Making the Adjustments

To open a photo for editing in the Adjust tab, click its thumbnail in the Organizer. Alternatively, you can drag a file from Windows Explorer and drop it on the Adjust window or use the File ❯ Open menu.

With the file open, examine the histogram above the tools. Use the histogram to help you interpret the photo. In this case (see Figure 6.31), the lighting looks good. There is a small gap between the darks in the photo and the left edge of the histogram. That means that there is extra room for shadows to be darkened. This photo shows a dearth of midtones. That's understandable, as the background is white (highs) and the camera is black (lows).

Although you may decide to take another path, I prefer skipping the tools beneath the histogram (Crop, Straighten, Red Eye, and so forth) and going through the other options in order, from the top down.

First up, then, is the Smart Photo Fix. Press Suggest Settings and see what PaintShop Pro's quick solution is. As shown in Figure 6.32, the recommended settings increase the brightness a bit, leave the shadows alone, brighten the highlights, increase the saturation of the photo, and trim both ends of the photo's spectrum.

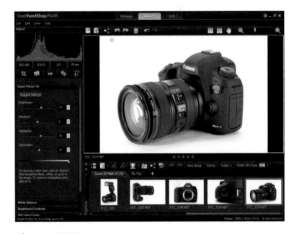

Figure 6.32
Use the suggested settings as a reality check.
© Corel® Corporation, All Rights Reserved. © 2013 Cengage Learning®, All Rights Reserved.

Although the results aren't horrible, this is a case where PaintShop Pro doesn't know this is a photo of a black camera on a white background and therefore is supposed to be dark and bright at the same time. I like the look of the original photo better than this.

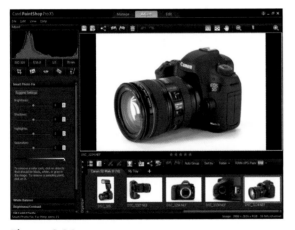

Figure 6.31
Use the histogram to analyze and troubleshoot.
© Corel® Corporation, All Rights Reserved. © 2013 Cengage Learning®, All Rights Reserved.

If you want to, adjust the settings to suit your taste or press the Undo arrow. If all looks fine, try boosting the saturation to try more troubleshooting. I temporarily increased Saturation to 74, as shown in Figure 6.33, to see if the white balance of the photo was correct. The increase in saturation reveals a green background tint and blue camera tint that weren't as apparent before. That's a problem (albeit minor), as the camera should be black and the background white.

Therefore, as shown in Figure 6.34, I moved the Temperature slider towards the Warmer side and the Tint slider towards Purple. Notice the appearance of the camera is now truly a dark gray. This is confirmed by looking at the histogram. The red, green, and blue peaks in the histogram have lined up with each other, indicating a nice strong gray towards the dark end of the spectrum. That's exactly as it should be.

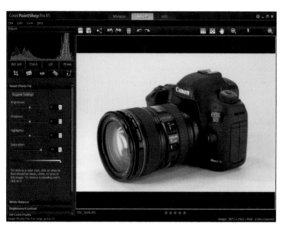

Figure 6.33

Boosting saturation to evaluate white balance.

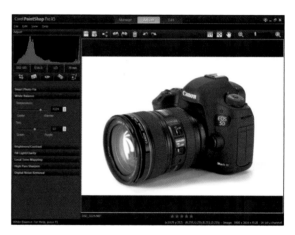

Figure 6.34

Correcting color tints with White Balance.

To correct white balance problems, click the White Balance option and drag the Temperature and Tint sliders around until you see something that looks good. In this case, I wanted to correct both a cool (or blue) tint that was plaguing the camera and a green tint that crept into the background.

As you work with your photos continue moving down the list of options, clicking the title of each setting to expand it. Remember, this isn't a contest to see how many tweaks you can make to a photo. It's okay to make one or two or ten. The number is irrelevant, save for the fact that overediting increases the risk of revealing your work and ruining the photo. Be happy when you don't have to do much.

One note of caution: When you select a new tool or option, the settings you have in the currently selected item are applied. Therefore, if you are experimenting and leave something goofy in Smart Photo Fix when you click on, say, Brightness/Contrast, it will stick. It's best to zero the settings out if you've decided not to use a particular feature.

In this case, the color looks fine, as do the brightness and contrast. There's no need to stop and play with those settings. If you want realistic photos, there's no overriding need to mess with Fill Light/Clarity or Local Tone Mapping. However, they can fix photos with poor contrast by clarifying edges and pulling out details.

If you want to know what a setting does, grab the control and max it out. Then move it to its minimum. That way you can see the entire range of the effect.

The last two adjustments to consider are High Pass Sharpen and Digital Noise Removal. Now, in many ways, these are important controls. However, consider the final size and resolution of your image before you get too carried away. If the final size is going to be small, there is no need to oversharpen or remove every speck of noise at this level. If things look reasonable when you're looking at the entire photo in PaintShop Pro, try removing some softness from the photo and eliminating any glaring noise, but don't overdo it. No one will ever notice when it's reduced and displayed on the Web.

For this photo, even a small amount of High Pass Sharpen made the noise worse and did not noticeably increase the sharpness (see Figure 6.35). If this is the case, don't bother with it!

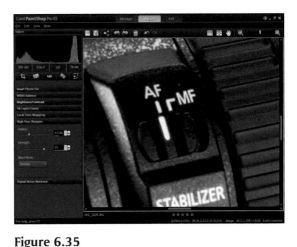

Figure 6.35
Sharpening is not effective here.

Tackling Dust

Now it's time to dust. This is the dust problem that plagues digital photos when you're taking really nice, high-resolution shots of stuff. Dust settles on everything. Try dusting your subjects off with a cloth or using a puff of compressed air, but unless you're setting up in a NASA Clean Room, fighting dust is a battle that you'll have to continue in software.

Since this study is using the Adjust tab, there's only one way to remove the dust: the Clone brush. If you are working in the Edit tab, you also have the Blemish Fixer and some of the more esoteric Add/Remove Noise options to choose from. For this study, I've eschewed my normal procedure of creating working and clone layers. All the action happens on the photo layer.

Select the Clone brush from the small toolbar beneath the histogram and adjust the settings as you would in the Edit workspace.

In this case, the camera body and lens have a small amount of dust. There are also a few overzealous pixels (the ones that get stuck on are the biggest problem) and other imperfections in the background to clone out.

First, the camera body. Zoom in to work, and set the size of the brush larger than the dust particles you want to remove. This surface is deceptively complex. In cases like this, you have to see where the gradient flows from dark areas to lighter areas and clone along it (see Figure 6.36), just as you would a face or other surface.

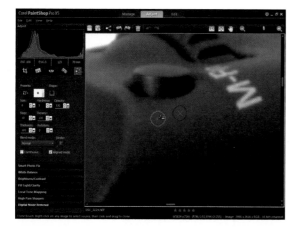

Figure 6.36
Matching the light gradient.
© Corel® Corporation, All Rights Reserved. © 2013 Cengage Learning®, All Rights Reserved.

If you're working with an area that has a lot of small specks, like you see in Figure 6.37, make the brush very small. Right-click carefully to match tones around the area you're covering up, and be careful not to pick up any specks and transplant them.

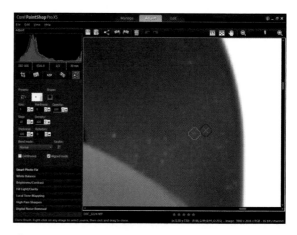

Figure 6.37
Cloning carefully in tighter spaces.
© Corel® Corporation, All Rights Reserved. © 2013 Cengage Learning®, All Rights Reserved.

In the case of the lens rings (many zoom and focus rings have ridges), clone with the ridges (see Figure 6.38), not across them. You can often right-click once to establish your source and keep it for several ridges.

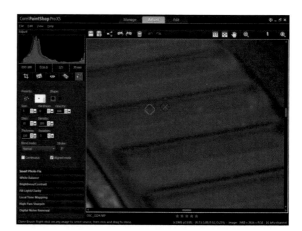

Figure 6.38
Clone with features like these lens ridges.
© Corel® Corporation, All Rights Reserved. © 2013 Cengage Learning®, All Rights Reserved.

Zoom in and out to finish work on the camera; then inspect the background to make sure it doesn't have any major problems. In this case (Figure 6.39), there were a few spots on my white paper background.

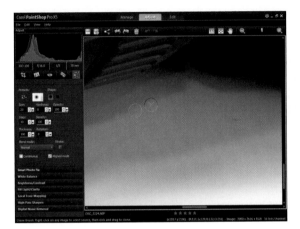

Figure 6.39

Watch out for dust or marks on the background.

© Corel® Corporation, All Rights Reserved. © 2013 Cengage Learning®, All Rights Reserved.

Finishing the Photo Study

If necessary, straighten and crop the photo and then save it as a new image. If you need to resize it to put it on the Web, you'll have to switch to the Edit workspace and choose Image ❯ Resize. Save your photo first. When you switch to Edit, it will be opened automatically.

The finished photo, shown in Figure 6.40, is clean, neat, looks good, and provides a great view of the camera.

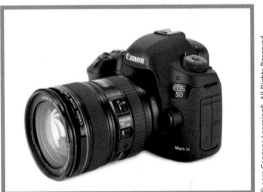

Figure 6.40

A product shot worthy of eBay.

Photo Study 24: Dealing with Background Texture

FIGURE 6.41 IS A CUTE SHOT of our oldest son, Ben. It was taken in 2003, when he was about 9 months old. We had this taken in the mall by one of those professional chains. We would walk by the store on our way somewhere else, and they would invariably ask us in for a free sitting. We took them up on their offer a few times, and were always happy with the results.

You may not get digital files from a studio. They want you to pay for prints, which can deteriorate over time. When I decided to scan this photo and preserve it as a digital image, I realized how much was wrong with the original. It had scratches and pits all over it. I also realized that studio prints like this sometimes have a texture to them that can interfere with the scan and make the digital image even harder to retouch.

Reducing Size to Experiment

The surface texture and other imperfections are a major problem for this photo. This one doesn't look easy, and promises to be downright tedious. There are times when I sit at the computer for hours trying different approach after different approach, searching to find just the right combination of things to restore or retouch a photo. I tell myself that I'm not wasting time—I'm solving a puzzle.

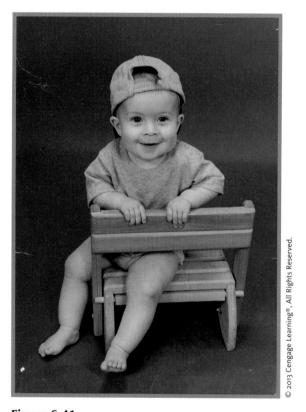

First Things First

Most of the time, I find it helpful to clean up photos with more damage before I make any sweeping brightness, color, noise, or contrast adjustments.

Figure 6.41
Scratches, specks, and texture problems abound in this studio print.

You can treat some surface texture problems like noise, so that's how I am going to approach restoring this photo. Since I originally scanned this photo at a very high resolution, making constant noise adjustments to the overall photo takes a lot of processing power and time. Do. Wait. Undo. Wait. Do. Wait. Undo. Wait. Wait some more. Believe me, I've sat here and done a lot of waiting.

Try this alternate technique to experiment with different solutions when working with huge photos. It should save you a lot of processing time. Here's what to do:

1. Open up the photo in PaintShop Pro's Edit workspace.

2. Select the Selection tool (Rectangular type) from the Tools toolbar.

3. Look around. Zoom in and out. Find a good area to serve as a representative sample of the overall texture or noise problem.

4. Use the Selection tool to select a small portion of the photo (the area you identified in step 3).

5. Copy the area using Ctrl+C.

6. Select Edit ❯ Paste as New Image.

7. Save the new image as an experimental working copy. Now you've got a smaller image to work with that won't take forever to apply a number of different noise removal techniques to and compare them against each other.

Figure 6.42 is a close-up of an area that has part of the background and Ben's ear. I chose this as a good representative sample of the background texture, imperfections, and photo detail. I can see where the texture and specks stand out and how the noise reduction will affect both areas.

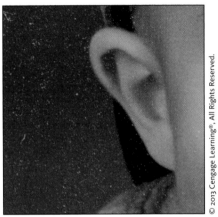

Figure 6.42
The test area.

Cleaning Things Up

Although this technically isn't noise, PaintShop Pro has a number of different ways to tackle these types of problems. Deciding which one is best for a particular photo takes time and determination. This section is a grab bag of techniques, most of which you'll immediately look at and say "Ugh!" or "What?" That's because noise can be notoriously hard to remove without damaging the image (the Ugh!) or make you wonder if it's doing anything (the What?).

One Step Noise Removal

This sounds promising. One step! What could be simpler? Apply it by selecting the Adjust menu and choosing One Step Noise Removal. Figure 6.43 reveals the result. It's hard to tell, but there is noise that has been reduced on Ben's ear and cheek. The specks, however, are still prevalent.

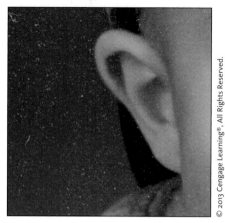

Figure 6.44
Hard to tell if anything changed here.

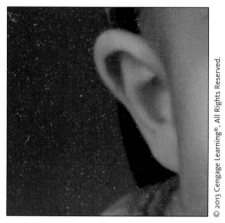

Figure 6.43
Good on the cheek, but ineffective against specks.

Edge Preserving Smooth

Another selection available from the Adjust ❯ Add/Remove Noise menu, Edge Preserving Smooth sounds promising. I had to ratchet the setting up to 20 to get it to do anything for this image. Figure 6.45 shows the result, which I thought was iffy at first, but to be honest, it's growing on me.

Despeckle

Despeckle is also part of the Adjust ❯ Add/Remove Noise menu. That's a perfectly reasonable place to expect to find tools that will help you remove specks, film grain, and noise. Figure 6.44 shows the result.

It doesn't seem to have done much for this photo. Keep trying on your own photos, because you never know when this will be the exact thing you need.

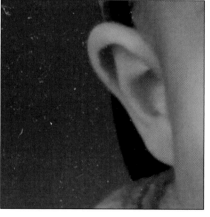

Figure 6.45
Edge Preserving Smooth removes noise and some detail.

Texture Preserving Smooth

Texture Preserving Smooth is the same as Edge Preserving Smooth, only completely different. In this case, it tries to preserve the texture of a photo inside the edges, as opposed to protecting the edges. For edges, think focus and sharpness. For textures, think, well, texture. It's the surface material. Choose Texture Preserving Smooth from the Adjust ❯ Add/Remove Noise menu.

Figure 6.46 shows the results of applying the maximum Texture Preserving Smooth adjustment. It has done a reasonable job of not oversmoothing the image, but the specks are worse than Edge Preserving Smooth.

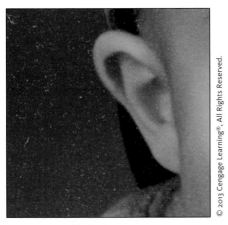

Figure 6.46
Texture Preserving Smooth is not so good in this case.

Salt and Pepper Filter

Another possible solution to the crisis is the Salt and Pepper Filter from the Adjust ❯ Add/Remove Noise menu. The only problem is that I don't see any salt or pepper (ha ha). Figure 6.47 shows the results. There is a definite effect, but I'm not sure I like it. You can alter the speck size and the filter's sensitivity to specks in the dialog box, but this was about the best I could do with this photo. (The settings I used were 5, 4, yes, and yes.)

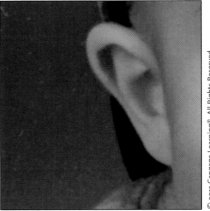

Figure 6.47
Good, but not perfect.

Median Filter

The Median Filter (choose Adjust ❯ Add/Remove Noise ❯ Median Filter) is often quite good at removing film grain or noise in a photo. In this case, I'm fairly happy with it, but it has enough flaws (too many specks) that make me not want to use it. This is often the situation when you are restoring or retouching photos. It's sometimes very difficult to find a good solution, and there is often no solution that works the best. Figure 6.48 shows the result of the Median Filter applied with a Filter aperture of 7. Going any higher resulted in a blurry, blotchy photo.

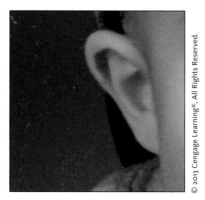

Figure 6.48
*The Median filter has a harder time on
specks unless you go overboard.*

The Combo Platter

You always have the option of masking out your
subject and applying different levels of noise
reduction (or sharpening, or Levels adjustments, or
whatever you want) to it versus the background.
Duplicate the background layer (or your interim
working layer) as many times as you have different
areas you want to apply different levels (or types)
of noise reduction to. In this case, I created one
layer for the backdrop and another for Ben. I plan
to optimize the noise reduction for each texture.

Figure 6.49 shows the Layers palette at the stage
where I completed the mask around Ben. The layers and a description of their function within the
file (from top to bottom) are the following:

> ▶ **Group - Ben:** This is the layer group formed
> when I created a mask to hide the back-
> ground on Ben's layer.

>> • **Mask:** This mask hides the part of the
>> layer just beneath it in this layer group.
>> Black hides and white reveals. I used a
>> combination of techniques to get the
>> mask, in order to cover what I wanted
>> to hide.

• **Ben - lighter smoothing:** This is the layer
that will show Ben. I can apply a different
amount of noise reduction here (Median
Filter, but not as strong as what I used on
the backdrop) and hide the backdrop
on this layer, allowing a lower layer (with
more noise reduction) to show through.

▶ **Backdrop - heavy smoothing:** This is the
layer that I want to use for the backdrop.
It has heavier smoothing that does a better
job of taking away the specks. The same
amount on Ben would have taken away all
his detail. Notice that I don't need to mask
anything out of this layer because Ben's
layer is on top of it.

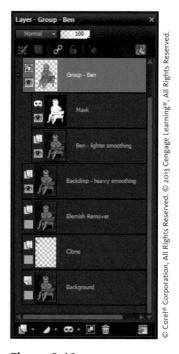

Figure 6.49
*Selectively applying noise reduction
to different areas of the photo.*

▶ **Blemish Fixer:** This layer was an interim step. I used it to remove larger blemishes in the backdrop before I smoothed it. It was created by copying everything beneath (a merged copy) and pasting it as a new layer. I turned this and the next two layers off to indicate they were completely covered up by the upper layers. Their purpose now is to enable me to backtrack to any part of the process.

▶ **Clone:** This is another working layer. It has all the clone work I did on the backdrop and Ben.

▶ **Background:** This is the original photo layer, straightened and cropped.

Finishing the Photo Study

Figure 6.50 shows the final photo. This was a very challenging study because of the number of pits, specks, scratches, and other surface imperfections, not to mention the odd surface texture caused by being a professional studio print. However, a combination of cloning and blemish fixing, with different levels of smoothing made possible by a mask, made the photo much better.

For Ben's layer, I used a slight amount of Digital Noise Removal and Unsharp Mask after the Median Filter. These seemingly contradictory adjustments took out specks, smoothed his skin, and sharpened the edges—in that order. In the end, I edited the mask to allow the smoother backdrop to show through in darker areas, even on Ben. That helped eliminate the last specks on his layer, and it goes unnoticed because of the way the shadows fall and where the focus changes from being sharp to blurry due to the depth-of-field effect caused by the lens' aperture.

After getting things smoothed and masked the way I wanted, I selected all (Ctrl+A), performed a merged copy (Ctrl+Shift+C), and pasted that as a new layer to lock everything in. I think I went over the image one more time with the Blemish Fixer and Clone brush, removing any obvious problems. Always go back and clone or use the Blemish Fixer to touch up. I was able to knock out the remaining specks quite nicely, and any imperfections that are left lend to the authenticity of the photo (look at the scuff marks on the backdrop). As a last step, I used Levels to brighten the photo.

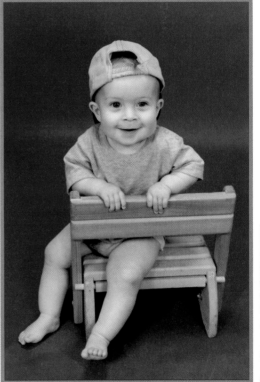

Figure 6.50
Looking good with the original background.

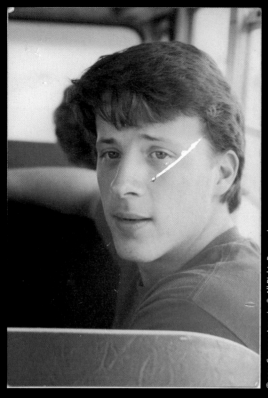

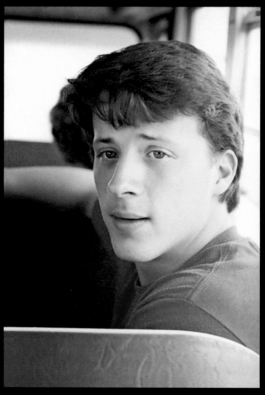

Repairing Scratches, Tears, Creases, and Holes

7

TACKLING PHYSICAL PROBLEMS is challenging but also fun and very rewarding. One of the reasons I love working with these problems is my affection for using the Clone brush. It's something *you* have to do, unlike a dialog box or menu choice. The computer can't. Using the Clone brush takes skill, daring, and creative courage to go plopping down stuff where there isn't any to begin with. Follow along with me as I use the Clone brush and other tools to retouch and restore these damaged photos:

▶ **Photo Study 25: Fixing a Large Scratch**—A large scratch across my cheek ruins this photo of me from high school. Compare how effective the Clone brush is with the Scratch Remover.

▶ **Photo Study 26: Repairing Border Problems and Tearing**—It's a fact that older photos are prone to wear and tear, especially around the edges. Not a problem, because restoring a torn border is pretty easy. Film tearing is a less common problem. Learn how to tackle both issues with the Clone brush in this photo study.

▶ **Photo Study 27: Repairing a Mounted Photo**—Some old prints were cut into ovals and pasted onto sturdy cardboard mounts. It's impossible to separate them. Learn how to repair the frame and the photo in this study.

▶ **Photo Study 28: Filling a Hole**—This photo has a small hole torn in the bottom center. Learn how to repair it with the Clone brush. Aside from the obvious aesthetic reasons for fixing holes and tears, you can print the restored photo and handle it without fear of damaging the original further.

▶ **Photo Study 29: Mending a Torn Photo**—This photo has been torn in half and taped back together. Learn how to put photos like this back together and hide the tape so the photo looks like it was never torn.

▶ **Photo Study 30: Mending a Partial Tear**—This old photo has a tear running most of the way across it. One problem is that the tear travels across my wife's great grandmother's dress—which has a pattern I have to be careful to follow.

▶ **Photo Study 31: Dealing with Tears, Creases, and Stains**—This study features a photo of the Leaning Tower of Pisa. Follow along with the basic steps of restoring a print photo that has been physically damaged.

▶ **Photo Study 32: Restoring a Missing Corner**—Learn how to creatively re-create a missing corner in this advanced photo study.

Photo Study 25: Fixing a Large Scratch

FIGURE 7.1 IS A PHOTO OF ME in high school. I think I was on some sort of band trip when one of my friends took this. I really like this shot, and am thankful to be able to show my kids some photos of me from my youth. They get to see my past and get a glimpse into their future.

Unfortunately, there is a large scratch running up my cheek. It looks horrible, but is actually quite repairable due to its location. Notice that it is in an area where there's not much intricate detail. Although there are subtle variations in skin tone and lighting, it's just skin. If the scratch were across my eye, nose, mouth, or ear, it would be much harder to fix.

Removing Scanner Artifacts

There are hard-to-see artifacts created by the scanner in this photo. The most obvious one runs right across the top of my eyes and is a few pixel rows high. These artifacts run horizontally across the photo in different areas. I carefully smoothed them with the Smooth brush to reduce their visibility for this study.

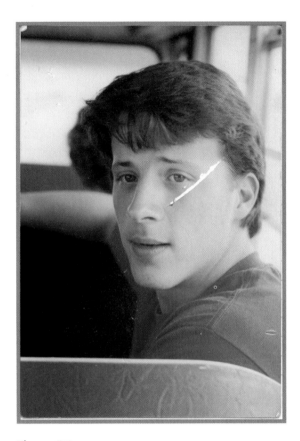

Figure 7.1
This photo is very fixable.
© 2013 Cengage Learning®, All Rights Reserved.

Trying Scratch Remover

This seems like a good time to try out the Scratch Remover. I'm applying it to the scratch in Figure 7.2.

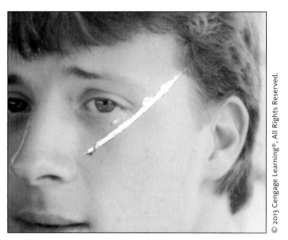

Figure 7.2
Trying one large Scratch Remover.

Increase or decrease the width of the tool to match the scratch. I've chosen a rather large width to get the entire scratch under control, which was 55 pixels. Figure 7.3 shows the result, which is fairly bad.

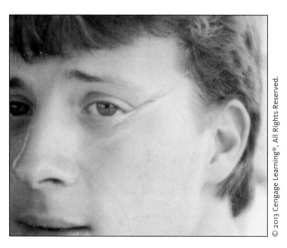

Figure 7.3
Blending problems are prominent.

I'm rather surprised at how bad this looks. I thought it would look reasonably good, but it had major problems with my eye and hair.

You could try to apply the Scratch Remover across the scratch, as shown in Figure 7.4.

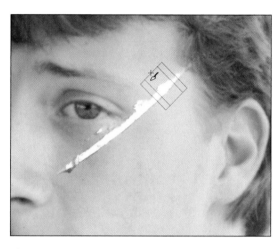

Figure 7.4
Going across a scratch is not effective.

Figure 7.5 shows the result. Hardly anything happened. That's because the Scratch Remover relies on blending the outer regions of the tool's swath toward the center. Take another look at Figure 7.4. The tool has a central area that should cover what you're trying to fix. The outer border is what the tool pulls from (like a clone source) in order to blend into the center.

When you go across a scratch instead of along it, you're pulling the scratch in and blending it along its own axis of imperfection, which defeats the entire purpose.

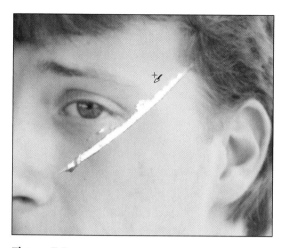

Figure 7.5

Little change here.

In the next photo study, you'll see that smaller applications of the Scratch Remover seem to work pretty well. I am using several small strokes with the Scratch Remover in Figure 7.6, and there is definite improvement over the large swath of the original.

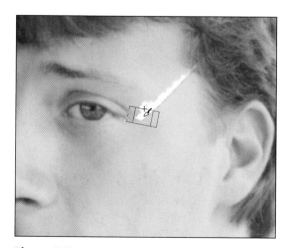

Figure 7.6

Scratch Remover in smaller applications.

One reason I prefer the Clone brush to the Scratch Remover in photo restoration and retouching is the ability to separate what I'm doing to a new layer and blend it in later. Since you can't do that with the Scratch Remover, make sure that you're using a duplicate layer so you can go back easily to prior steps if you need to.

Cloning

Cloning is also a viable technique to remove scratches, but your technique has to be up to the task. Figure 7.7 shows what can happen if you don't get an exact match from the source to the destination. This is the pinnacle of cloning "wrongness." If this happens, undo and then start over. Keep at it until you get it right. Sometimes I have to select a source area two or three times (maybe even more) to get the right hue and lightness at the source to match the destination. You may also have to adjust the brush size, depending on the size and shape of the source area you're pulling from.

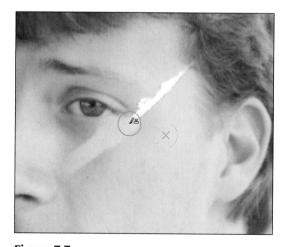

Figure 7.7

Matching shades is very important.

I've done just that in Figure 7.8. Even though my original source was pretty close to the destination (as shown in Figure 7.7), it wasn't a good match. The source was clearly lighter than the destination area.

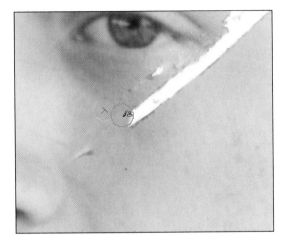

Figure 7.8
Clone along shade lines.

Keep Trying!

I consider myself pretty good at this stuff, but trial and error remain part of the equation. Experience and talent mean a lot, but they don't guarantee that every time you right-click to select a source area it will automatically be a perfect match with the destination area. There will be times when the color gradient is subtle enough that it will take getting it wrong a few times to find the right source spot.

Pay attention to subtle changes in hue and what direction gradient "flows." This will keep the trial and error phase to a reasonable minimum. Another thing to keep in mind is that this source may only be good for a very small area at the destination, meaning you need to continually move and adjust your source spot for areas of photos like this. At this magnification, this portion of my face is a very complex shape that has subtle lighting differences that result in a continually changing landscape.

I don't want you to think, though, that this is always super hard or impossible to get right. It's probably harder for me to explain than it is for you to do.

I am using another good technique in Figure 7.9. I've moved my source spot over to the other side of the scratch in order to find a good match for where I plan to clone. Work both sides of a scratch like this to make sure you are getting the tone right.

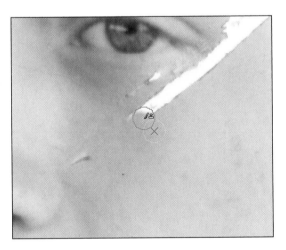

Figure 7.9
Now from the other side.

Another trick is to zoom in to see some of the more microscopic cloning that you need to do. You don't need to do this on the larger elements, but in Figure 7.10, I've zoomed to 600% to get at a line of damage that runs parallel to the main scratch. You can see that the line hasn't broken the surface of the film but instead looks like something on top of it. My brush size has been scaled down to 5 pixels to fit in this area. You can also see that I've got my source selected just above the destination. This was the best area to get the right "flow" of my skin tone.

Try and develop a habit of zooming in and out to inspect your work. You will find a "sweet spot" for each level of damage you're trying to fix. If you zoom in closer, you'll feel claustrophobic, but if you zoom out you can't see the right level of detail. Whatever your current working view is, closer inspections are always a good idea to catch problems you might miss at a lower magnification. The cumulative effect of fixing a large number of very tiny problems can be dramatic.

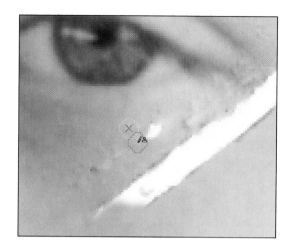

Figure 7.10
Smaller brush for a tiny area.
© Corel® Corporation, All Rights Reserved. © 2013 Cengage Learning®, All Rights Reserved.

Dabbing

Remember to alternate your technique based on the situation at hand. Sometimes, "dabbing" is better than laying down a long stroke with the Clone brush. In fact, you should hardly ever select the Clone brush and start painting away like you would a normal brush. Use short, small strokes and don't forget to dab.

I've got one final tip for you to consider. When you're done cloning, check your work by creating a temporary Levels adjustment layer. Set the Levels adjustment to something wacky that brings out any possible deviations in tone and delete or hide this layer when you're done inspecting your cloning work. I'm setting this temporary layer up in Figure 7.11. I dragged the dark and middle adjustment diamonds upward, which has made the After preview window look pretty dark. That's okay. It's not supposed to look good. You're supposed to be able to see changes in tone that might have been imperceptible under normal lighting conditions.

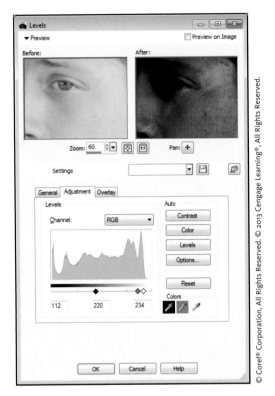

Figure 7.11
Use a Levels adjustment layer to check your work.

Notice where the scratch used to be in Figure 7.11? It's not there anymore. That's good. But I can see where I've cloned. That's not ideal. In fact, when I arrived at this point, I studied the photo very closely because it really bothered me. I came to the conclusion that I was seeing a couple of things. First, my cloning successfully covered the scratch. When I compare where the scratch was with the tone of my cheek elsewhere, it blends in very nicely. When the photo was scratched, the rubbing that caused the scratch also caused additional damage that wasn't as obvious. That's the reddish tone you see in Figure 7.11, which was made more visible by the temporary Levels adjustment layer.

In my final restoration, I repaired the rub marks where I could, but I was content to leave some visible. More repair work in this case would be more visible than the original damage.

Finishing the Photo Study

My final work is revealed in Figure 7.12. I took the main scratch on my face out, but left in some smaller imperfections in the shadows to my front. I got the photo to the point where I really liked it, and I didn't want to overdo it.

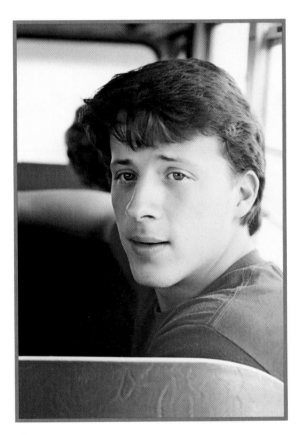

Figure 7.12
Magic Bus, circa 1983.

Why didn't I fix absolutely everything? It's the real world. We've all got deadlines, other projects, a life, wife, husband, significant other, kids, pets, other interests, and finite resources. I want to make this real—not some fantasy book where I promise you the sun, the moon, the stars, but oh-by-the-way, you'll never be able to replicate what you see here in a thousand years because it's all fake!

You can do this, and you will. That's what this is about. But consider this: finish what you start. Don't get caught in the trap of working on one photo until you think it's perfect—and never finish it. That's a pipe dream. Do the best job with what you have, and recognize the point when you have to stop.

The Expectations Game

Manage your expectations and those of others. If you are restoring photos professionally, come to terms with what you can do, how long it will take you, and what it's worth to you. Clearly communicate those terms with your clients. Sit down and have a heart-to-heart talk with them. (If yours is an Internet-based business, then have some of this information available on your Web site.) Discuss what you need from them, what they can expect from you, what the final product might look like, how long it will take, and how much it will cost. Don't over promise! If it's a terribly damaged photo and you think a light touch is about the only thing that will look good, don't let them think they're going to get a perfect photo back. As you restore the photo, make a conscious decision to remember why you take a certain approach so you can explain it to your clients. Take notes, if necessary, so you don't forget.

Photo Study 26:
Repairing Border Problems and Tearing

FIGURE 7.13 IS A PHOTO of Mary Anne, my mother-in-law. When I first saw it, I thought she was in college, but it turns out she was only 16 and a junior in high school. Kids in old photos seem to always look older than they were. My mom looks 25 in her high school yearbook.

I spoke with Mary Anne about this photo recently, and she said her father took it. She is standing outside of their rented farmhouse, which is now gone. Today, the land is part of a public school.

The photo has obvious charm, but the physical damage is threatening it. The film is tearing along the border and within the body of the photo. In addition, the photo has lost some of its pizzazz and has specks and other dust problems that should be fixed along the way.

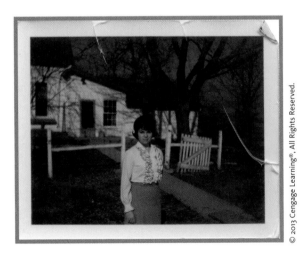

Figure 7.13
Vintage 1960s, complete with rough spots.

Cloning Do's and Don'ts

This is a good time to go over cloning do's and don'ts because the Clone brush is your primary tool to repair physical damage. The Clone brush copies material from one part of the photo to another. The general workflow is as follows:

1. **Select the Clone brush from the Tools toolbar.**

2. **Make changes to the tool's options, such as the brush size, hardness, opacity, and whether to "Use all layers" or not.** Make these changes in the Tool Options palette.

3. **Identify what you want to cover.** This is called the *destination*. Pay attention to the surrounding details because you will need to match them when you choose a source.

4. **Move your cursor to the photo and identify the source spot.** Then right-click (you can also Shift+click) to set that into the brush. Pay attention to the "grain" of the details and match the source color gradient, texture, and brightness with the destination you've previously identified.

5. **Paint the source material onto the destination with the Clone brush.**

6. **Reselect sources frequently so that you don't create obvious duplications.** Switch sides of a flaw as you clone and move at different angles so you don't create linear patterns.

Normally, I clone using a separate layer on top of the Background or current working layer. This preserves the original (or my interim working layer) image, and if I'm not happy with what I've cloned I can erase it, even well after the fact (for example, after closing and then reopening the file). It also opens up a lot of blending options. I can alter the opacity of the clone layer, soften the entire layer, or select the Soften Brush and selectively blend the cloned material with the original photo.

Choosing the correct brush size is important. There are times when you want a tiny brush to get into small areas. I've used Clone brushes of one pixel many times to clone individual pixels. Be careful with small brushes. Cloning with a small brush tends to be more easily recognized. Larger, soft-edged brushes blend in better.

Changing Sizes

If you're cloning, and it doesn't seem to be working well, take a look at brush options like size and hardness. Change them to see if that's the problem.

There's More to a Brush Than You Might Think

You can also change a brush's Thickness, Rotation, Style, and other parameters from the Tool Options palette. These options can come in handy if you're cloning over differently shaped and tilted areas. If that's not enough, open the Brush Variance palette and go crazy.

I also clone with the brush hardness set below 50, more often toward or at 0. This helps the new material blend in because there are no hard edges. If you haven't guessed by now, blending is an important part of cloning.

Working Around Edges

Using the Clone brush near edges requires that you closely monitor where the edge is in relation to your source and destination. I've positioned my source spot (the circle with the X in it) too close to the edge of the photo in Figure 7.14. When I selected my destination, my movement upward with the Clone brush copied the photo border. If you must select a source spot close to the edge, keep a disciplined hand when you brush and be aware of the "don't go that way" direction.

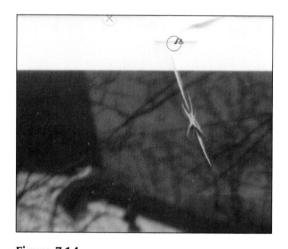

Figure 7.14
Source too close to outer border.

Figure 7.15 shows a similar problem, only reversed. Instead of transferring the outer edge of the photo, I'm transferring the boundary between the border and the picture. In this case, I've set the source spot too close to that boundary and let my brushing stray too far down.

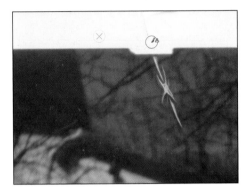

Figure 7.15

Source too close to photo edge.

If you want to protect an area of the photo from dangers like this, make a selection and clone inside it, as shown in Figure 7.16. You can make a nice, straight cloned border without fear.

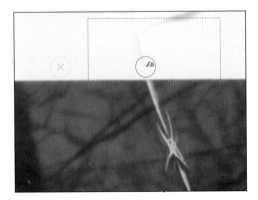

Figure 7.16

Protect the photo with a selection if needed.

If you've got a steady hand and a soft brush, you can routinely clone close to edges as you see me doing in Figure 7.17. The keys are practice, technique, the right brush hardness (softer is more forgiving and easier to blend), and a pen tablet. It doesn't take forever to learn and master. Pay attention to what you're doing, and you will learn very quickly. Developing a good technique makes you more efficient and saves time and effort.

One timesaving tool that I use to clone with is a pen tablet. A pen is more intuitive and natural to hold and use as a brush than a mouse. Additionally, the pen that I use is pressure sensitive, which means that I can press down very lightly with a larger brush and barely clone, or press harder, and the brush squishes more.

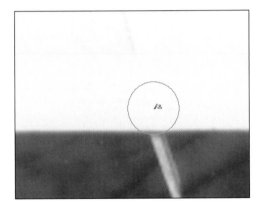

Figure 7.17

Freehand cloning with soft brush edge and a pen tablet.

I know it sounds like I own stock in pen tablets. I don't, but I want you to realize how much help they are. If you're going to casually restore photos, you might not need one. But, if you're going to be doing this a lot, especially professionally, invest in it. Pronto.

Another cloning technique, especially on borders like that shown in Figure 7.18, is aligning the source spot exactly (either horizontally or vertically) with your destination. You might have to select a source, clone, undo, and redo several times to get the correct alignment. The material in the corner (referring to Figure 7.18), up past where the bend is, is new. I've transplanted it from the edge below. I left it undone so you could see it in progress. The key here was to precisely align the right edge of the source well below the destination. The edge looks straight and original because I've precisely aligned the source and destination vertically. Setting the source well below the destination area gives me room to move the brush up.

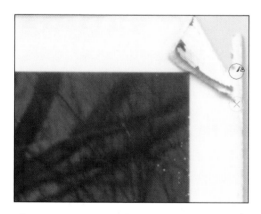

Figure 7.18

Start down to go up.

Cloning Areas Separated by Lines

Figure 7.19 shows the importance of good situational awareness as you clone in a busy area. Notice the tree branches that run from the top right to the lower left? They separate sky and smaller, fuzzier branches. If you break the lines of the large diagonal branches, it will be obvious.

Pay attention to these details. You can clone in the area between the diagonal lines first, or work on the branches first and return later to fill in the gaps. The point is to see how they divide the photo into regions that you need to work in. Here, the separating lines are the larger branches. In another photo, it could be power lines or a swing set or a sidewalk.

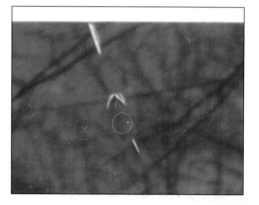

Figure 7.19

Cloning between branch lines.

I've come back and cloned the branches that run diagonally across the photo in Figure 7.20. That completes this portion of the photo. I've been careful to watch how things "flow" in this area. In fact, that dictated how I used the Clone brush.

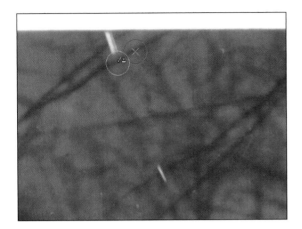

Figure 7.20
Finish up along the branch.

In Figure 7.21, I'm cloning in the lower-right portion of the photo, along the ground. See the different textures? The split has run between different shades of grass, making it particularly hard to match things up. I clone from one side of a split like this and then go back and work the other side. This helps balance the change in texture.

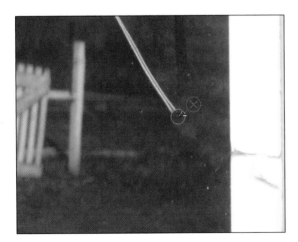

Figure 7.21
Some textures are hard to match.

Figure 7.22 shows the border area between the far background and the sky. I've chosen a source spot along this line so that I can take care of the split in the photo along the border between the two textures (grass and sky) first. Then I'll go back and tackle the rest of the split from the top and then the bottom.

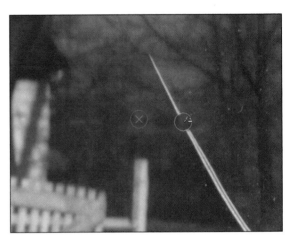

Figure 7.22
Always clone along a border between textures.

Trying Scratch Remover

There are plenty of applications where the Scratch Remover does a fantastic job, but this is pretty complex stuff. If the sky were a uniform blue and not covered with branches of different levels of detail, it would be dandy. Here, I don't expect it to work well.

Look at Figure 7.23. I've zoomed in on one of the splits and am in the process of applying a large swath of Scratch Remover.

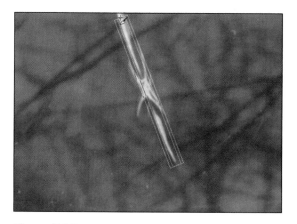

Figure 7.23
Trying the Scratch Remover.

Figure 7.24 shows the result. Bad. The blending is too much for the tool to handle.

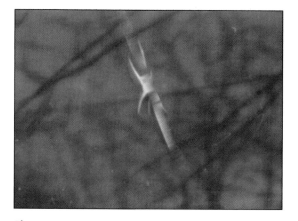

Figure 7.24
Not for this application.

I tried to tackle the split with the Scratch Remover in smaller chunks in Figure 7.25. I can still see the blending, however. It isn't as blatant as Figure 7.24, but you can see the pixelation that runs from the center down to the right. It looks like someone's appendix scar. If you increase the width of the Scratch Remover to something much larger, say 120 or so, the result will look much better, but you'll still have some blending issues because of the trees (whether you use short or long strokes).

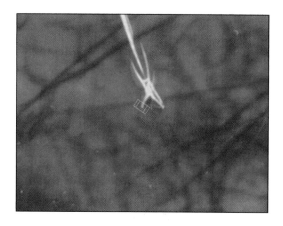

Figure 7.25
Smaller applications work better.

Fixing the Border

One viable technique for fixing border problems is to clone good parts over the damaged parts. You've seen that in some of the previous figures. I often fix all the border problems in a photo this way, especially if I want to preserve a vintage look.

If you want a bright border, you can select the photo area, invert the selection so that only the border is selected, and then use the Lighten brush to "white out" everything. For a subtler effect, lower the opacity of the brush.

Finishing the Photo Study

In the end, I used the Clone brush to fix all the splits, scratches, border problems, specks, dust, and dots in this photo. It's pretty straightforward, really. Find something that needs to be fixed, zoom in, select your brush, adjust the size, select the source, and clone. Although it gets routine, you've still got to pay attention to borders, textures, shades, and colors while you clone.

Figure 7.26 reveals the final, restored photo. All the tears have been mended, the other scratches and marks have been cloned out, the border looks great, and I tweaked a few other aspects of the photo. Namely, I made a histogram adjustment and fiddled with the curves to make the photo lighter and more vibrant, reduced the noise, and then sharpened the photo.

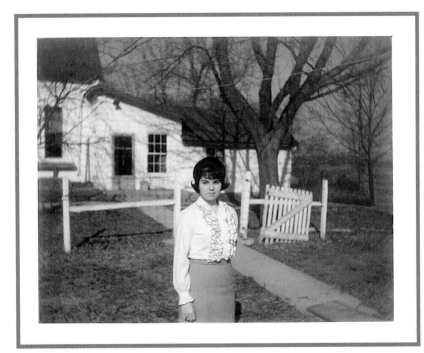

Figure 7.26
It was the Age of Aquarius.

Photo Study 27: Repairing a Mounted Photo

FIGURE 7.27 IS A PHOTO of my wife's great aunt, Blanche. This was taken in the early 1900s by a commercial photographer named Charles Groty. The photo paper was cut into an oval shape and fixed to the heavy card stock by his studio. Although the cardboard has been worn, the photo is in fantastic shape.

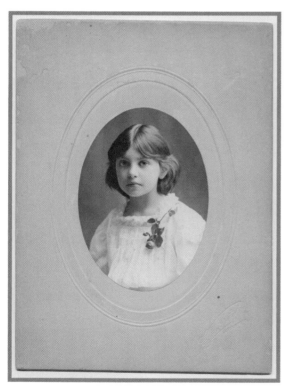

Figure 7.27
This photo can't be removed from the mount.

Choosing an Approach

There are two distinctly different approaches to retouching photos like this. One is to focus on the photo and ignore the border or cardboard. I do this quite often with older photos whose borders are torn or too scalloped to restore in a reasonable length of time. In this case, though, the mount, with the photographer's name embossed in the lower right, is part of the narrative.

The fact that the photo is oval also complicates things. You could restore the oval photo and replace the mount with a solid color. When done, print it, cut the oval photo out of the paper, and then remount it on a new backing. You could also keep the paper rectangular and put the photo under an oval mat.

Alternatively, you could try to clone the background and turn the photo into a rectangle or crop it drastically.

In this case, I want to try and restore the appearance of the cardboard mount as well as the photo itself. That way, the photo and mount are kept together. I still have the option to cut the oval photo out and remount it, or place it under an oval mat.

Life Histories

When restoring old photos, you can often follow a person's life from childhood to maturity, and possibly into old age. The girl in this photo study is the woman on the left (she is number 2 in the initial photo) in Photo Study 33, which can be found in Chapter 8, "Moving, Adding, or Removing Objects."

Repairing the Mount

I prefer doing physical repair work first. The results are normally cut-and-dried—it either works or it doesn't. Then I make brightness, contrast, and color corrections, which are normally more subjective and likely to change after looking at the photo for a long time. If I reversed my process, I would have to re-clone everything if I wasn't happy with my initial lighting changes. It's easier to have a finished clone process and then experiment with the other changes.

So, I will first turn my attention to the cardboard mount. It has several problems.

There are several spots and stains scattered about. Clone imperfections like these are just like marks or small dust spots. Next, there are areas of wear and tear, mostly on the top half of the mount. Those that are located in open areas, as shown in Figure 7.28, are also pretty easy to fix. Pay attention to the texture and tone of the cardboard and make sure to match the surface texture and tone. Some areas display more wear than others. Don't clone a perfect patch in the middle of a bare spot.

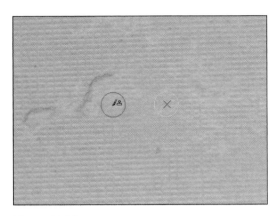

Figure 7.28
Clone with the texture of the mount.

There are also worn areas in the oval area just outside of the photo. In this case, the texture is more uniform. The challenge here, as shown in Figure 7.29, is to clone with the curve. The large bare spot I am working on in the figure isn't that hard to repair. The area up and to the left will be harder because the bare area is the width of the raised curve. Carefully select source areas near the target and be sure to match the shadows.

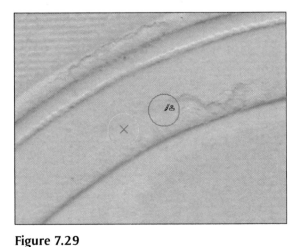

Figure 7.29
Clone along the curve carefully.

The corners are also damaged. They are worn to varying degrees, and the surface texture has been worn away in spots. Carefully clone along the top, as shown in Figure 7.30, and up from the side, to create the angle of the corner. It doesn't have to be perfect. Do the best you can to fill the bare spots, though.

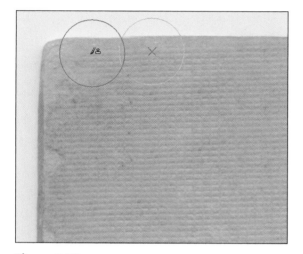

Figure 7.30

Carefully touch up the corners.

Restoring the Photo

Although the photo of Blanche is in good shape, I think it can be slightly improved. Before I do, take note of the fact that the card stock is definitely yellow. However, the photo itself is much closer to gray. Don't let situations like this tempt you to overcorrect the photo, as if it were yellowed with age. In this case, it's not. I want to brighten everything up a bit, but not completely whiten it.

To begin with, I'll use a Curves adjustment layer. I am using the dropper to select the black portion of Blanche's iris in Figure 7.31. This helps set the correct brightness by setting the black point. The result is a bit lighter.

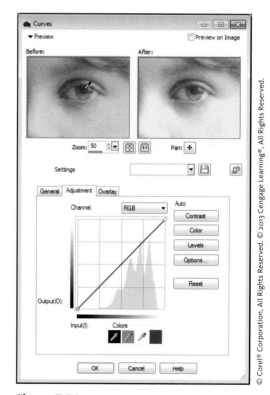

Figure 7.31

Brightening with Curves.

In Figure 7.32 I am using another adjustment layer to add contrast. I don't want to overdo it. I like the general appearance of the photo.

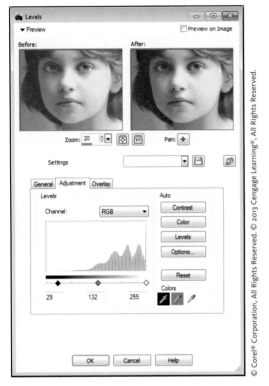

Figure 7.32
Adding a touch of contrast with Levels.

What Not to Do

Although I've only made small adjustments so far, even they are debatable. I will continue to think about them and review them as I work on the photo. If necessary, I can adjust the strength of each adjustment, lower their opacities, or toggle them off entirely.

As I continue to look for ways to improve this photo, I am struck by its physical texture. It is on the bumpy side. Sometimes that can be removed by using noise reduction. As Figure 7.33 shows, applying moderate Digital Noise Removal smoothes her hair too much. Always remember that if you add problems as you correct problems, you aren't making any headway. In this case, then, I will live with the bumpiness.

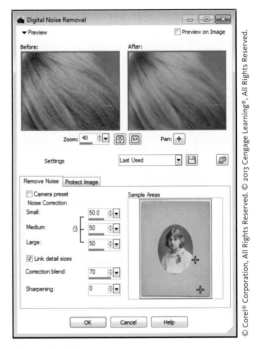

Figure 7.33
Digital Noise Removal smoothes too much.

It's also apparent that this isn't the sharpest photo ever. The solution to that is to sharpen it, right? Wrong. I am trying to do that in Figure 7.34. For the sharpening to matter, I would have to increase its strength so much that the texture of the photo would become distracting. After all, it's becoming sharper, too!

As I continued looking for ways to improve the photo, I thought about adding definition to the photo. Enhancing clarity or contrast can appear to sharpen photos without actually sharpening then. Figure 7.35 shows you what boosting Clarity would look like.

It's not bad; however, I think it takes away from some of the magic of the original.

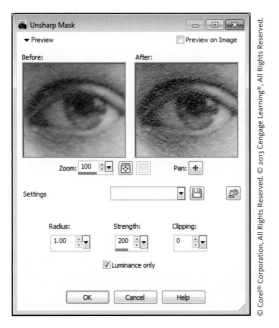

Figure 7.34
Unsharp Mask sharpens the surface of the photo too much.

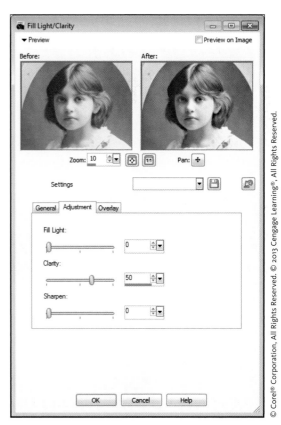

Figure 7.35
Trying to add definition by boosting Clarity.

The moral of this story? Look for every way to improve your photos, but realize that you can often do more harm than good. When you find that happening, back off and don't force it. It's better to have a slightly soft photo than a sharp photo with every change in surface texture magnified and enhanced. In this case, all that was required were slight tweaks to the brightness and contrast. Anything else I did made other issues worse or changed the photo into something it wasn't.

Finishing the Photo Study

The final photo is seen in Figure 7.36. Although the photo is the center of attention, it looks better with the cardboard mount touched up a bit. This is a charming photo. Now that it has been scanned in and retouched, we have a good copy preserved from further damage.

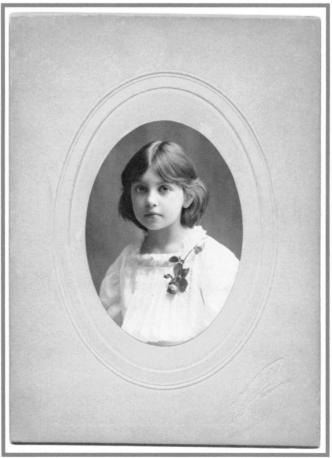

Figure 7.36
Preserving a touching photo.

Photo Study 28: Filling a Hole

FIGURE 7.37 IS A PHOTO of my mother-in-law's mom, Louise, and Louise's father, Dwight. Their family used to go to Michigan for summer vacations, and as near as we can tell, this photo was taken during one of those times. Louise looks around three or so, which would date this to approximately 1928.

At some point during the life of this photo, a hole was torn in the bottom center of the picture. Quite apart from restoring an old photo for aesthetic reasons, photos with torn edges are always in danger of being torn more. Once you restore them, you'll be able to print out new copies for viewing and handling while the original is stored safely away.

Prioritize

If you have boxes of photos to restore, tackle the torn ones first so they don't keep degenerating.

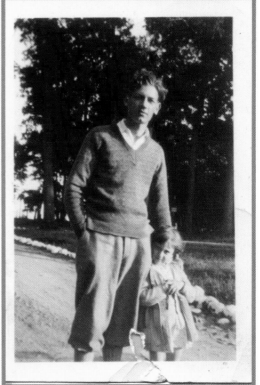

Figure 7.37
Notice the hole at the bottom?

This photo is a classic example of a fairly minor touch-up that will make an enormous positive difference to the photo.

Working the Pants Leg

I'm going to walk you through a rather detailed look at fixing this (think play-by-play), starting with the pant leg.

My first cloning operation on the pant leg can be seen in Figure 7.38. In instances like this, I generally choose to work from the inside out, which is why I've started at the top of the hole where the pant breaks from shadow to light. Borders like this, shadows and light, are just as important to nail down as texture and color borders. In this case, I'm very fortunate to have a good amount of existing material to work with.

I think in terms of pieces when I restore photos. You can break the bigger picture down and down and down—until you're left with very manageable tasks. The first task here was to fix the line of the pant leg, which bordered between shadow and light. Check. Next, the task was to fill in the shadow area and complete the bottom of the pant. Roger. Notice how each of these pieces has a border that separates it from other parts of the job? Affirmative.

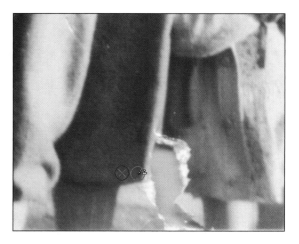

Figure 7.39
Finishing the bottom of the pant leg.
© Corel® Corporation, All Rights Reserved. © 2013 Cengage Learning®, All Rights Reserved.

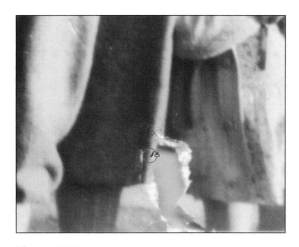

Figure 7.38
Cloning along the pant shadow.
© Corel® Corporation, All Rights Reserved. © 2013 Cengage Learning®, All Rights Reserved.

Now all I need to do is finish the pant leg, and that part is done. Figure 7.40 shows the final cloning on the pant leg in the light area.

Now that I've got the border between light and shadow, I'm going to fill in the shaded part of the pant leg, moving carefully into the hole and filling it in. Figure 7.39 brings you up to date. It's looking really good. I'm excited!

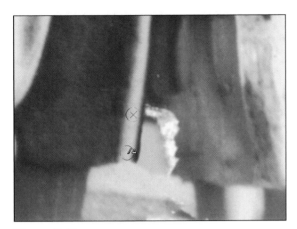

Figure 7.40

Finishing the pant leg.

Starting the Ground

I've finished Dwight's torn pant leg, so it's time to go on to another piece. I'll work on the ground a bit. I am, again, cloning along a border in Figure 7.41. This time I am working on the ground where it turns from darker to a lighter tan. I will work this area briefly so that when I turn to Louise's skirt, I can finish the ground as I finish her.

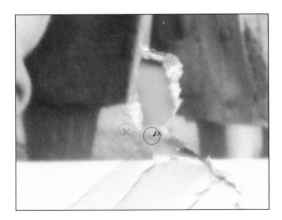

Figure 7.41

Pay attention to shading.

Now for the Coat

I am starting to clone the bottom of Louise's coat in Figure 7.42. (I thought it was her dress for a long time, but this is her coat.) This time I am working from the outside border in. I'll grab a bit of the coat from the right and pull it over, making sure to bring the ground along.

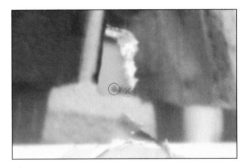

Figure 7.42

Extending the coat.

Next, I'll focus on another border. This time I want to get the border between Dwight's pant leg and Louise's coat done. I may clone "over" some existing material. No matter. I'll take care not to disturb my finished pant leg, but some of the border area can be refined. I extended the shadow between the pant and the coat down and inward in Figure 7.43.

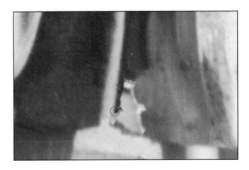

Figure 7.43

Bringing down the shadow.

If you want to be extra careful about things, you can consolidate your work along the way. I like working with the photo on the Background layer, and I never disturb it. I create a new raster layer on top of the Background layer and make sure that "Use all layers" is enabled when I select my Clone brush. Make sure you've selected this clone layer when you start to work; otherwise, you'll be putting down paint on the layer you want to protect. It's simple to consolidate. Perform a merged copy by pressing Ctrl+Shift+C, and then paste that merged copy as a new layer on top of the clone layer by pressing Ctrl+V. This is your new working layer. You've just consolidated your work, and it's protected. Create a new clone layer (an empty raster layer) once again and go back to cloning. You can do this as many times as you need, up to the amount of memory you have.

It's time for me to get back to work on that coat. It's pretty tough in the interior. There are folds and shadows galore here. Tricky indeed. Figure 7.44 shows my progress.

If it doesn't look right, give it a little time. Don't start over immediately. There are times I clone tough areas like this, and it doesn't look good at first, but it comes around if I keep at it.

Figure 7.45 shows the filled-in coat, and I'm doing some touching up. I'm working with the "grain" of the coat, which is to say, vertically. What may have looked a little dodgy in the beginning fits right in after a little work.

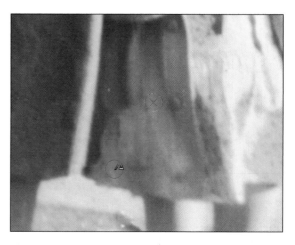

Figure 7.45
Finishing the fill.

There are two final steps that are tricks of the trade and can make cloning much better. First, I'm going to push some paint around with the Push brush (a handy tool) in Figure 7.46.

My primary purpose is to blend my cloned work. It's still on a separate layer, but I'm pushing the paint around to blend it. I've lowered the opacity to 28, so it's a pretty light touch.

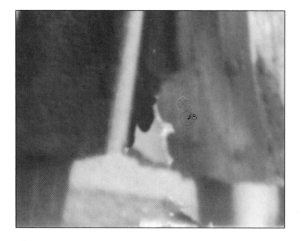

Figure 7.44
Starting to fill in.

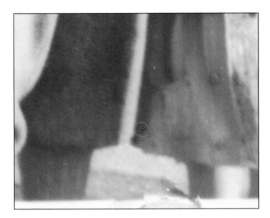

Figure 7.46
Using the Push brush to blend.

Finally, I will use the Soften brush in Figure 7.47 to soften the work that I just completed. I turned off the photo layer so you can see what I'm doing a little better. I've turned down the opacity of this brush, too. It's set at 34.

Softening is different than pushing paint around. Soften takes the edge off of things. It smoothes the borders and creates more of a gradient between different colors.

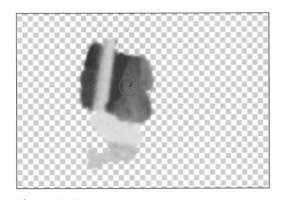

Figure 7.47
Softening the cloned material.

Finishing the Photo Study

Figure 7.48 shows the finished photo. This is a photo where everything came nicely together. I want to make sure and point these out, too! I had enough time, it wasn't too badly damaged, and the final print is as nice as one could expect. The hole is gone, and I also fixed the other specks and scratches in the photo. Plus, I enhanced the contrast and color balance.

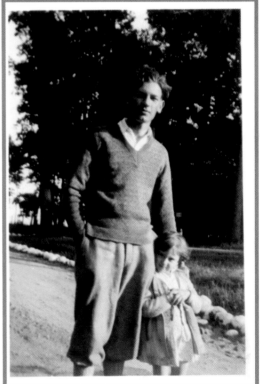

Figure 7.48
Even small repairs are very gratifying.

Photo Study 29: Mending a Torn Photo

MOST PHOTOS IN THIS BOOK have reasonably interesting stories behind them, but this one (see Figure 7.49) is an exception. The one somewhat interesting factoid I have to share is that the flowers next to the house are orange "Ditch Lilies" (aka Tiger or Orange Lilies). There you have it.

This photo has been torn in half and taped back together. I propose to fix that, without taking the halves apart prior to scanning (which could damage this photo further, but is not a bad idea if you can do it). I'll scan it in "as is" and repair it digitally.

Prepping the Patient

Before I move on to fixing the tape, contrast, sharpness, color, and other problems, I will stitch the photo back together.

To make repairs such as this, follow these steps:

1. **Choose the Freehand Selection tool from the Tools toolbar and change the type to "Point to point" in the Tool Options palette.** I'll use the selection tool to select the top and bottom of the photo separately.

2. **Select the top or the bottom of the photo.** I'm starting with the bottom in Figure 7.50. Make sure to select an area well on the other side of the taped border. You'll erase this extra area later.

3. **Copy this selection.**

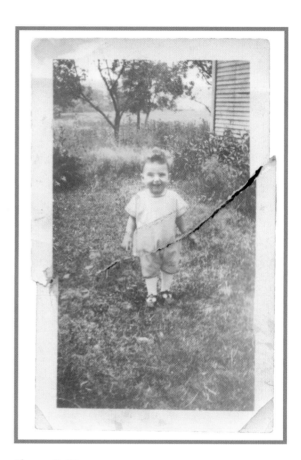

Figure 7.49
Old, yellowed, torn, and taped.
© 2013 Cengage Learning®, All Rights Reserved.

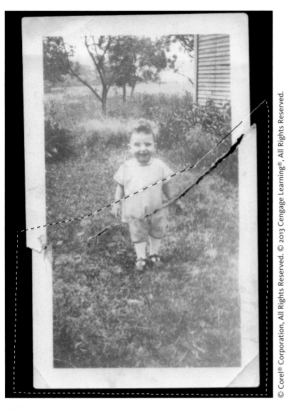

Figure 7.50
Select the bottom.

4. **Paste the selection into a new image using Ctrl+Shift+V, as shown in Figure 7.51.**

5. **Enlarge the canvas since this new image contains roughly half of the overall photo.** Choose Image ▶ Canvas Size and double the vertical size of this file to make room for the other half of the photo. Make sure that the "Lock aspect ratio" setting in the Canvas Size dialog box is off so you'll be able to enlarge the canvas significantly more in one dimension than another. Don't worry if the canvas ends up being too large (which is better than too small). You'll crop out the unneeded space later.

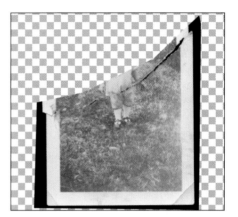

Figure 7.51
Paste as new image.

6. **Go back to your original file and select the top half (or the opposite of what you just did) of the photo this time.** (See Figure 7.52.)

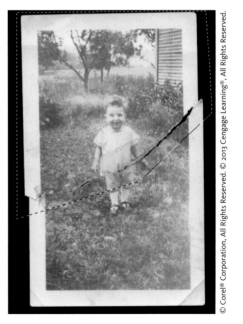

Figure 7.52
Select and copy the top.

7. **Copy the selection.**

8. **Switch to your new image and paste this as a new layer, as shown in Figure 7.53.** I've pasted this as the top layer and moved the two layers in a rough approximation of where they will end up.

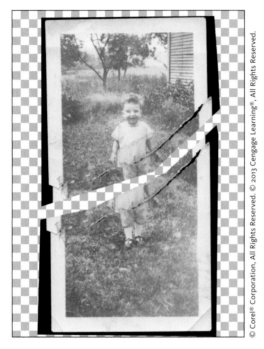

Figure 7.53

Paste as New Layer in New Image.

9. **Now I need to straighten my two layers.** I'm going to use the long vertical side to straighten the bottom of the photo, as seen in Figure 7.54. Select the Straighten tool from the Tools toolbar and line up the two end points. Make sure that "Rotate all layers" and "Crop image" are off. I've hidden the top layer to make it easier to see what I'm doing. Make sure that you've got the right layer selected when you apply the Straighten tool.

10. **Now for the top: if you hid the top, unhide it now and hide the lower layer.** Then select the Straighten tool, as shown in Figure 7.55. I'm using the opposite side as a reference this time, but it's still a long side. You'll get better results if you can choose the longest edge you have. Make sure that your Straighten tool options stayed the same; then apply.

11. **Save your work in the appropriate location on your hard drive with a proper name.** Make sure that you save it as a .pspimage so the layers are preserved.

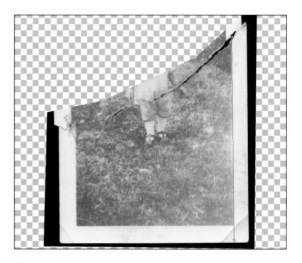

Figure 7.54

Straighten the bottom.

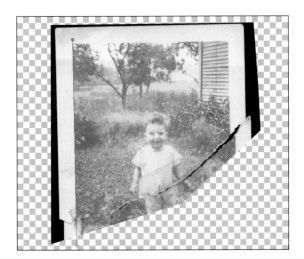

Figure 7.55
Straighten the top.

That's it, doctor. The patient is prepped for restoration!

Joining the Pieces

Let's set the stage. A torn photo has been taped back together, and you're going to restore it. You've scanned it in and then digitally separated the two torn pieces with the power and majesty of PaintShop Pro. They've been straightened, and now you're ready to begin joining the pieces, which is the second phase of this three-phase operation.

1. **Hide one of the layers; then select the other layer to work on.** It doesn't matter which one.

2. **Select the Eraser and choose a size and hardness appropriate to the area you want to erase (which, in this case, is on the opposite side of the tear).** When I'm erasing a lot of material, I start out with a large eraser that's 100% hard and then move smaller and softer the closer I get to the edge. I may take two or three passes to get close to the edge. In this case, I can go right to a smaller, softer brush.

   If you would rather use a mask, create a Show All mask on each layer and use the Eraser to mask the material you want to hide. (Note that this is my personal preference; you can also use the Paint brush and paint black on the mask to hide the material.)

3. **Begin erasing material from the opposite side of the tape, as shown in Figure 7.56.** Work your way carefully across, trying not to erase anything from the "keeper" side. Don't worry about the rough edge of the torn paper border. You'll clone this out eventually.

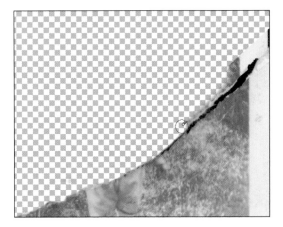

Figure 7.56
Erase extra bottom area.

4. **When you're done with this layer, hide it, show the other, and repeat the process, as shown in Figure 7.57.** I'm working on the top of the photo by erasing everything from below the tape and tear line. This is cool stuff!

Occasionally, show the other layer (in step 3 as well as 4) to make sure that you're not overerasing.

There are many ways to fix borders that don't match perfectly after the fact. For example, you could clone new material, create a rectangular selection and lighten the outside to form a new border, or crop the photo. If your subject doesn't line up, then you're toast. You'll do more damage trying to fix that (self-created) problem than you would ever do fixing a border.

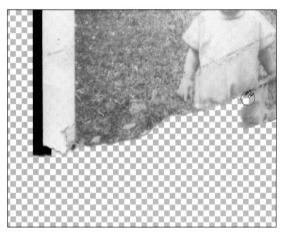

Figure 7.57
Erase extra top area.

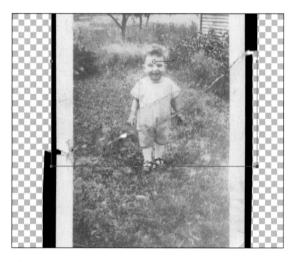

Figure 7.58
Align the two layers.

5. **Now for some magic: show both layers and then select the content of the top layer with the Pick tool and move it into position, matching the edge of the bottom layer, as seen in Figure 7.58.** If you get it close and want to verify its position, zoom in. You can also use your arrow keys to nudge the selection in any direction you choose. In particular, look to match the subject of the photo first; then check out the border. Never choose a straight border over your subject.

6. **Now it's time to stitch them together.** Create a layer to clone with on top of the two content layers.

7. **Make this clone layer active.** Then select the Clone brush and clone the edges of the photo together along one side of the photo, as seen in Figure 7.59.

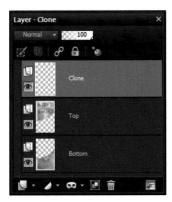

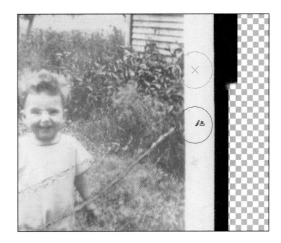

Figure 7.60

Getting the other side.

Continuing to Clone

This is the third phase of restoring this photo and hiding the tape. I will hide the tape with the judicious use of the Clone brush. I am cloning grass over the taped area to the left of the young boy in Figure 7.61.

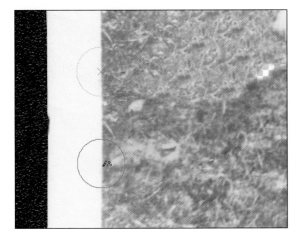

Figure 7.59

Clone them together.

8. **Repeat on the other side, as seen in Figure 7.60.**

With the pieces fit together, the subject successfully lined up, and the photo border fixed with the Clone brush, I'm ready to move to the center of the photo.

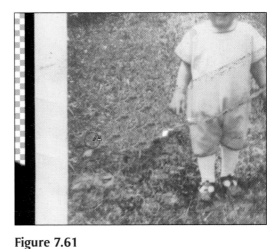

Figure 7.61

Working the middle.

I am continuing to clone, and have moved on to his wrist in Figure 7.62. I need to be very careful here because there is little room to work, and the gradient of his wrist needs to match perfectly.

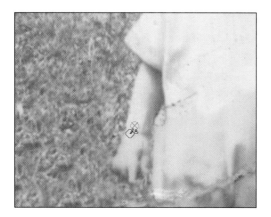

Figure 7.62
Careful along the arm.

If cloning tape away is problematic in a portion of the photo, desaturate the area with the Saturation Up/Down brush. This takes the color out of the tape and leaves the detail of the clothes behind, as seen in Figure 7.63.

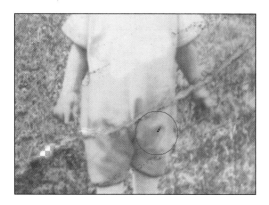

Figure 7.63
You can also desaturate.

Finishing the Photo Study

This was another rewarding photo to restore. The difference between the before (Figure 7.49) and after (see Figure 7.64) shots is amazing. When you can put together a photo that has been torn in half and then taped back together, you start to see the world of possibilities that are open to you.

After I got the photo together and cloned much of the tape and other problems away, I worked on the brightness, contrast, and color with histogram adjustments, fade corrections, and some desaturation.

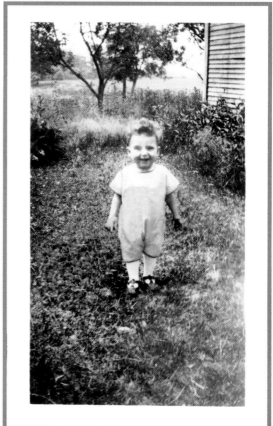

Figure 7.64
Smiling child recovered.

Photo Study 30: Mending a Partial Tear

THE CUTE COUPLE IN FIGURE 7.65, also shown in Photo Study 33 in Chapter 8 (they are on the far right in that shot), are my wife's great grandparents. They are sitting on their porch, laughing about something. This was taken only a few years before John senior's death. His wife, Clara, lived another twenty years.

This is a nice example of a good snapshot from the early 1940s. Clara's face is sharp and clear. Although a bit on the bright side, the exposure is not too bad. The real problems are the numerous small scratches that plague the photo and the large tear. The tear begins on the left and runs three-fourths of the way across the photo. It happens to travel through areas that promise to be hard to fix. It will be important to match John's cane and Clara's dress with any cloned repair.

Getting Started

The first few steps in restoring this photo involve rotating it so that it is straight, cropping out the border and beginning work on the scratches.

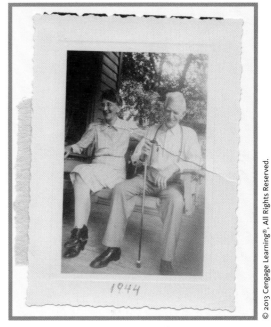

Figure 7.65
This charming photo has a long tear running across it.

I've zoomed in and am placing one end of the Straighten tool in Figure 7.66. In this case, I decided to use the top edge of the photo—not the border. Notice that the end point extends beyond the corner of the photo. I prefer to place the tool this way versus trying to put the point on the exact corner. This gives me a better perspective to make sure the tool lines up with the edge of the photo.

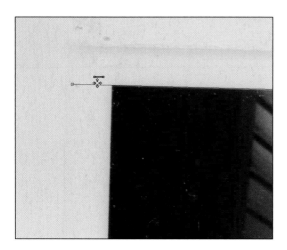

Figure 7.66
Straightening the scan.

I have decided to crop this photo and lose the border. That's a subjective decision on my part. The edges are scalloped and you can see remnants of tape that are still attached to the back of the photo. Rather than try to work around or fix these issues, I am simply going to cut them off. I won't crop to the photo, however. There is an indentation about a quarter of an inch larger than the photo that I will use as the edge of my new border. That way I keep some of the original. You'll see this reflected in the final shot of this photo.

Although you can jump right in and start working on the scratch, I prefer handling the easier problems first. That means creating a clone layer and working out all the small scratches and spots on the photo that aren't part of the tear. You have to be careful in areas with a lot of problems, as shown in Figure 7.67. Take special care not to transplant specks from one area to another. I find it best to work out the specks first. This gives me more room to work out the longer scratches.

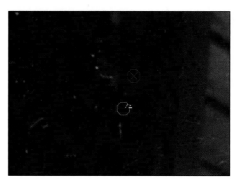

Figure 7.67
Carefully cloning out scratches.

Cloning the Tear Out

With the rest of the photo repaired, it's time to tackle the tear. This one has three distinct areas.

First, the tear extends into the dark area on the left of the photo. There is also a slight discoloration that should be removed. It runs on top of the tear and is slightly blue or purple. This part of the operation, shown in Figure 7.68, is pretty straightforward. Pay attention to the tone of the dark area and match your source and destination. Not all dark areas have the same tone!

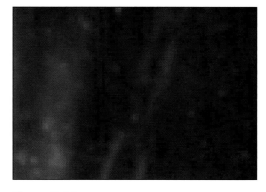

Figure 7.68
Repairing the tear in the dark area.

The second area of the tear is around John. The most challenging part of repairing this region is his cane. The curve makes it very hard to match a source area with the destination. I have completed work on the top, as shown in Figure 7.69, and have begun working toward the end.

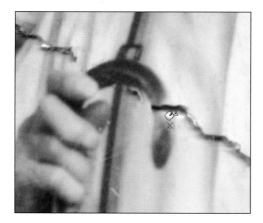

Figure 7.69
Carefully reconstructing John's cane.

The final area to repair is across Clara's dress. This is challenging for two reasons. First, her dress has a pattern to it that must match. If you didn't pay attention to this, your work would really stand out. Second, the brightness makes it hard to see the exact pattern of her dress.

To make it easier to see, I used a temporary Levels adjustment layer in Figure 7.70 to darken the photo and add in contrast.

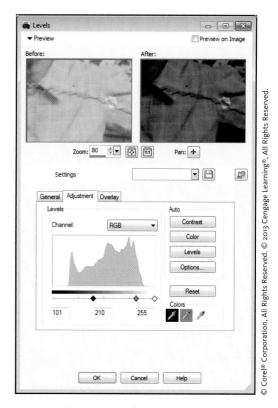

Figure 7.70
Using a temporary adjustment layer to see the dress pattern.

With that in place, it's possible to use the same technique that I showed you in Photo Study 21 (Chapter 6, "Removing Specks and Dust"). Set the Clone brush to work on the active layer only, select the photo layer, identify a source spot with a right-click, select the destination layer, and then paint on new material with the brush. I'm doing just that in Figure 7.71.

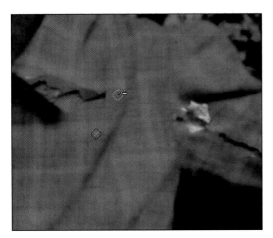

Figure 7.71

Match the patterns up as best you can. Alternate using the adjustment layer and cloning normally as you see fit.

I won't kid you. This ended up being much harder than I expected. I finished by gently using the Soften brush on the cloned regions across the dress to soften the edges. This made my repairs blend in so well they are almost imperceptible.

Final Touch-Ups

With all the physical problems taken care of, the photo can be tweaked and finished. I began with a Curves adjustment layer to see what I could do with brightness, color, and contrast. On the whole, the photo is a bit too bright, and has a hint of yellow to it. The problem with darkening is that it makes the photo look dull.

Figure 7.22 shows my compromise. I clicked on a white area in the photo to remove the yellow color cast, and then tweaked what the dialog box suggested I do to both ends of the spectrum. If the result looks too harsh, it can be further blended by lowering the layer's opacity.

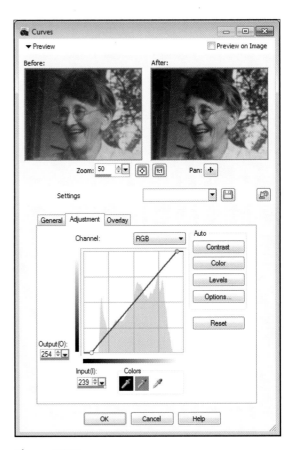

Figure 7.72

Curves to correct brightness, color, and contrast.

As always, look for other ways to improve your photos. In this case, I am seeing what a moderate amount of High Pass Sharpen will do in Figure 7.73. I think it looks better, but will be careful to analyze its impact in relation to all the other repairs. It's often better to leave something alone that has a questionable impact. However, small improvements do add up.

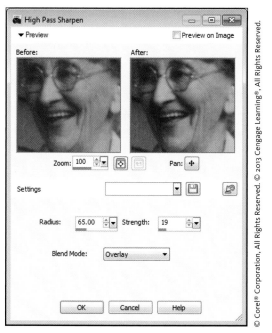

Figure 7.73
High Pass Sharpen helps a bit but is optional.

Finishing the Photo Study

Figure 7.74 shows the final result. This photo shows a fine balance between fixing important physical problems and gently improving the brightness, color, and contrast.

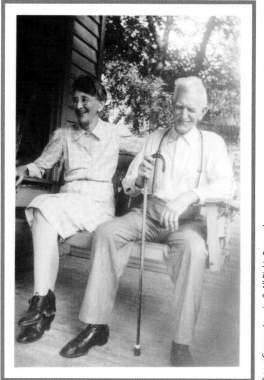

Figure 7.74
Another family photo rescued and preserved.

Photo Study 31:
Dealing with Tears, Creases, and Stains

FIGURE 7.75 IS A PHOTO MY WIFE'S grandfather took when he was in Europe during World War II. He saw his first combat in North Africa, and his unit was involved in the invasion at Anzio in 1944. He continued to serve in Europe until the end of the war.

While Bud was in Italy, he found the time to take this photo of the Leaning Tower of Pisa. It's a compelling photo of an immediately recognizable landmark, taken during a historically significant time in modern human history. The topper is that someone in our family took the photo. I can't think of a better candidate for photo restoration.

Getting Started

Before you begin to work, take a close look at the photo with a critical eye toward what is wrong and can be fixed. In this case, there is a huge blob of gunk, or whatever it is, staining the sky. That's going to have to go. There are several creases and cracks in the finish. I think I can fix those. The border is looking shoddy. Check. And, in general, it's faded and yellowed. Lots of physical damage, but nothing looks insurmountable.

Critical Viewing

Learn to look critically at photos. You're going to need this skill to see what's wrong with a photo. There are times when it will be immediately obvious, but at other times the problems will be more subtle. Imagination and some experience will help you get into this groove.

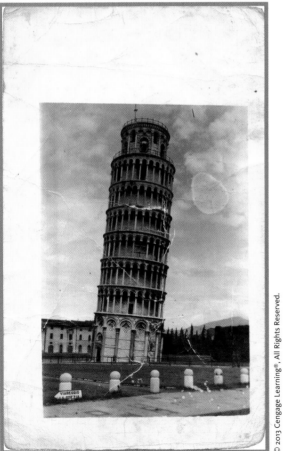

Figure 7.75
Wartime photo of the tower at Pisa, Italy.

Having identified several flaws and turned them into my restoration goals, the following steps took me through the process of restoring this wonderful photo from start to finish.

1. **Scan the photo.** This photo was scanned at 600dpi and 24-bit color. It's a fairly small photo to begin with, so 600dpi was not too unwieldy.

2. **Open the photo in PaintShop Pro and straighten it, if necessary.** I straightened it a bit. You'll find that most photos, even modern 4×6 prints, aren't perfectly straight on all sides. In this case, I chose one of the long sides of the photo itself, not the border, to use as a straightedge. Save the file as a .pspimage in order to preserve the original scan.

3. **Next, I went to work on cleaning up the photo border.** It's a fairly easy way to get started on a photo and work your way up to the harder parts. This border is yellowed and cracked with age. There are several approaches you can take. You could create a new border, crop the old border out entirely, or lighten the original border. After I duplicated the Background layer, I lightened the border with the Lighten/Darken brush (see Figure 7.76) on the new working layer. Notice that I selected the border area to keep the brush out of the photo. If you don't want a solid white border, you can lower the opacity of the border working layer to blend it in with the original. That is an effective way of minimizing the damage but retaining some of the original border.

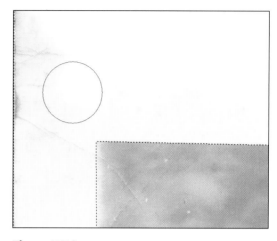

Figure 7.76
Use the Lighten brush to wipe away an old photo border.

4. **Next, I addressed the sky, with the exception of the large, gunky spot.** I used the Clone brush to cover up the most obvious creases and spots. (There were so many that I eventually had to choose to stop.) This photo didn't have a dust or a speck problem. For large Clone brush operations (as is the case with this photo), I usually create a new raster layer to use as my Clone brush destination.

5. **With the majority of the sky repaired, I moved on to tackling the gunk.** I used the Clone brush to cover up this unsightly stain (see Figure 7.77). I needed to be very careful not to be obvious about it. Larger sections of cloning can be much more visible than smaller areas if done improperly. I used the Soften brush to make the edges of my clone work less visible. This was one of the harder parts of the entire project.

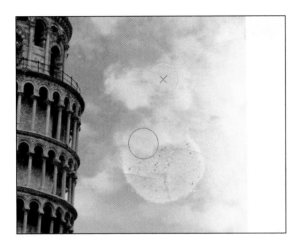

Figure 7.77
Go away, gunk.

6. **I worked on the grounds (see Figure 7.78) next.** This included the pavement at the front of the photo, the trees on the right side, and the buildings on the left. Once again, the Clone brush was my friend.

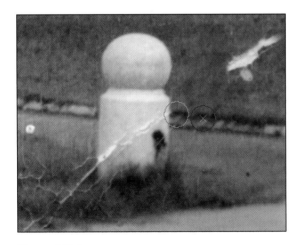

Figure 7.78
Focus on getting the right texture as you clone.

7. **I made a lot of progress up to this point, but hadn't touched the central feature: the tower.** The tower (Figure 7.79) proved to be a more time-consuming process than the rest of the photo. In situations like this, take your time and don't feel like you have to repair everything in one sitting. The key to restoring the tower was to vary the size of the brush so it was not too large and to pull the right source material from columns and spaces that had the same shadows and tones. I pulled material from areas above, below, and to either side of the feature I was restoring. It takes a bit of practice to get this part right.

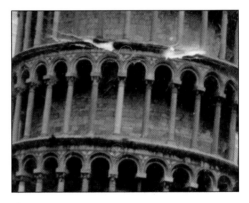

Figure 7.79
Imaginative cloning.

8. **The final touches were next.** I left these for last because I wanted to be able to adjust a clean photo. Since this is a black-and-white photograph, I reduced the yellow cast very slightly with Fade Correction.

9. **Next, I increased the sharpness with Unsharp Mask (see Figure 7.80) very slightly.** I didn't overdo it. A stronger setting brought out extra noise and made the remaining imperfections stand out.

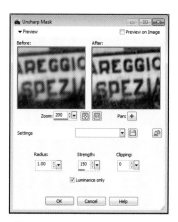

Figure 7.80
Sharpening focus.
© Corel® Corporation, All Rights Reserved. © 2013 Cengage Learning®,
All Rights Reserved.

10. **Finally, I created a Curves adjustment layer (see Figure 7.81) to brighten the tower slightly.**

11. **With work on the photo done, I saved a final version.**

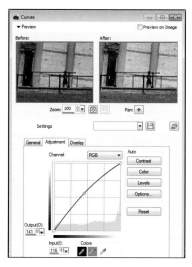

Figure 7.81
Brightening with Curves.
© Corel® Corporation, All Rights Reserved. © 2013 Cengage Learning®,
All Rights Reserved.

Finishing the Photo Study

As you look at the finished photo in Figure 7.82, I want to point out that I did not try to restore every pixel of this photo. First, that would have been too time-consuming. Second, as you have seen, there are times when it is impossible. You may have to step back and say "it's done," even when there are still flaws. At those points, you may actually do more damage to the artistry of the original photo if you continue, as well as making it obvious to everyone that you've attempted to retouch it. That's a bad thing. It's better to stop at the point where your hand is still invisible. Make the photo better, not worse.

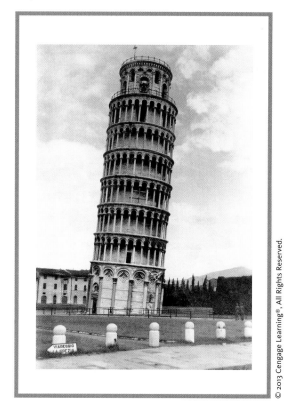

Figure 7.82
The restored Leaning Tower of Pisa.

Photo Study 32: Restoring a Missing Corner

THIS PHOTO, TAKEN AND developed in 1954, is another of my wife's family (see Figure 7.83). Louise, the young girl in Photo Study 28, is back again, this time as a grown woman with a family. Bud, her husband (previously seen in Photo Study 11, Chapter 4, "Solving Color Problems"), is also here. Mary Anne, featured in Photo Study 26, is the young girl on the left. She's got an older sister and a younger brother in this photo.

This photo has been through some tough times. It's got a pretty good chunk missing out of the lower-left corner, and it looks like it's been wadded up, as evidenced by all the creases. This goes far beyond normal wear and tear. That makes it perfect for this chapter!

Tackle the Border First

The first thing I'm going to do is get the corner fixed. There is a pretty hefty chunk missing. I could use the Clone brush and copy the existing borders, but it's actually much faster and easier to copy another corner and rotate it so that it fits in place.

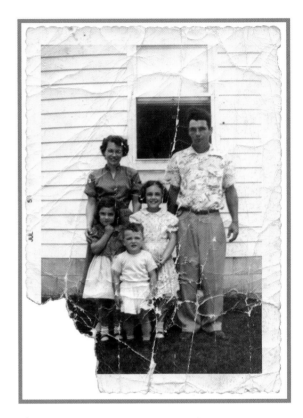

Figure 7.83
Mangled family portrait.
© 2013 Cengage Learning®, All Rights Reserved.

I've selected the bottom-right corner with the Selection tool in Figure 7.84.

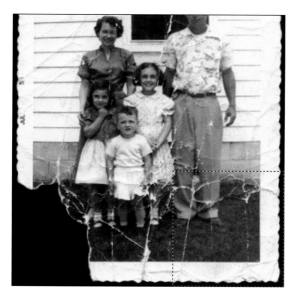

Figure 7.84
Copy the opposite corner.

I pressed Ctrl+C to copy this selection and Ctrl+V to paste it as a new layer, deselected it, and then used Image ❯ Mirror to mirror the pasted material horizontally. After it was mirrored, I moved the new corner to cover the missing space, as shown in Figure 7.85.

Ctrl+Shift+P

If you want to streamline the process, make your selection and press Ctrl+Shift+P to promote it to a new layer. You don't have to copy and paste it that way. You can then deselect it, mirror, and move the material.

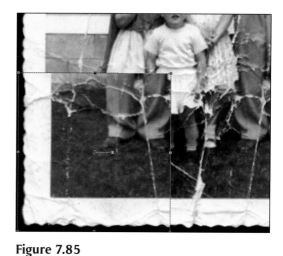

Figure 7.85
Paste and mirror.

You can see that the old content is still inside the "new" corner. Don't worry. It takes very little effort to delete it. It doesn't even matter that the inside border is a bit off. The important border to align here is the outer border, which will ensure that the new corner blends in. This photo has a scalloped edge, which makes it a bit trickier.

With the replacement corner aligned (it's a separate layer than the Background photo layer), I returned to the Selection tool and selected the interior of the new corner to delete it, as shown in Figure 7.86. I matched the inner border of the photo frame with what was selected in this step.

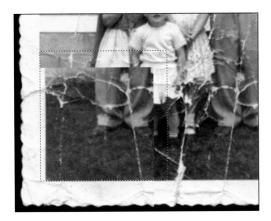

Figure 7.86

Select and delete unwanted material.

After I selected the proper area, I pressed the Delete key to send it to oblivion.

All I need to do now is touch up the "joints" where the new corner and existing border overlap. I am using the Clone brush to remove the obvious signs that this corner was pasted in Figure 7.87. I'm not worried about restoring the corner fully. That will come later.

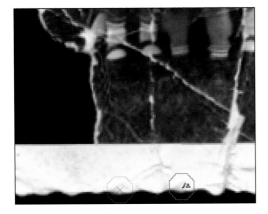

Figure 7.87

Touching up.

Filling In

The outer border is complete. Now for the hard part—filling in the missing area of the picture.

There will be times when this will be impossible. In some of these cases, restore the border and the rest of the photo but do not re-create the missing material. Fill the area with a neutral shade of gray. This is similar to the way some architectural restorations (like the Coliseum in Rome) are handled. New material is clearly new. People can see there was a missing corner, it's not distracting, and you can handle the restored photo without fear of damaging the original any further.

For this study, I decided to put grass in the missing corner. I am beginning the process in Figure 7.88.

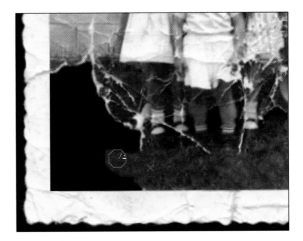

Figure 7.88

Cloning grass.

My source area is on the other side of the photo from the destination, as seen in Figure 7.89. There's no grass anywhere else that I can use to try and fill in the missing area.

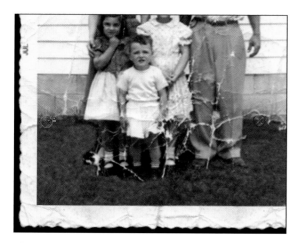

Figure 7.89

Taking material from the other side.

After the new grass was planted, I used the Burn brush to create a shadow behind Louise, as seen in Figure 7.90. This made the cloned area look more realistic. I lowered the opacity of the Burn brush to 10 to blend it in naturally.

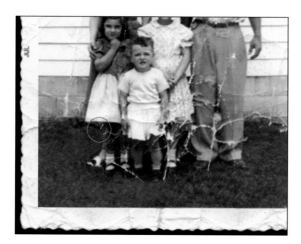

Figure 7.90

Using the Burn brush to create a shadow.

Finishing the Photo Study

The fully restored photo can be seen in Figure 7.91. This was a tough one, and the corner was only the tip of the iceberg. After fixing the corner, I made as many other repairs as I could. I retouched the siding of the house, the window, the grass, everyone's faces and hair, and other areas. I also made contrast and color adjustments, plus worked on the border.

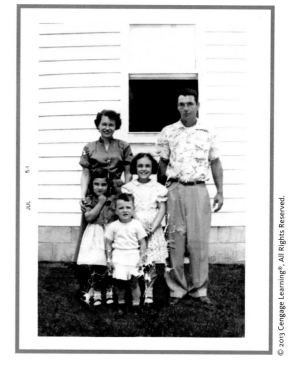

Figure 7.91

Large jobs are great, too.

I want to conclude this chapter by making the point that whether the job is very large or relatively minor, restoring and retouching photos should be fun and rewarding. Although photo restoration will challenge you as a creative artist and push your technological limits, PaintShop Pro is an economical and powerful tool. Be positive and don't get down on yourself.

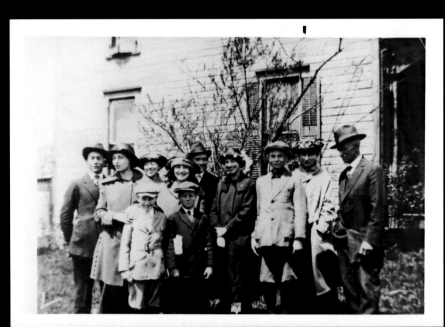

Moving, Adding, or Removing Objects

8

ALTHOUGH THIS CHAPTER WILL CHALLENGE YOU, being able to move, add, or remove something (including writing and other marks) from a photo is very fun stuff. Believe it or not, you probably already know or have learned many of the technical skills needed to complete these tasks by now. If you can copy, paste, erase, and clone—you're off to a good start. Of course, a lot depends on the photos. As you'll see, some are very hard, while others are much easier to work with.

▶ **Photo Study 33: Taking Out Photo Notations**—This photo has a bunch of numbers above people's heads and a tear that runs from left to right. It's a great exercise in cloning. You'll learn how to adjust your technique to fit each notation and make this photo look as good as new.

▶ **Photo Study 34: Erasing Crayon and Pen**—This old photo has a number of different marks and writing on it that make it an excellent (and difficult) example. You'll learn how to use the Color Changer and the Change to Target brush to try and remove or minimize these additions.

▶ **Photo Study 35: Removing Marker and Ink Smudges**—Sometimes the best way to get rid of marks on a photo is to separate the photo into HSL channels. This makes the marker stand out much more clearly than the original photo. Then it's a simple matter of sending in the clones.

▶ **Photo Study 36: Moving a Teddy Bear**—This is an older photo of my son sleeping on the couch with one of his teddy bears. The bear is tucked up under his pillow and looks a little out of place in the original. This is a classic case of moving something around in a photo so that it looks better.

▶ **Photo Study 37: Removing Odds and Ends**—It's not the end of the world when odd things make it into a photo, but it's fun to be able to improve the overall composition without changing things too much. In this study, the object is to remove the distractions. .

 ▶ **Photo Study 38: Adding a Person to a Photo**—This photo study is a bit more advanced than the others. Here, you'll learn how to add someone to a photo that she wasn't originally in, and make it appear that she was always there. The process is very similar to moving an object, only you're moving it from one photo to another.

 ▶ **Photo Study 39: Creating Montages**—Montages are incredibly fun to make. I could easily fill a good-size chapter with those I've made over the years of our family's faces, of us sticking our tongues out, of our kids, and of our pets. If you can copy, paste, and erase, you can montage.

Photo Study 33: Taking Out Photo Notations

FIGURE 8.1 IS A CLASSIC FAMILY SHOT with a lot of people from different generations in it. It has notations on it to indicate who everyone is. Some of the numbers are on the house. Others cover parts of people's hats or are in the trees. There's also a pretty long tear in the photo, which runs from the upper left-center clear to the right edge of the picture.

It amazes me how these photos tie together. You'll run into the same thing when you restore your own family photos. Take a close look at the women numbered 3 and 4. They are in the next study, which was taken between 15 and 20 years earlier. Their names are Grace (3) and Jo (4).

This type of visible genealogical information makes this photo especially significant. Photos like this are invaluable when researching family trees. If you restore photos professionally, keep in mind that these photos often have special emotional and historical significance to their owners. You play a special part in preserving their family treasures.

Even though there are marks on the siding of the house, on windows, shutters, hats, and branches, this photo presents a fairly straightforward cloning operation.

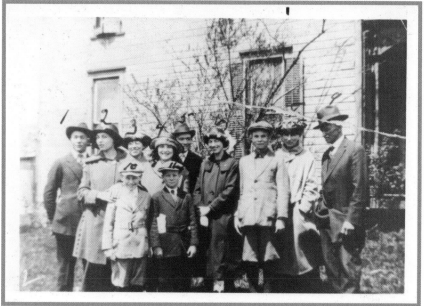

Figure 8.1
An impressive family photo, complete with notations.

Creating an Adjustment Layer

Since this was such a bright photo, I created an Adjustment layer to darken the photo so I could see things. Figure 8.2 shows the Levels adjustment layer with the sliders tweaked to give the photo better definition. The point here is to make the problems more visible, not to make the photo look better. Hide or delete Adjustment layers that you use for this purpose after you're done cloning.

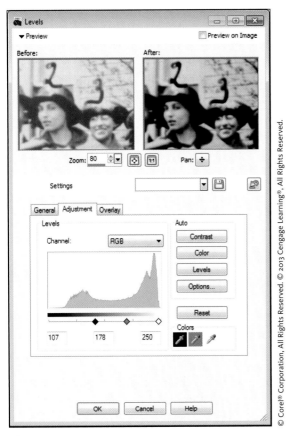

Figure 8.2
Creating a Levels adjustment layer to see better.

Cloning the Problems Away

To review the setup, the working environment at this point in the study includes the Background photo layer, a blank layer to clone on, and a Levels adjustment layer to make it possible to see the work. Turn off the Clone brush's Use All Layers option so it doesn't pick up material from the Adjustment layer. That's critical.

Get into the habit (this applies only when you have an Adjustment layer like this) of looking at the Layers palette (see Figure 8.3) to confirm what layer the source is coming from and what layer you're cloning onto. If you go too fast, you'll make mistakes. First, select the photo layer and right-click the source. Next, select the empty clone layer and apply the brush. Think of it this way. You want to pick up material from the photo layer and deposit it on the working clone layer.

I cloned with the siding of the house to cover the number 1 (see Figure 8.3). When cloning in these types of areas, make sure to keep your source and destination areas aligned with the siding.

I'm cloning in the window above a woman's head in Figure 8.4. You can faintly tell where the tone of the window frame is different than the window. Noticing things like that will help you improve your technique. Find the changes in tone as you clone and work *with* them, not *against* (or oblivious to) them.

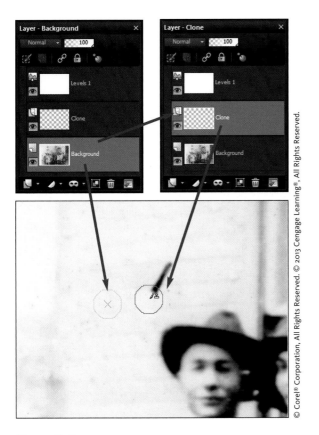

The work wasn't too hard in the window. It got much harder when I moved down to the hat. For situations like this, zoom in and make the brush smaller. I was able to pick up material from below the bottom of the number 2.

Figure 8.5 shows where I am cloning above Grace's hat. Here, the challenge was to move along the grain of the siding while picking up branches and leaves. If you clone the whiteness of the siding here, it will look out of place.

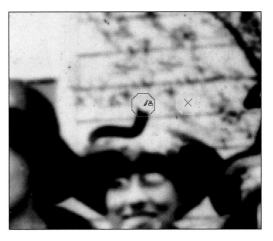

Figure 8.5

Cloning siding with leaves.

Ah, now for a real tricky part. In Figure 8.6, I'm cloning a number out of a window shutter. This is harder because of the fine details, but not impossible. I picked up details from above and to the side, while paying attention to where all the lines were (that's the tricky part). In the figure, I'm pulling detail from the central vertical frame down. It has to match the horizontal shutter shadow on both sides. The outer frame is easier, but it also needs to match the siding on the house.

Figure 8.3

Cloning along the siding.

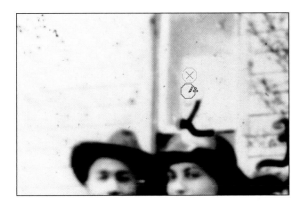

Figure 8.4

Cloning with the window.

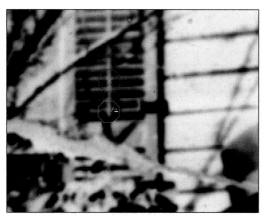

Figure 8.6
Extra care is required for the shutters.

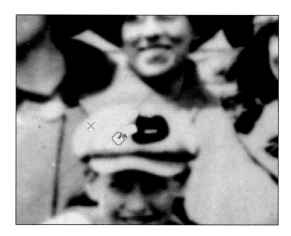

Figure 8.7
Follow the shadow lines.

I've moved on to a young boy's hat in Figure 8.7. We're not completely sure whom this is, but he's got a dapper hat on. The problem is, his hat has a lot of subtle shading so I can't just plop material down. I've got to examine the hat closely and see where the best tone match is; then I'll have to try it out and see if it works. I'm cloning in an arc here, from near the brim of the hat up and toward the center. That matches the shape and tone of the hat where you can see my source spot.

If you can't match the tone perfectly, return with the Soften brush and soften the material on the clone layer. That helps blend things in tremendously. I used a pretty light touch (opacity of 50) to soften it in Figure 8.8.

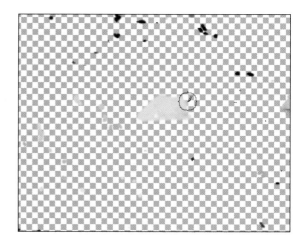

Figure 8.8
Softening the cloned area.

I've also found that the Soften brush (remember, this is on the clone layer, not the photo layer) can lighten cloned material. If you work at it too much, you can start to see the original photo through the clone layer. If that happens, undo and come back a little softer. If you need to, clone a darker patch and then come back with the Soften brush.

Finishing the Photo Study

Photos like this are a lot of fun and rewarding. You feel like you've accomplished something when you look at them afterwards. If there is a lot of work to do, tackle things in stages and break the stages down into steps. For example, I normally start with easy things and then move on to harder tasks. I get on a roll accomplishing things, which boosts my enthusiasm and confidence. In this photo, that meant I started with a few easy numbers before switching to the background. I came back to the harder numbers a bit later and then worked the tear. I finished by scouring every inch of the photo at a high magnification, looking for any imperfections I could fix.

In addition to getting rid of the numbers and fixing other surface imperfections, I tweaked the brightness, contrast, and sharpened the photo to finish the restoration. The final photo is shown in Figure 8.9.

Be Flexible

You don't always have to remove everything you come across. You can restore a photo like this a few different ways. You can also preserve the numbering as an alternate version. That's the convenience of having a digital file to work with and the advantage of keeping track of what you're doing in the file by using layers and saving tool presets.

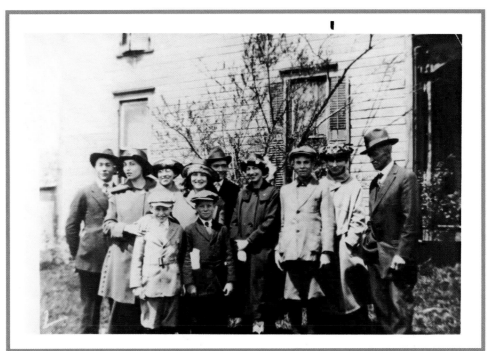

Figure 8.9
Completely restored family lineup.

Photo Study 34: Erasing Crayon and Pen

FIGURE 8.10 IS A PHOTO of my father-in-law's mother, Grace, and her siblings, taken in (as the writing shows), 1919. Grace, our daughter, is the namesake of the woman in this photo, who is about 24 here. The playful young girl on the right is "Grandma Jo," my father-in-law's aunt and Grace's sister.

Seeing old family photos is a powerful reminder of history of people and events. This photo was taken before the roaring twenties, before the Great Depression, and before women had the right to vote. This photo was taken before television, during the inventions of automobiles and airplanes, before spaceflight of any kind, before microwaves and cell phones and computers and most of what we have around us today. They didn't have to decide between cable and satellite TV or between Windows and Macs.

Technique Bonanza

PaintShop Pro has more than a few options when it comes to removing ink and writing on photos. The Color Changer tool (organized with the Flood Fill tool on the Tools toolbar) and the Change to Target brush are two tools that might be successful here. After trying those, I'll move on to saturation options, changing the tint of the colors, using the Clone brush, and finally, the Paint brush.

Removing Color Information

One way to get rid of color marks on a black-and-white photo is to either desaturate the area or to desaturate the whole photo. To convert the entire photo to grayscale (I prefer this Americanized spelling of gray over the UK practice of spelling of grey with an e, which is what PaintShop Pro uses), choose the Image > Greyscale option. The result is shown in Figure 8.11.

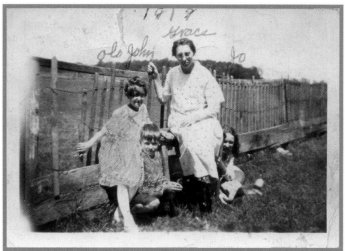

Figure 8.10
Colored ink mars a classic old-time photo.

The color is certainly gone; however, it feels like some of the character of the photo has been lost. The red spots and smudges are still there, but rather than red or blue, the marks are gray.

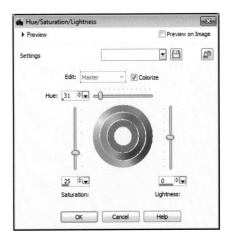

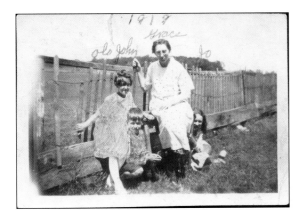

Figure 8.11

Desaturation throws all color information away.

Another desaturation option is to choose the Adjust ❯ Hue and Saturation ❯ Hue/Saturation/Lightness menu. This opens the Hue/Saturation/Lightness dialog box, which allows you to globally or selectively desaturate the photo. You can also check Colorize to impart a colored tint effect. Figure 8.12 shows the result of choosing a Saturation of 25 and Hue of 31 with the Colorize option checked. That's not bad.

You can also colorize a photo by selecting the Adjust ❯ Hue and Saturation ❯ Colorize menu and entering Hue and Saturation options in the Colorize dialog box.

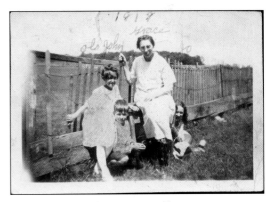

Figure 8.12

It's possible to colorize with Hue/Saturation/Lightness.

You might think that the Saturation Up/Down brush would make fast work of the color in this photo. Figure 8.13 shows the result. The problem is the sepia tone that needs to be maintained. Desaturating selected areas makes them stand out like a sore thumb because they have no color at all, while the rest of the photo does. If you lower the brush's opacity, you can't remove the color.

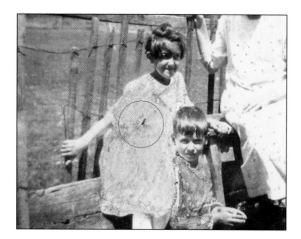

Figure 8.13
Selective desaturation is too much.

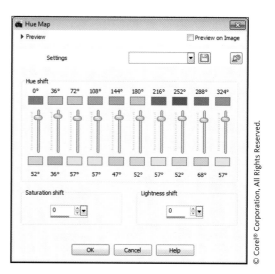

Figure 8.14
Selectively changing the photo's hues.

Hue

Altering the hue of the marks is another possible solution. In this case, you could try turning the reds and blues to a shade of yellowish brown. Select the Adjust ❯ Hue and Saturation ❯ Hue Map menu to open the Hue Map dialog box. This command enables you to selectively change hues of the photo from one value to another. That's one of the cool things about working with digital photographs. Every pixel is a set of numbers that can be mathematically changed.

Figure 8.14 shows the dialog box. The color swatches along the top are the hues of the color wheel. They represent the colors in the photo. In the center are sliders that you move up and down to change the hue of the bottom swatch to whatever hue you want. You can also lower or raise the photo's saturation or lightness. In this case, I changed all the hues to various shades of yellow and desaturated the photo to tone down the color intensity.

Figure 8.15 shows the result. Not that bad.

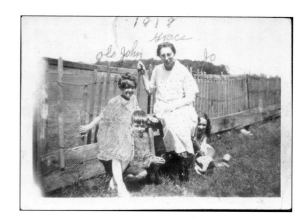

Figure 8.15
There are still color issues, but this is better.

Color Changer

The Color Changer tool made its appearance with the release of PaintShop Pro Photo XI. Older color replacement tools like the Flood Fill tool (which admittedly, isn't the only way to change colors, and has also gotten better) were designed to operate simply: see blue (within a certain tolerance), replace blue. Only one replacement shade of blue per customer, please. They were great for changing a color range to a specific color, but not so great for replacing a color range with a color range.

The Color Changer tool is optimized to replace a range of similar colors. You specify a tolerance and edge softness from the Tool Options palette. That's nifty.

It's easy to use this tool. First, select the Dropper and click on the photo to load the color you want to use to replace into the Materials palette (see Figure 8.16).

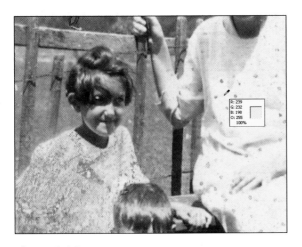

Figure 8.16

Sampling the color to replace with.

Next, switch to the Color Changer, modify the Tolerance and Edge Softness if necessary, and click on the color you want to replace in the photo, as shown in Figure 8.17.

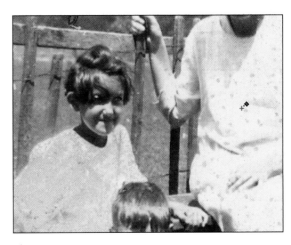

Figure 8.17

Washing those reds away.

Notice a few things from Figure 8.17. First, the areas of color that get changed do not have to be adjacent, providing they are connected by pixels within the color tolerance. They can be on opposite sides of the photo, and the Color Changer will replace them. The red in the young girl's dress was changed to off-white (roughly, I will get to that), even though I clicked in Grace's dress. This has benefits but also drawbacks. If you're working in a photo where the colors are very similar (as this one is), you will get more color replacement than you may want. Try lowering the tolerance in those cases.

Second, the off-white color that replaced the red did so reasonably intelligently. It's not just a blob of solid color. The bad thing is that it didn't completely eliminate the red from this photo. I will still have to use the Clone brush, as seen in Figure 8.18, to completely remove the spots.

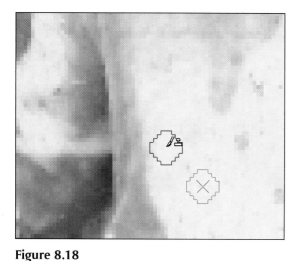

Figure 8.18
Cloning to finish.

Change to Target

I want to try a different technique on John's shirt. It's been pretty well inked over, with globs of thick color interspersed with less dense patches. This time I will use the Change to Target brush.

Set the foreground color in the Materials palette to the color you want to change to with the Dropper tool, as I'm doing in Figure 8.19. Look for something in the photo that has the same tone you want to use as a replacement color. The area on that wooden post will do.

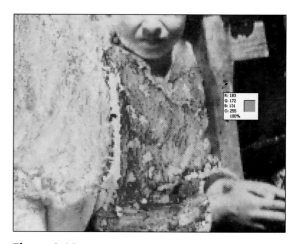

Figure 8.19
Taking another sample.

Next, change to the Change to Target brush and modify the brush size and hardness to suit the area where you are working, as I have done in Figure 8.20, brushing the area you want to recolor.

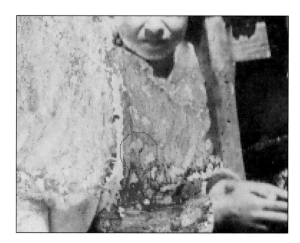

Figure 8.20
Using the Change to Target brush.
© Corel® Corporation, All Rights Reserved. © 2013 Cengage Learning®, All Rights Reserved.

Be careful when you paint with the Change to Target brush. It isn't a "smart" tool. In other words, some tools analyze what you click on and then change a range of similar pixels within a certain tolerance, like the Color Changer tool. The Change to Target brush doesn't work like that. With it, your brush covers whatever you're painting over with the target color.

In Color mode, the Change to Target brush modifies the color (a combination of hue and saturation in this instance) but not other properties (like lightness, which is where much of the detail is). Normally, that's nice. In this instance, it's not so good. After changing the color of John's shirt, it still looks like someone has drawn on it. I softened the final texture with the Soften brush, as shown in Figure 8.21, to correct that.

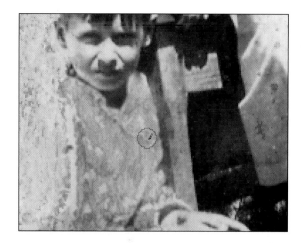

Figure 8.21
Softening to smooth the effect.
© Corel® Corporation, All Rights Reserved. © 2013 Cengage Learning®, All Rights Reserved.

Finishing the Photo Study

In the end, this isn't the type of photo you can make look brand new. The coloring covers up important details too effectively. Altering the color or saturation doesn't eliminate the clumping, nor does it uncover details underneath. In effect, you have to reduce the glaring problems but know where to stop before you ruin the photo.

Figure 8.22 shows the final result. Aside from cloning out the writing, I used the Change to Target brush to alter the color on people's clothing. I cleaned up with the Clone brush and repaired many imperfections around the photo. I also emphasized the edges a bit with Clarity, sharpened the photo with Unsharp Mask, and used Levels to increase the contrast a tad. Finally, I took some of the yellow out of the photo by desaturating it a small amount, but I left a good part of it in because I thought it added to the character.

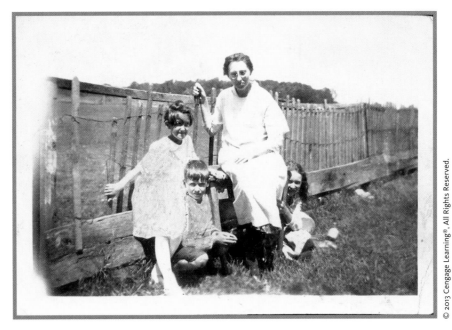

Figure 8.22
Attractively restored.

Photo Study 35:
Removing Marker and Ink Smudges

FIGURE 8.23 IS ANOTHER PHOTO of me from high school. I was a drum major of our marching band, which explains my white uniform when the others are in green. I am playing my alto saxophone on this song. One of the highlights of my marching band experience was participating in the 1982 Macy's Thanksgiving Day Parade in New York City.

This photo was taken by one of the photographers of our local newspaper. Some years later, I was able to scan it and keep this digital copy—thankfully, because the original photo seems to have been lost.

I like the composition of this photo and the fact that the farther you look into the background, the more out of focus everything is. (You're seeing a shallow depth of field, which is caused by having a wide aperture in the lens and standing close to the subject. You can simulate this in PaintShop Pro by choosing the Adjust ❯ Depth of Field menu.) The challenge with this photo is to remove the marker and what looks like smudged ink without taking anything away from such a good photo.

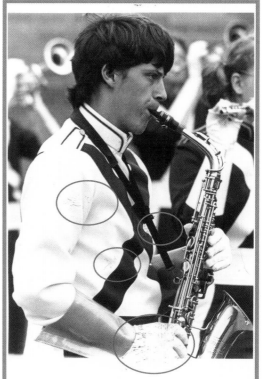

Figure 8.23
Smudged marker has damaged this photo of me.

Splitting HSL Channels

For problems like this, try splitting the channels to HSL. There are a few reasons why you might want to do this. First, it may be easier to repair the damage to a photo using the H, S, and L channels, as opposed to the normal photo. Second, splitting channels is often the best way to see the damage in the first place (and may be the best way to repair it once you see it). That's the case here. You always have the option to experiment and discover which method works best for you on a specific photo.

I wrote a description of color and HSL in Chapter 4, "Solving Color Problems." Here's a recap. HSL stands for Hue, Saturation, and Lightness. These are three "channels" that store information about a picture. They work like the Red, Green, and Blue channels, which you're probably more familiar with. RGB is purely color information, whereas HSL is more. Here's how it breaks out in simplified terms:

- ▶ **Hue**—the color of the pixel.
- ▶ **Saturation**—the intensity of that color from gray to the pure color.
- ▶ **Lightness**—the lightness of the pixel.

Each of these channels is independent of each other, which means you can change the color of something in the photo without compromising its intensity or lightness. Or you can change lightness without altering saturation, or saturation without altering hue, and so forth.

To split a photo into its component HSL channels, select Image ❯ Split Channel ❯ Split to HSL. The result is shown in Figure 8.24.

As you can see, splitting the H, S, and L channels results in three separate images, not layers within your working photo. When you switch channels, select the appropriate image in the PaintShop Pro workspace.

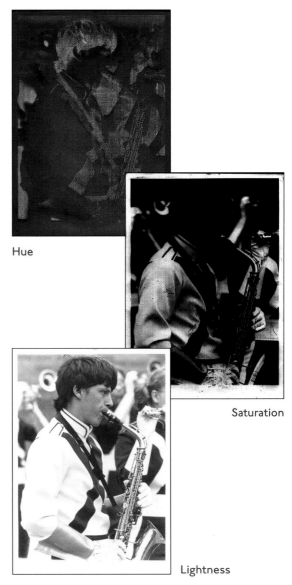

Hue

Saturation

Lightness

Figure 8.24
The three separate HSL channel images.

That's what is happening in Figure 8.25. I have selected the Hue channel image and am working in a sea of gray that represents the hues of the photo. This area is on the right side of my chest. The little white spots are marks and imperfections on the photo that I need to clone out. They stand out like sore thumbs.

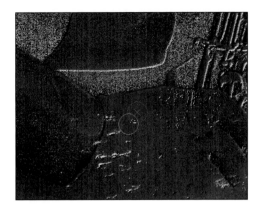

Figure 8.26

The more difficult hand area is still easier when using channels.

Figure 8.25

Cloning away easy-to-spot imperfections in the Hue channel.

I am still in the Hue channel in Figure 8.26, but I've moved down to my hand. This is another area where there are heavy markings. Using the Hue channel makes it far easier to spot them and clone them out. This particular area is harder to fix than my chest, but it's still very practical.

Let's look at my chest area again (see Figure 8.27). The differences in tone stand out, despite the fact that this channel is very consistent. Notice the subtle shadows of my uniform in the Hue channel.

Don't let your guard down when working with channels. Pay really close attention and stay within the same range of tones. I can see the folds of my uniform, so when I clone, I'm going to go with that "grain." My source spot is within this region, and I am moving down and to the right, following the fold of the shirt.

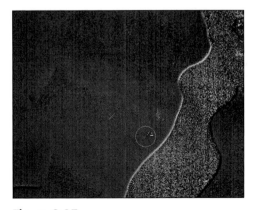

Figure 8.27

The texture is almost imperceptible.

Figure 8.28 shows the center of my uniform, still looking at the Hue channel. My neck strap travels from the bottom right to the top center. You can tell the difference in hue between my white uniform (the left center of this figure), the black markings on the uniform (the X), and the marker that I am cloning out, which stands out as a brighter white, just below the Clone brush.

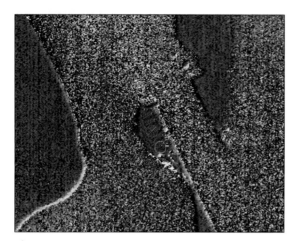

Figure 8.28
Carefully working in small areas.

Figure 8.29 shows my right shoulder and arm in the Saturation channel. The marker is visible as dark lines. I am cloning it out carefully, following the folds of my garment where the shadow lies.

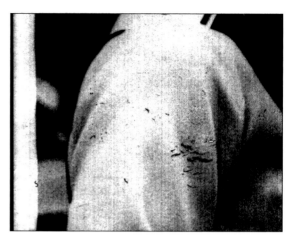

Figure 8.29
The marker is easy to spot in the Saturation channel.

I've zoomed in closer and am working in a more deeply shadowed area in Figure 8.30. Always be careful to match source and destination areas.

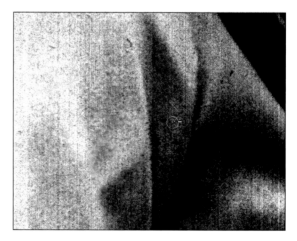

Figure 8.30
Working along shaded areas.

Figure 8.31 shows the back of my right hand in the Saturation channel. You can see more detail here than in the Hue channel, which complicates matters a bit. However, because the photo is essentially in black and white, I can get away with things I wouldn't try with a color photo. In other words, if I wanted to "paint" this area one shade of gray, it would work just fine. The glove would be saturated equally, and it wouldn't look strange or out of place.

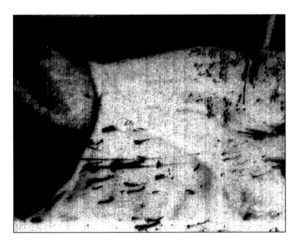

Figure 8.31
Smaller brush for the hand.

Some of the flexibility I had while working in the Saturation channel is unique to the area I am working in with this photo. It's black and white, essentially, and the glove is fairly uniformly saturated.

The damage stands out, whereas the glove blends in and almost disappears. I could have removed all saturation information from the photo, but I don't like throwing information away. Remember, black-and-white photo prints may not be true grayscale, and they may contain very subtle tints and coloration that can add to the character of the photo.

Finally, I want to show you a Lightness channel example.

Figure 8.32, the Lightness channel image, looks essentially like the unsplit photo. Cloning works pretty normally in the Lightness channel. Just remember where you've cloned away marks in the other channels and check those spots to see if you need to work them in this channel.

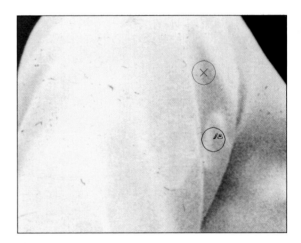

Figure 8.32
The Lightness channel completes the trifecta.

Splitting and Combining

You can split and combine channels as many times as you need. For example, if you're working with HSL channels and need to quit (but you aren't finished), combine the split channels by selecting Image > Combine Channel > Combine from HSL. Next, select the newly combined image and press Ctrl+C to copy it. Then paste that as a new layer in your working .pspimage file. Save and close your file. When you come back to work on it, split that layer into its component channels and continue working on the separate channels. This technique enables you to stop and start when you need to without losing your work in the split channels.

Finishing the Photo Study

After finishing my work in the channels, I combined them by selecting Image > Combine Channel > Combine from HSL. This provided me with a single image, just like the scanned original, only without the marks. I then continued to work on the photo to make it better.

Figure 8.33 shows the final result, which also included noise reduction and contrast adjustments. Splitting the channels made all the difference in the world with this photo. It made seeing subtle problems and fixing them easier. That's what this is all about.

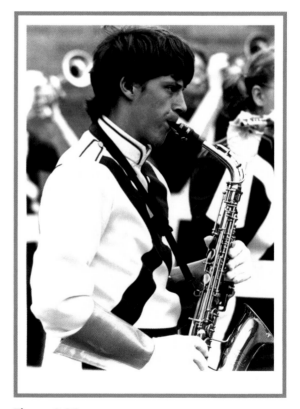

Figure 8.33
The spots are gone.

Photo Study 36: Moving a Teddy Bear

OUR KIDS LOVE THEIR TEDDY BEARS and pillows. In this photo from 2006 (see Figure 8.34), my oldest son, Benjamin, is napping on the couch with his pillow and one of his smaller bears, Baby Grace.

Baby Grace would look cuter if she were under the blanket with Ben. This is a perfect opportunity to show you how to move something around in a photo.

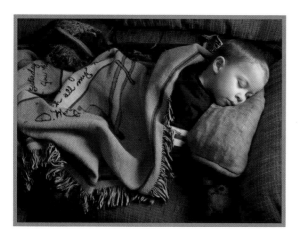

Figure 8.34
Cute, but could be composed better.

Getting Started

First, I duplicated the Background layer so I wouldn't accidentally clone on it or otherwise change it. That new layer serves as my new working layer and photo background. Next, I had to copy the bear. I use the Freehand Selection tool in Point to Point mode for selection operations like this. (Modes are accessible in the Tool Options palette at the top of the screen.) The Freehand Selection tool in Freehand mode takes more effort to use quickly, and the extra around the edges will be erased anyway. There is no need to be fancy with selections like this as long as you get the entire subject. I've made my selection of the bear in Figure 8.35 with the Freehand Selection tool in Point to Point mode. This mode lets me click at each point of the selection polygon so I can go rapido. Comprende?

Freehand Conventions

From this point forward, I will write Freehand Selection tool in Freehand mode as *Freehand Selection tool (Freehand mode)*. I will shorten Freehand Selection tool in Point to Point mode to *Freehand Selection tool (Point mode)*.

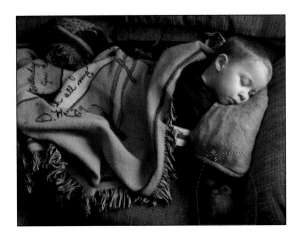

Figure 8.35
Lasso that bear.

I copied the bear using the standard keyboard shortcut (I'm a sucker for Ctrl+C) and then pasted it as a new layer (Ctrl+V). This is the working layer for the bear. Next, I had to erase around it. (You can also mask the extra material out if you'd like.)

Ctrl+V and Paste

Some older versions of PaintShop Pro had Ctrl+V as a shortcut for Paste as New Image. If you prefer the older behavior, modify the keyboard shortcut accordingly.

I've hidden the Background layer in Figure 8.36 so you can see the bear and where I was erasing. It's a good idea to center what you're erasing so you can zoom in and see all the edges. If you need to erase a lot, start with a large eraser and set the hardness to 100%, and then work your way down to a small brush at 0% hardness for the final pass. There wasn't much to erase here, so I used a soft eraser from the outset.

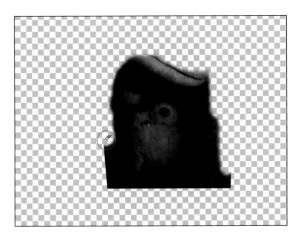

Figure 8.36
Don't wake the bear while you erase.

Erasing is one of the most important aspects of this exercise. If you don't get a good clean, soft border (not sharp—sharp will stick out like a sore thumb) around your subject, it will be obvious when you position it. Use short strokes as you erase so you don't lose a lot of work if you have to undo later. Notice that I haven't rotated the bear or positioned it yet. I'm concentrating on erasing the border. That's it.

Covering Up

With the subject prepped and ready to position (remember, it's been copied and pasted to a new layer), put it aside and start covering the original up. For this photo, that involved extending the couch fabric to cover the original bear. I could have used the Clone brush, but I decided to copy and paste a section of the couch instead. The texture of the couch made it hard to clone without being obviously repetitious.

To copy and paste a small strip of couch fabric, select the trusty Freehand Selection tool (Point mode) and make a selection of the couch to copy, as shown in Figure 8.37. Look for an area that will make a good match to repeatedly paste and blend. There are some shadow problems here, but I will minimize that later by applying an overall shadow to the area. In this case, I wanted to match the texture and pattern alignment exactly, while going for the general tone. Had I not been able to grab this area, I would have looked for another photo that had the couch in it, or walked out of the computer room and into the living room and taken another photo for that express purpose. You can do that, too!

After making the selection, I copied and pasted it as a new layer. You can paste it several times or once and then duplicate that layer several times. It's your call. I pasted the couch material eight times. (This is a good example of thinking outside the box to solve a problem; you should be thinking this way as well.) Then I arranged the pieces to fit the area, as you can see in Figure 8.38. Don't worry about borders yet. This step is to align and get the pattern set.

After you align the strips, select the top one from the Layers palette and choose Merge Down.

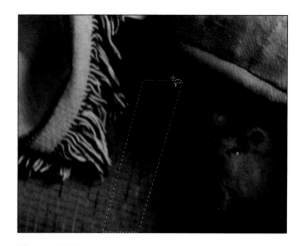

Figure 8.37
Carefully selecting along the lines.

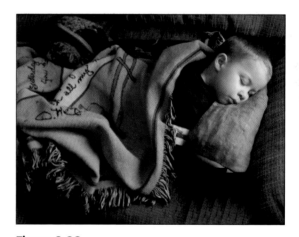

Figure 8.38
Transplanting couch texture.

(Right-click over the layer in the palette, choose Merge, and then Merge Down.) Do this until all the strips are merged. When you are merging layers, take special care. It is very important not to merge this layer with the Background layer.

The reason I merged these couch fabric layers together but did not merge them with the background was to be able to manipulate one layer (not eight) separately from the main photo layer. I erased all the ragged edges (see Figure 8.39), moved along the arm of the couch, and erased next to the pillow. It's important to remember that this "patch" is on a separate layer above the couch. As I erased the border of the patch, it "sunk" in and blended with the couch.

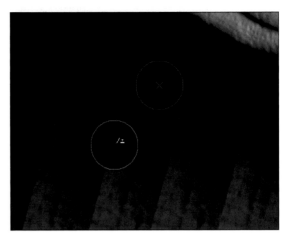

Figure 8.40
Couches sans borders.

With the cloning done and the original bear covered, it was time to put the copy of Baby Grace into position.

Fitting In

I kept the new Baby Grace layer hidden while I was covering up the original area, which kept things visually simple. With that completed, I was ready to make Baby Grace look like she was tucked under the blanket as opposed to the pillow.

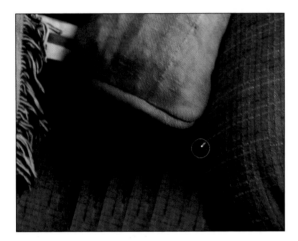

Figure 8.39
Erase to fit.

Next, I got rid of the straight edges that formed the border between the pasted patches. This was easily done with the Clone brush (see Figure 8.40). I was careful to match tones (colors, shadows, and lightness) and patterns.

It was a simple matter to grab the Pick tool and drag Baby Grace over to the blanket and rotate her to match the orientation of the new scene I wanted her in (see Figure 8.41). After positioning her, I blended her in with the Eraser. While it looks like I'm erasing the blanket in the figure, I was actually erasing around the bear on a layer above the blanket's fringe. It's funny how perception works sometimes.

During the blending stage, I was careful to observe how she blended in. I zoomed in and out to get a close perspective.

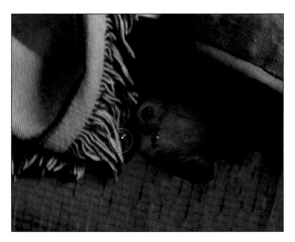

Figure 8.41
Erase border of Baby Grace to create the illusion.

Almost done.

Shadows are an important aspect of getting things to blend and match. They can also cover up things that you can't get to look right. For this photo, I darkened a few areas to help cement the illusion. First, I used the Burn brush (at a pretty light setting: opacity 10) and stroked around Baby Grace (see Figure 8.42). This gave her a sense of belonging in her new position. I also darkened the couch below her to make it look as if she were casting a shadow. I also darkened the area of the couch she came from to hide some texture and tone mismatches.

That completed the reposition. I selected everything, performed a merged copy, and pasted that to a new layer on top of everything else to be able to make global adjustments to a single layer.

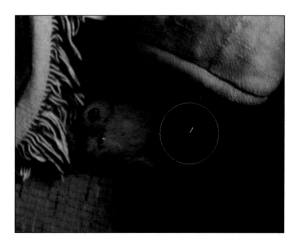

Figure 8.42
Burn shadow on the couch.

Final Adjustments

Always remember to tweak things. Although the main point of this restoration was moving the bear, that's only one part of the overall retouching job. In this case, I consulted Smart Photo Fix. With minor alterations (lowering the suggested increase in brightness and choosing new black and white points in the photo), the result was a bit livelier than the original.

After this, I smoothed things out a touch using Adjust ❯ Add/Remove Noise ❯ Edge Preserving Smooth. Dark or poorly lit digital photos often have more noise than well-lit photos, especially if the ISO is raised to brighten the exposure. This photo has an ISO of 50, so that wasn't causing the noise. More than likely, it was the camera's noisy sensor, whose internal noise characteristics were more evident when it captured dark regions.

This smoothed the blanket and the couch too much, however, so I masked out everything but Ben's face on the smoothing layer (see Figure 8.43) and then made that layer group semi-transparent to blend it in better.

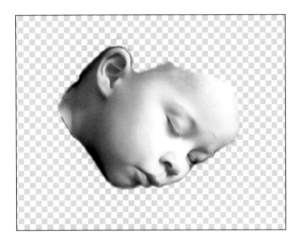

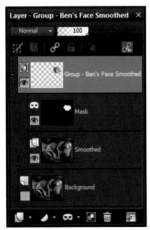

Figure 8.43
Selective smoothing with a mask.
© Corel® Corporation, All Rights Reserved. © 2013 Cengage Learning®, All Rights Reserved.

Finishing the Photo Study

Figure 8.44 shows the final result. Baby Grace looks better under the blanket than where she was originally. Before I moved her, she was aligned vertically and was at odds with everything else in the photo.

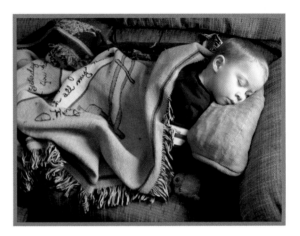

Figure 8.44
Ben and Baby Grace hibernating one afternoon.
© 2013 Cengage Learning®, All Rights Reserved.

Restoration and Retouching Ethics

Danger! You could write a lot of damaging things with this word processing program! Use this program wisely!

That's silly, of course, and you wouldn't see a note like this in a word processing book. Pictures are powerful things, however, and PaintShop Pro gives you the ability to alter them quite a bit.

I trust you to know where the ethical lines of photo retouching are and not to cross them. Something to think about.

Photo Study 37: Removing Odds and Ends

Figure 8.45 shows a lighthearted family portrait (sans the photographer, me) taken in 2009. Anne and the kids were playing, and everyone fell down on the floor. I had my camera at the ready because I was experimenting with white balance bracketing down in the (very yellowish) basement, taking pictures under the fluorescent lights.

It's got some odds and ends I can use to show you how to remove odds and ends. There's a green square stacking toy by Ben's head, a Hot Wheels toy (where you rev up motorcycles and let them fly) next to Sam, and some stuff on the couch to the top left. There are also spots on the rug I can remove.

Sounds like a perfect fit for this chapter.

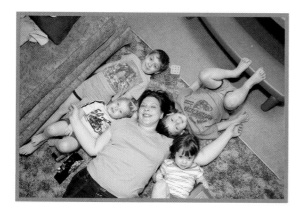

Figure 8.45

Lots of extras to remove from this photo.

Stay Flexible

In the process of experimenting with the photo's framing, I realized I could crop out a lot of the distractions and focus more tightly on everyone's faces. Figure 8.46 shows where I planned to crop the photo.

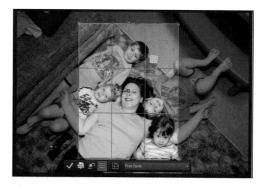

Figure 8.46

The planned crop.

That meant my initial plans had to change. I went back and carefully reviewed the things I wanted to remove. The Hot Wheels toy was outside of the crop so I could ignore it. The green cube was still in the shot, as were the couch and the spots on the rug. No changes to my plan there. I realized, though, that the crop would make everyone more prominent in the photo. In other words, cropping out their legs and floor meant faces and upper bodies were visually more dominant and important to the photo. Therefore, I decided to remove the cuts and scrapes on everyone, remove Jake's knee by replacing his arm (he's wearing the orange shirt), replace Grace in this photo with her from another shot taken at the same time, and take the couch out.

If you rotate and enlarge the photo layer with the Pick tool instead of rotating and cropping the entire image, take note of the Scale percentage (this was 174.54). If you copy and paste material in from another photo, you can scale the new material by entering the same value in the Pick Tool Options palette. You still might have to tweak things, but you'll be closer to where you want to end up.

Standard Cloning

For this photo, I cloned out the green cube and the couch. Both had a few tricky spots worth mentioning. The green cube overlays the edge of a rug, which is angled. Cloning along this angle resulted in a mismatch between the sides, as shown in Figure 8.47. You can see where the two diagonal edges of the new rug don't match up.

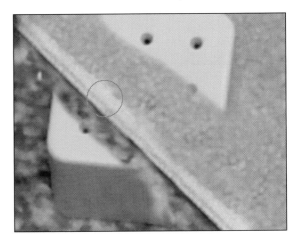

Figure 8.48
Matching the angle carefully.

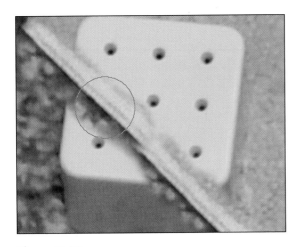

Figure 8.47
Cloning mismatch on an angle.

In cases like this, don't worry about cloning from either side and meeting in the middle. Clone from one side all the way over. I cloned a new border from the cube all the way to Ben, as shown in Figure 8.48.

The couch posed a different problem. Namely, my first attempt to clone it out was too obvious (see Figure 8.49). I made the mistake of not cloning any of the lighter spots on the carpet.

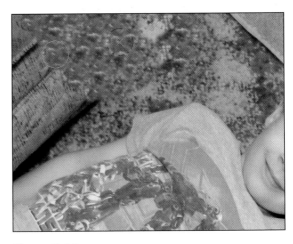

Figure 8.49
Pay attention to textures and patterns.

I started over and took special care to randomize my source selections, making sure to pick up light and dark areas. Likewise, don't neglect things like shadows. The couch cast a darker shadow on the carpet close to Ben's arm. I was careful to clone over this with lighter material so it didn't look like a shadow was being cast from nothing. Figure 8.50 shows the result.

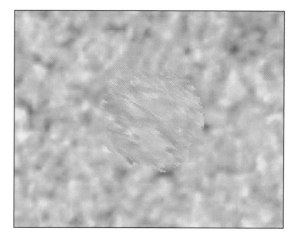

Figure 8.51
Watch carefully how the Blemish Fixer blends.

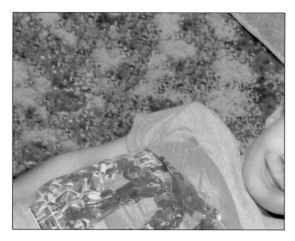

Figure 8.50
Much better match the second time around.

Removing Blemishes

I often use the Blemish Fixer mode of the Makeover tool to take out spots, scrapes, and cuts on people. Pay attention to how the tool blends. Figure 8.51 shows a blend problem, probably caused by the image scale. (I scaled instead of cropped.) In this case, I would undo and go for the Clone brush.

Replacement Material

Jacob's arm and knee bothered me, so I decided to make it look like his left arm was straight. That meant I had to remove the knee. I tried cloning his arm to extend it, but it never looked right. I realized I had a few other photos I took at the same time to choose from, so I looked them over to see if I could copy his arm from a different photo and transplant it here.

I did, and it worked. I drew a rough, freehand selection around his left arm in another photo and copied and pasted it into my working file. After rotating and scaling the new arm (this is when knowing the scaling percentage comes in handy), I still had to resize it slightly to match the scale of this photo. Next, I erased what I didn't need and blended it in. In the end, it worked perfectly.

In Figure 8.52, I have placed the rotated and scaled new arm next to the original so you can clearly see they aren't the same. (As an aside, this is a good example to show you the merit of taking several photos of the same scene. You can pick and choose parts from different photos and combine them into the best photo.)

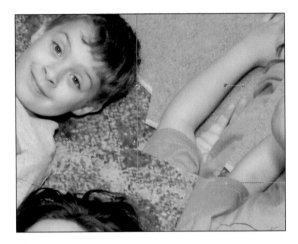

Figure 8.52
Matching Jake's new arm.

The other transplant involved Grace. She has an odd expression in the original photo. Having looked at the photo from which I copied Jake's arm, I realized I preferred her expression in that one. I applied the same technique to selecting and transplanting her as I did to Jake's arm, although hers was a bit more complicated.

For starters, I could have tried to copy and paste her face or her head and replace her expression. Well, I did try, and it never looked right. Faces are connected to heads, and heads are connected to bodies. Mixing and matching faces or heads is pretty hard. It's far easier to replace an entire body.

Therefore, I made sure to get Anne's green shirt in the selection (knowing I would need that to blend in) and all of Grace. After copying and pasting it into the working file, I used the Pick tool to scale her upward (make the layer you're enlarging semi-transparent so you can see what you're doing), and then I positioned her in the right spot.

I erased around her (see Figure 8.53) to blend her in, which is to say that I was mostly erasing Jake and Anne's shirts. Figure 8.53 looks like I'm erasing Jake's eye, which is correct. The material I'm erasing surrounds Grace and is meant to blend her in with the surroundings. It's not perfect (you can tell when you toggle the new layer on and off), but you really can't tell from looking at the new material that anything is wrong.

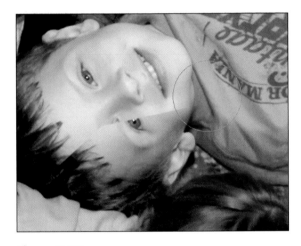

Figure 8.53
Erasing to blend Grace in.

Finishing the Photo Study

I finished the photo study by running the photo through Levels to brighten it and improve contrast, and then I whitened everyone's teeth and performed One Step Noise Removal. I typically save these adjustments for last when working with photos like this. Otherwise, it's too hard to match new material to the original. Figure 8.54 shows the final result. This photo went from a slightly cluttered family shot into a tightly focused and yet fun family portrait.

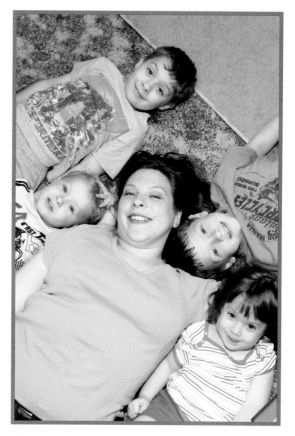

Figure 8.54
The slightly altered family portrait.

Photo Study 38: Adding a Person to a Photo

FIGURE 8.55 SHOWS TWO PHOTOS from 2002 that my wife and I took of each other. Each of us posed with our son, Benjamin, sitting in his car seat on the kitchen table. The obvious problem is, we couldn't be in the same photo! She couldn't be in the picture she took and I couldn't be in the picture I took.

These photos stood out from the very beginning as good candidates for moving one of us to the other photo. They were taken at the same time, with the same lighting, and from basically the same vantage point.

I used one of the photos as a "base" layer and copied the other person in to blend them together.

Adding Anne

First, I took Anne from her photo (see Figure 8.56) and added her to my "base" photo. I used the Freehand Selection tool (Point mode) to select her. I decided to move her (rather than move me into her photo) because she was sitting off to the side and there was less of her covered up by the car seat. That meant it would take less effort to put her in a new photo. If you look at my chest (see Figure 8.55), much of it is covered by the car seat. If I were to move myself, I would have to create a large area from out of thin air or try to put myself behind something to cover that missing area up. Those are tricky operations.

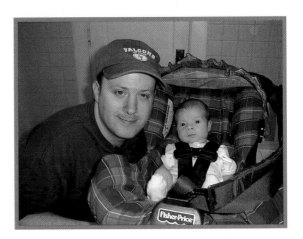

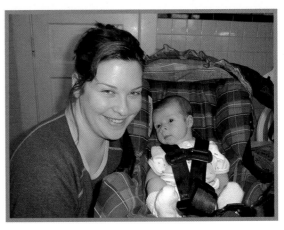

Figure 8.55
We needed someone to take our photo together.

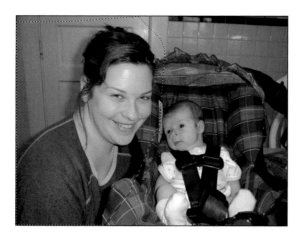

Figure 8.56

Select and copy the subject from the other photo.

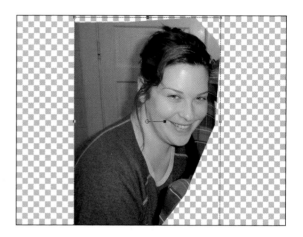

Figure 8.57

Paste her in the "keeper" photo.

I was fairly liberal with the amount of wall and pantry door I included with Anne in the selection. This is about moving her over, not making a perfect selection on the front end. Don't waste your time with that. I also saw that I could use the extra space. First, when I started erasing around her (again, you can mask instead of erase), the extra border width (in general, not the wall just yet) gave me a chance to get the right eraser size and hardness, which helped when I blended her in. Second, I used some of the extra material to match her size and perspective to mine, because the photos were not taken from exactly the same vantage point. (That means we weren't scaled exactly the same.) They were close, which makes this possible, but not exact.

I copied her and pasted that image into a new layer in my photo, as shown in Figure 8.57. You see the extra wall and door space that I have included with her in this figure. Those linear features are perfect for aligning and scaling the two parts of the photos.

Next, I lowered the opacity of Anne's layer to about 80% and used the Pick tool to align (move), size (using the outer handles), and rotate (matching the tile on the wall) Anne's layer to match mine.

I'm rotating and scaling her layer to match mine in Figure 8.58. Can you see the door hinges? I've got hers to the left of mine. Although her layer is less opaque, it looks stronger than mine because she is on the top layer. I used the hinge and the doorjamb to get the vertical alignment right, and the tile lines and size to get the rotation and scale. The tile sizes matched near the top, but they didn't line up as well near the bottom. That's proof that the scales of her photo and mine are a slight mismatch.

The reason I went to this extreme to figure out our scale is to make sure we looked good together. It would look weird for her head to be out of proportion with mine. Things like this don't need to match perfectly, but you want them to be close.

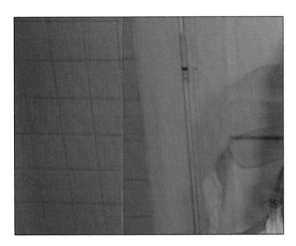

Figure 8.58

Adjust using reference points for scale and perspective.

Erasing and Positioning

Next, I erased around and positioned Anne in the context of the photo. I started erasing the border around her in Figure 8.59 with the Eraser. I made a few passes with the Eraser, and on each pass I zoomed in closer to catch more details.

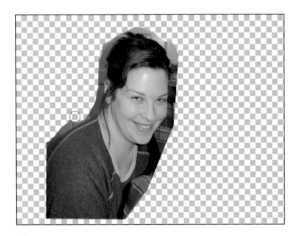

Figure 8.59

Erasing is critical.

Hair is hard to erase well, so I will share a little trick I use in these situations. First, don't worry about erasing a few straggling hairs. Just erase them. They aren't worth the trouble of trying to save. Second, you want to have a fuzzy border around the hair. That's what natural hair looks like anyway. The trick is to take a large Eraser that is 100% soft and lightly touch it outside of the area you are erasing to gently eat away at some of the opacity of the pixels that border the hair.

I moved Anne into position in Figure 8.60 with the Move tool. Remember, you should finish any changes to perspective and scale before you position.

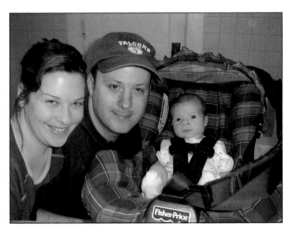

Figure 8.60

Position before making final adjustments.

The big stuff is done, but there are still some important things to fix. Anne's shirt is missing material that makes it obvious she doesn't belong in this photo. I need to add it to finish her.

Adding New Material

I've got another photo taken at the same time with Anne sitting at a slightly different angle to the camera, which picks up the front of her shirt better. This creates valuable source material for me to copy and paste. I selected an appropriate section of the shirt to copy and paste as a new layer in the base photo in Figure 8.61.

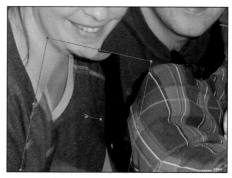

Figure 8.62
Go semi-transparent when positioning.
© Corel® Corporation, All Rights Reserved. © 2013 Cengage Learning®, All Rights Reserved.

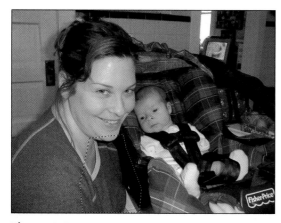

Figure 8.61
Copying extra material from another photo.
© Corel® Corporation, All Rights Reserved. © 2013 Cengage Learning®, All Rights Reserved.

I'm aligning the new layer in Figure 8.62 by making it semi-transparent and moving it around with the Pick tool.

The orientation of the new material was different enough from where I wanted to place it that I had to choose what to align. In this case, the neckline and the seam on her left shoulder were the best choices. They formed the border of what I wanted to replace. I aligned the new shirt material and am erasing what I don't need in Figure 8.63.

Next, I had to do some retouching to make the new layer match her neckline. I am just starting to use the Clone brush in Figure 8.64 to line up the seam by cloning gray material over the mismatch.

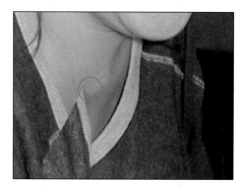

Figure 8.63
Erase unneeded material.
© Corel® Corporation, All Rights Reserved. © 2013 Cengage Learning®, All Rights Reserved.

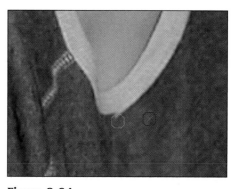

Figure 8.64
Getting ready to clone.
© Corel® Corporation, All Rights Reserved. © 2013 Cengage Learning®, All Rights Reserved.

Figure 8.65 shows the result. You cannot tell that this neckline and shirt were from two different photos.

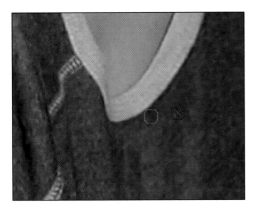

Figure 8.65

Now it matches perfectly.

© Corel® Corporation, All Rights Reserved. © 2013 Cengage Learning®,
All Rights Reserved.

Final Adjustments

I'll finish with my usual flourish. I selected all, copy merged, and pasted as a new layer. This locked in all the changes to a single layer that I used to make global adjustments.

Next, I carefully softened the bright spots on our faces and removed a few blemishes. Then I did some minor noise reduction. Finally, I used Levels (as shown in Figure 8.66) to get better contrast and made a color correction to take some yellow out of our faces (Adjust ❯ White Balance).

Finishing the Photo Study

This one's done (see Figure 8.67). I didn't use more than a handful of tools for this entire photo study, but the results were dramatic. We were in two photos, and now we are in one photo. It's not about how many tools you use or how easy or hard they are—it's about the photos and the results.

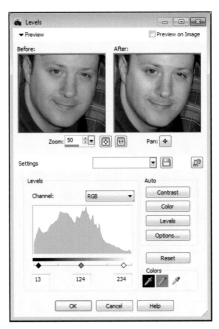

Figure 8.66

Don't forget to check Levels.

© Corel® Corporation, All Rights Reserved. © 2013 Cengage Learning®,
All Rights Reserved.

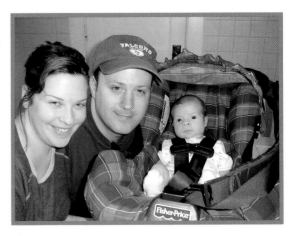

Figure 8.67

A successful operation, doctor!

© 2013 Cengage Learning®, All Rights Reserved.

Photo Study 39: Creating Montages

FIGURE 8.68, TAKEN IN 2012, shows my son Sam leaping off the elevated sidewalk of a local bridge onto the main, lower walkway. Don't worry, cars aren't allowed on this historic bridge. Anne and I were out taking pictures with a new lens I was testing, and getting kids to jump and play around is one way of creating some fun action to capture.

As you might have surmised by now, we have four kids. Having one jump around as I take his or her photo creates a line. They all want to join in and show off! Taking several pictures of each child creates a large pool of source images for a fun montage.

Workload and Time

Let me say right up front: this can be a lot of work. It's not that difficult once you get the hang of it, but the more source photos you use in your montage, the more you'll have to copy, paste, mask, erase, and blend.

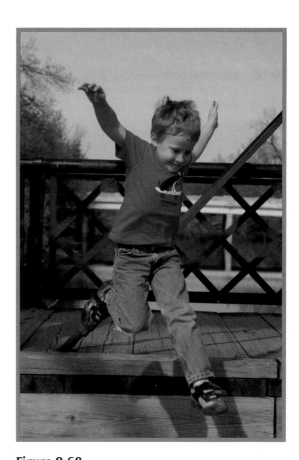

Figure 8.68
Sam leaping.
© 2013 Cengage Learning®, All Rights Reserved.

Prep

First, I needed to get my photos together and decide which ones I was going to use. (I call them the *source photos*.) Then I decided which one would serve as the background. I chose the photo of Ben for the background because there was ample space on both sides of him to position the other kids. He would also look better in the back because he hadn't completed his lift-off. Next, I opened them all up in PaintShop Pro; then I copied each source photo and pasted it into the background file as a new layer. My plan was to mask out what I don't need instead of erasing it. This is not the only approach. Alternatively, you could select, copy, and paste the objects rather than the entire canvasses they appear on. That approach would keep the file size smaller. However, my plan was to use the same adjustment layers to make identical adjustments to these photos later.

Select and Mask

With the prep work completed, I selected each child on his or her source photo layer. I used the trusty Freehand Selection tool (Point mode) for this, as shown in Figure 8.69. I gave myself a good border. The point is to quickly create a mask to show the selection and then refine it at your leisure.

When you have selected the source you want to see, select the Layers ❯ New Mask Layer ❯ Show Selection menu. (You can also use the buttons at the bottom of the Layers palette.) This creates a group with the source layer and a mask inside it.

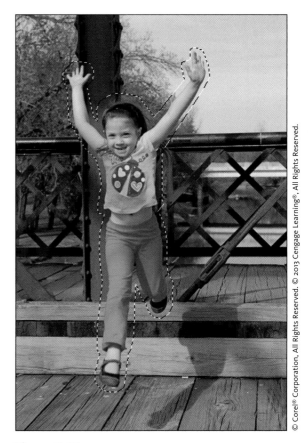

Figure 8.69
Within each source image, select the subject to show.

In turn, create a selection around each object you want to see in the final montage. Turn the other layers off and make sure you have the proper layer selected as you create the Show Selection mask for each. The next step is to start refining each mask.

Refining the Masks

It starts getting harder and more time consuming here. The task at hand is to refine each mask so that the source object (in this case, my kids) fits seamlessly into the new photo. This requires effort and patience.

Remember, I use the eraser with the background color set to black when I "paint on" a mask and hide material. I think of myself as "erasing" what I don't want to see. Others, however, use the Paint brush with the foreground color set to black. Use whichever way makes the most sense to you. The results are identical.

Before working on the masks, make sure that you have selected the right layer. To make things easier to see, I hide everything but the layer I am working on for these first few passes.

I make three main passes at each mask, each with a differently sized Eraser. I make the first pass (as shown in Figure 8.70) with a relatively large brush. If you have trouble seeing the edges, set the Eraser to 100% hardness. I eat away at the outer border, and am careful not to get too close to the subject.

Size Is Relative

When I say "large brush," as opposed to medium or small, the actual size (in pixels) of the brush can vary, depending on the context of the photo and its resolution.

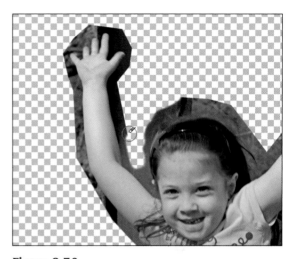

Figure 8.70
My first pass at refining the mask.

For my second pass (see Figure 8.71), I zoom in, shrink the size of the Eraser, and soften it, if necessary. I get close to the edge of the subject and erase very carefully. The soft brush edge helps blend the pixels from totally opaque to transparent.

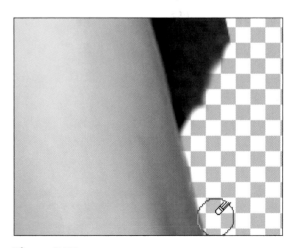

Figure 8.71
Magnify and continue with the smaller Eraser.

Finally, I make a third pass around each object with a very small Eraser. On this pass, I get into the nooks and crannies of fingers, corners, and between things. I'm working on Grace's elbow in Figure 8.72.

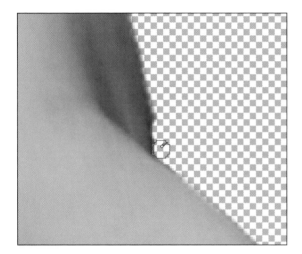

Figure 8.72

Third pass with the smallest Eraser.

© Corel® Corporation, All Rights Reserved. © 2013 Cengage Learning®, All Rights Reserved.

Montage

As you work on your masks, move the montage pieces into position. Experiment with different looks and depths. Figure 8.73 shows my final layout.

By the time you finish with the masks, you should be done laying things out.

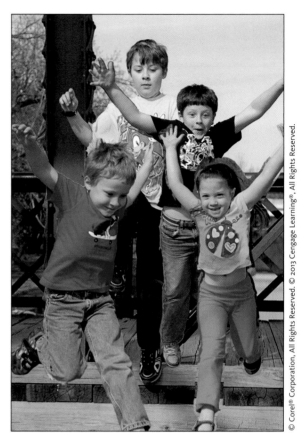

Figure 8.73

Arranging each child's position within the montage.

Check Mask in Context

These next steps are critically important. You can be very skilled with the Eraser (or Paint brush, as the case may be), but it is still important to check whether or not you've missed pixels and how they relate in context to what is in front or behind. I do this in three steps:

1. Check each layer against a white background.

2. Check each layer against a black background.

3. Show all layers and check against each other.

I create two new raster layers (they are temporary) for my initial checks. I fill one with white and the other with black and arrange them so they are above the Background layer but below all the montage layers. Choose one photo montage layer to start with and hide everything else but it and the white layer.

Figure 8.74 shows why I do this. I've zoomed in on Sam's hand, and you can see there are dark pixels that didn't get fully masked. Change your Eraser hardness to 100% and zap them.

Check each montage layer against the white layer.

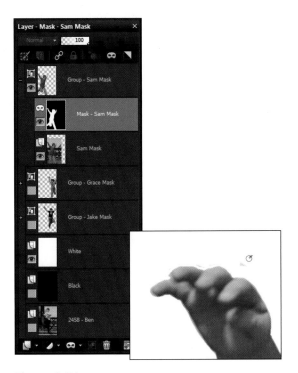

Figure 8.74

White background layer helps show dark leftovers.

© Corel® Corporation, All Rights Reserved. © 2013 Cengage Learning®, All Rights Reserved.

Next, hide the white layer and show the black layer. This time you're looking for light pixels that you missed. When you find them, mask them out (see Figure 8.75).

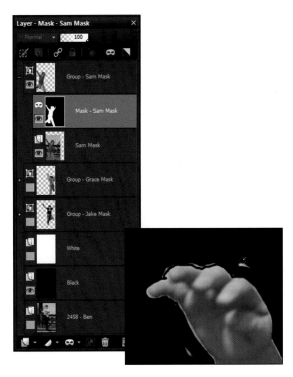

Figure 8.75

Black background layer helps show light leftovers.

© Corel® Corporation, All Rights Reserved. © 2013 Cengage Learning®, All Rights Reserved.

Finally, hide (or delete) both the black-and-white helper layers and show everything else. Then check edges against the photo montage. I am checking every edge that rests on another in Figure 8.76 to see how they blend. I moved closer and erased the border that looked lighter. These pixels were lighter because they were on top of a darker blue.

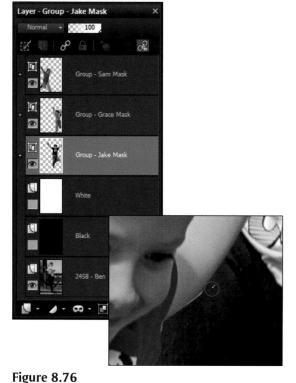

Figure 8.76

Next, check edges in context.

When they were on top of the white layer, I couldn't tell if this area needed erasing. Likewise, when they were on top of the black layer, it was not apparent that this border was too light. I had to check it in this configuration to see if I missed anything.

You can see why this turns into a lot of work. For this montage, the first three masking passes covered three objects, making nine passes. The next two passes with the white and black backgrounds amounted to six more. The final pass attended to three objects. That makes 18 total times around, carefully masking each time.

Brightness and Contrast

With all the masking and montaging done, I finished up with some small, but global, brightness and contrast adjustments. I didn't need to make separate adjustments to each layer because all my source photos were similar. After all, they were taken very close together, from the same basic direction, in the same lighting, and with the same camera settings. Adjustment layers made this a breeze.

I turned on all the photo layers with the kids in them and added a Curves adjustment layer (see Figure 8.77) and Levels (see Figure 8.78) adjustment layer above the photo layers. Using adjustment layers in this way enables you to adjust several layers with a single setting.

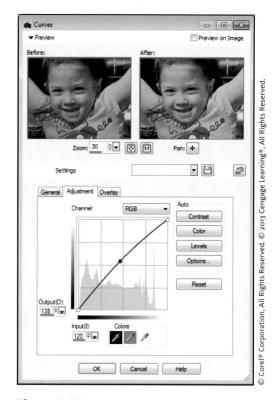

Figure 8.77

Enhancing midtones with Curves.

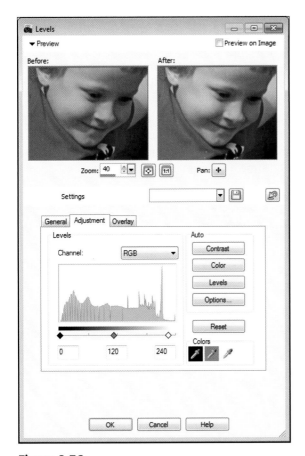

Figure 8.78

Brightening with Levels.

© Corel® Corporation, All Rights Reserved. © 2013 Cengage Learning®, All Rights Reserved.

Finishing the Photo Study

This is it. This is the final study of this chapter (see Figure 8.79). Photo restoration and retouching isn't always about taking scratches out or covering up imperfections in a photo. This study showed you that it can be a fun exercise in creating a montage from four different digital pictures.

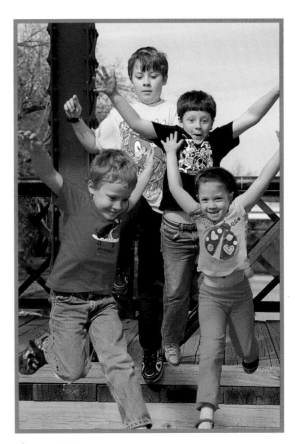

Figure 8.79

Putting lots of memories into a single photo.

© 2013 Cengage Learning®, All Rights Reserved.

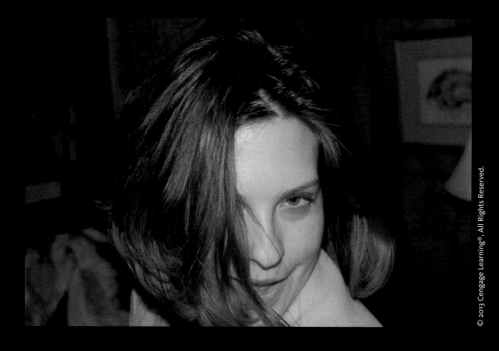

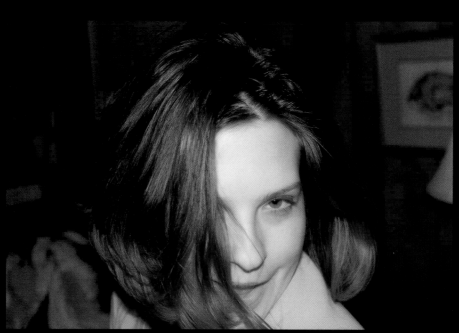

Retouching People

9

THE PHOTOS IN THIS CHAPTER SHOWCASE REAL PEOPLE engaging in real life. They aren't picture-perfect portraits shot in a studio. The studies illustrate the types of problems that tend to crop up in casual photography. You'll learn how to quickly fix that photo of yourself with dandruff or the precious one of your kids where they all have red eyes so you can enjoy the photos.

Aside from feeling good about fixing up photos, it's really fun working with people. It was fun for me to give myself a makeover. Err, well, a makeover in PaintShop Pro. I'm not ready to go spend the day at the spa with cucumbers on my eyes and mud on my face!

▶ **Photo Study 40: Removing Red Eye**—People look horrible with red eyes, and this problem can easily ruin a good photo. Learn how to use the standard technique for taking the red out of eyes, followed by one of my own techniques.

▶ **Photo Study 41: More Red Eye Techniques**—Learn how to use the Red Eye Removal command, which is both powerful and useful, in this photo study. Compare it to my technique.

▶ **Photo Study 42: Whitening Teeth**—Teeth that aren't gleaming white can be painfully exposed by photography. Learn the best technique for fixing yellowish teeth and touch up a few other things in this photo study as well.

▶ **Photo Study 43: Teeth, Eye, and Skin Touch-Ups**—This photo study illustrates the retouching trifecta: teeth, eyes, and skin. I'll polish my wife's teeth, intensify her eye color, and use the default skin smoother.

▶ **Photo Study 44: Glamorous Skin Smoothing**—Learn how to smooth and glamorize normal, everyday skin in this study involving a cute photo of my wife Anne.

▶ **Photo Study 45: Complete Body Makeover**—This is an astounding example of what you can do with PaintShop Pro and a little ingenuity. Learn how to make people lose weight, put on muscles, and get a tan in one photo.

▶ **Photo Study 46: Hiding Hair Loss**—This study shows you one technique to cover hair loss: applying new hair. Learn how to transplant hair from one photo to another.

▶ **Photo Study 47: Cleaning Up Nostrils**—Noses need to be clean to look good. This study shows you how to touch up around nostrils so people can look their best.

Photo Study 40: Removing Red Eye

FIGURE 9.1 IS A PHOTO OF MY youngest child, Samuel, from 2007. I'm taking the photo from behind Anne as she holds him over her shoulder. It was dark enough in the room that the flash went off, and sure enough, it caught him with red eyes. If you don't know, red eye is caused by the eye not reacting fast enough to the flash, which allows light to reflect off the blood-filled retina at the back of the eye. Animals aren't immune to this effect, and certain animals (cats, for instance) have a reflecting layer on the back of their eyes, which increases the problem. This layer is why a cat's eyes appear to glow in the dark.

There are a number of ways to get rid of red eyes in PaintShop Pro. I'll start by showing the Red Eye tool and then my own technique.

Duplicate Layers

This photo study, and many that follow, use my technique of duplicating the Background layer and applying changes, such as the Red Eye tool, to that duplicate working layer. This preserves a copy of the original photo within the working .pspimage file. If I hide all the intervening layers, I can quickly compare the top "after" layer to the bottom "before" layer and see the overall transformation.

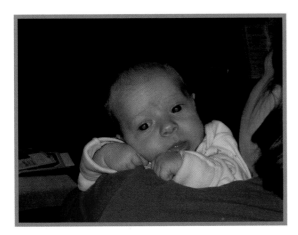

Figure 9.1
Attack of the serious red eye.

Using the Red Eye Tool

The standard method for removing red eyes in PaintShop Pro is to grab the Red Eye tool, which is located on the Tools toolbar. There is only one option to choose: the tool's size. I've selected the tool in Figure 9.2, sized it to cover the entire red portion of Sam's eye, and clicked on the red eye to apply. It did a pretty good job in the center, but there is still a red ring around his pupil.

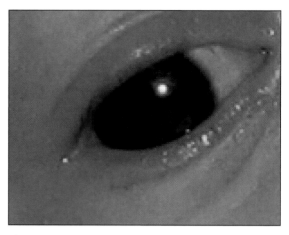

Figure 9.3
Further application is better.

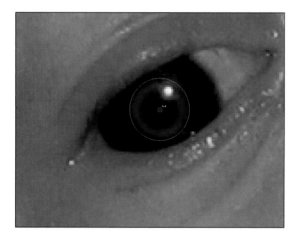

Figure 9.2
Red Eye tool does well, but not completely.

I kept clicking in the red area that was left behind in Figure 9.3 to see if I could complete the repair. I was able to make it better, but couldn't completely eliminate a red tinge.

You might think that if I made the tool larger, much larger than the red pupil, that it would take care of all the red. Unfortunately, this is not always the case. I enlarged the Red Eye tool to a diameter of 99 pixels in Figure 9.4 and applied it to the same eye as before. The result is essentially identical.

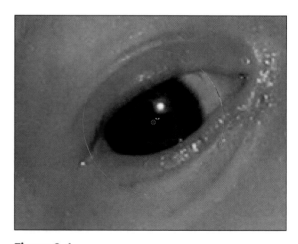

Figure 9.4
Larger tool does about the same.

An Alternate Technique

I'm not saying the Red Eye tool is useless or that you should never use it, but I want to extend beyond the simple basics of "click here" for portions of this book. There will be times when the Red Eye tool won't work the way you want it to, and you will have to figure out a way to get the job done. This section shows you a technique that I came up with and use when I absolutely have to get the red eye out.

First, duplicate the Background or working layer in case you want to erase around the effect and blend it in with the layer below. Then choose the Selection tool from the Tools toolbar and change the Selection type from Rectangle (which is the default) to Circle.

Using Different Selection Types

You don't have to use Circle if you don't want to. Some pupils appear elliptical, and you may need to draw around the pupil of someone's eye with the Freehand Selection tool. Use the type of tool that best fits your situation.

Then select the area around the red portion of the eye, as I have done in Figure 9.5. Get all the red, but don't stray too far outside of this area.

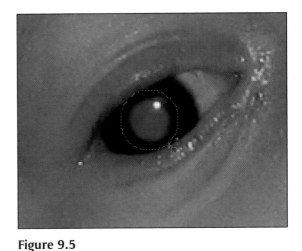

Figure 9.5
Select the red eye.

Now for the fun part. Take the red out of the eye with the Channel Mixer (Adjust > Color > Channel Mixer). Uncheck the Monochrome box at the bottom of the dialog box and select different Output channels to edit. Since this is a case of too much red, the Red channel is a great place to start.

Figure 9.6 shows the settings that I use most of the time. You might think you should just be able to pull the red percentage down and be done with it, but you can't. When I took red from 100% to 0% in this photo, the pupil looked too blue, and the glint was more cyan than white. I had to keep searching for the right combination, but I think I eventually found it. Leave the Green and Blue channels alone and set the Red, Green, and Blue percentages for the Red channel to 0, 125, and –15, respectively. (These numbers should work for most eye colors because you're taking the red out of the pupil, not altering the iris.) Be patient and keep fine-tuning if you need to. You can match the pupil's color to what it should be very precisely. By the way, if you take all the color out and make the pupil or iris absolutely black, you'll make people look like aliens.

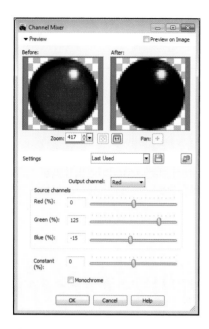

Figure 9.6
Tweak the Red channel.

I've accepted my Channel Mixer settings, and the result appears in Figure 9.7.

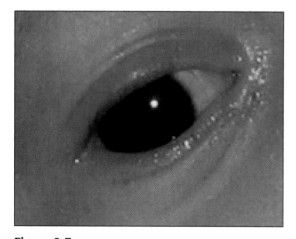

Figure 9.7
Red eye is really gone this time.

When I first removed red eye using this technique, I was astounded. I still am, really. The red is gone, and the pupil matches the rest of the eye. Notice that there's a light area on the inside of the iris, next to the pupil. That's the glint in someone's eye. Take a look at some good close-ups of eyes without red eye, and you'll see that this is the way an eye should look. Don't try to take that out of a person's eyes.

Finishing the Photo Study

Sam's red eyes were about the only dramatic thing wrong with this photo. I tried brightening the background, but in essence, that "flaw" puts more of the focus on Sam, which is what I want. When the background is brighter, the clutter on the table and the piano stands out more. So I removed the red eyes with my technique and performed a Histogram Adjustment to improve the brightness and contrast. Finally, I smoothed Sam's skin with Skin Smoothing (50). The finished study is shown in Figure 9.8. You should be able to complete retouching work like this quickly.

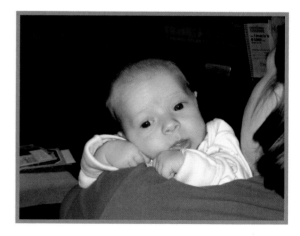

Figure 9.8
Ahh, that's better.

Photo Study 41: More Red Eye Techniques

MY SON, JACOB, IS SITTING on the couch watching television in Figure 9.9. This photo was taken on his birthday in 2008. He's got his bear, Jonesy, with him. Jake's red eyes are looking off obliquely to the camera, and his pupils appear elliptical. Red eyes that aren't perfectly circular can be more difficult to retouch.

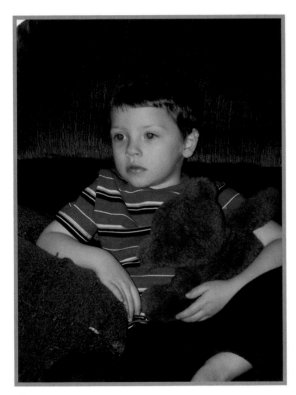

Figure 9.9
Cute photo marred by red eye.

More Techniques

In this photo study, I will show you four red eye removal techniques one after another. The first uses the Red Eye tool, the second the Red Eye Removal command, the third a variation of the Red Eye Removal command, and the fourth is my own technique.

Red Eye Tool

I selected the Red Eye tool from the Tools toolbar and applied it to Jake's eye in Figure 9.10. It has about the same effect as the previous photo study. Namely, it gets the red out of the center but leaves a red margin around the outside. In cases like this, enlarge the tool and try again. There are times you'll hit the jackpot, and it will look great.

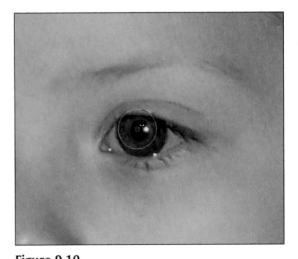

Figure 9.10
Red Eye tool on an elliptical pupil.

The Red Eye Removal Feature

There's an alternate method of removing red eye tucked in a place you may not think to look. It's called Red Eye Removal and is located in the Adjust menu. Figure 9.11 shows the Red Eye Removal dialog box. It's pretty intense, and there are a lot of settings that affect how it works. You can spend a lot of time practicing with this one.

I'll run through a series of steps to show you how to use Red Eye Removal. Many of the steps aren't sequential. In other words, you can follow most of these in sequence, or not, or find a sequence you prefer to use instead of this one. It's your call.

1. **Choose a method.** The options are Auto Human Eye, Auto Animal Eye, Freehand Pupil Outline, or Point-to-Point Pupil Outline. With the Auto methods, you have only limited ability to adjust the edges of the iris shape. With the Outline methods, you have more control since you manually draw around the pupil. If the eye is fairly circular, the Auto methods are more effective. For this example, I've chosen Auto Human Eye. I'll cover another method later.

2. **Select an eye in the left windowpane.** You'll see a circle, just like the Circular Selection tool, appear as you click and drag. The center point is where you click. Drag until it looks to be the right size and then let go. When you release the mouse button, the circle appears inside a box, as shown in Figure 9.11. You can resize the circle (which represents the eye's iris) by clicking and dragging the box around the eye's iris. You can move this box around by clicking on the inside and dragging.

If you click outside this eye's iris, you'll draw more circles, enabling you to perform multiple red eye removals at once. (You'll either have to zoom out or move the Preview window view to the other eye.) If you want to delete a selection, select the square and click the Delete Eye button.

The trick here is to get the selection box sized just right and the circle positioned directly over the eye. You'll see a preview of the effect in the right windowpane.

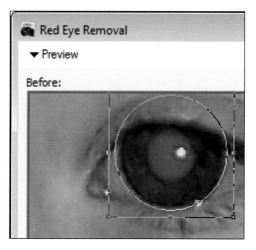

Figure 9.11
Draw box around the eye.
© Corel® Corporation, All Rights Reserved. © 2013 Cengage Learning®, All Rights Reserved.

3. **Now it's time to size the pupil (where the red is).** Do this with the Iris size control. Note that increasing or decreasing the value of the Iris size control doesn't change the outer diameter of the iris. It changes the pupil's size within the iris. You'll want this to be as exact as you can get it. Make sure to look at the right windowpane as you change the numbers. That's where the iris size preview shows up.

4. **At this point, take a look at the glint settings.** Check Center glint if the glint is in the center of the eye, or uncheck it if the glint is offset, as it is in this case. You can also modify its lightness.

5. **Next, change the Pupil lightness up or down.** This has a dramatic effect, moving from black to a light gray.

6. **You can also change the Feather and Blur settings.** Feather affects the blend between the iris and pupil, and Blur takes the entire eye out of focus.

7. **Next, drag the Refine slider left or right to match the overall shape of the eye and "completeness" of the iris.** PaintShop Pro will change how much of the iris and pupil are displayed. Compare using the Before and After windowpanes until you get the best coverage.

8. **Gray is the default color that Red Eye Removal will apply to the iris.** You can change what shade of gray you want from the Color list box (see Figure 9.12). Click on an iris that matches your subject more closely. You can also choose a different color entirely, like green or blue.

9. **Finally, click OK.**

Most of the time, the Refine control gets you pretty close to the overall shape of the eye, but it isn't always perfect. This is another reason why I duplicate the Background layer. I can erase the outer portion of the eye, the part the Refine control didn't remove, as shown in Figure 9.13. Jake's normal eye appears from underneath.

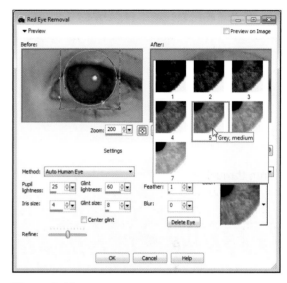

Figure 9.12

Choosing an iris hue and color.

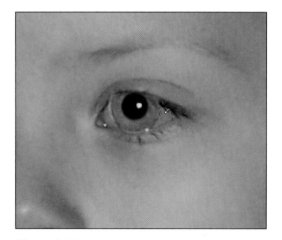

Figure 9.13

Trim away excess.

Freehand Pupil Outline

Now that you've seen how to use Red Eye Removal in Auto mode, the Freehand Pupil Outline mode will be easier to follow. I'll dispense with the steps and refer you to Figure 9.14.

Rather than selecting the eye's iris, the Outline modes prompt you to outline the pupil. This technique is best suited for pupils that aren't perfectly circular, as in this case. How you choose to outline the pupil is up to you. The difference is that in Freehand Pupil Outline mode, you're drawing around the pupil just like you would use the Freehand Selection tool (Freehand mode). For Point-to-Point Pupil Outline mode, click at points outside the pupil to draw around it.

The other options are mostly the same between this mode and the Auto modes. The differences are that you don't need to select an Iris size or Hue and you will need to select what type of eye you're working on. You'll make this selection in the Color section. The choices are Pupil, cat; Brown Pupil, dog; Black pupil, dog; and Pupil, human.

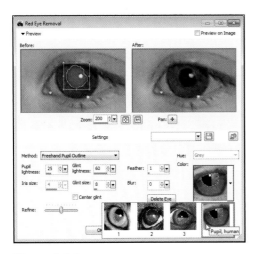

Figure 9.14
Using Freehand Pupil Outline.

I've made a freehand selection in Figure 9.14 and am changing the color to a human pupil. You can see the preview in the right side of the window.

The Channel Mixer

I've selected Jake's pupil in Figure 9.15 with the Selection tool. I changed the selection type to Elliptical to match the pupil. You can change the type to Circle or even switch to the Freehand Selection tool if you like. The important thing is to get all the red out and be working on a duplicate layer.

You can see that a portion of his eyelid is in the selection. Depending on their race (and other factors such as skin type and lighting), a person's skin will have different amounts of red. Jake's skin in this photo is pink. That might cause a little problem after I apply my color change. That's why I use a duplicate layer. I can erase or mask out the extra and rely on the Background layer to pick up the correct color of his eyelid.

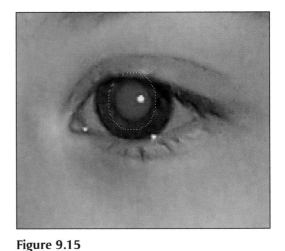

Figure 9.15
Select the pupil.

Next, I selected the Adjust ❯ Color ❯ Channel Mixer menu to open up the Channel Mixer dialog box, as shown in Figure 9.16. I altered the amount of red in the Red Output channel as shown. You may need to tweak this, depending on the red in the red eye and the overall color balance in the photo.

If it doesn't look right, check the other channels to make sure that the Green and Blue channels are at their default. If it looks wacky, you may have left-over settings. To correct that, choose the Default preset from the Settings menu (this corrects the other channels) and enter new percentages in the Red channel for Red, Green, and Blue.

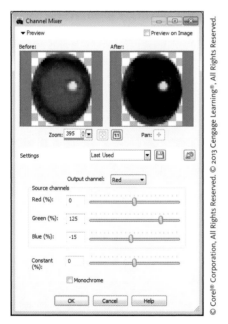

Figure 9.16
Alter Red output.

The result is shown in Figure 9.17. I deleted the portion of Jake's eyelid that was altered by the Channel Mixer so all you see is a perfectly retouched red eye and normal pink eyelid.

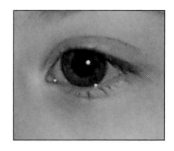

Figure 9.17
Great results.

Finishing the Photo Study

Figure 9.18 shows the final result. I've completed the red eye removal in both of Jake's eyes on a separate layer than the Background layer, erased the portions of his eyelids that were changed, selected everything and performed a merged copy, and then pasted the result as a new layer. Afterward, I used that merged layer as a basis to perform other adjustments. For this particular photo, I cleaned up parts of his pillow, darkened his skin with the Suntan Makeover tool, and cloned the top-left corner of the photo to extend the couch. After that, I lightened the photo a bit with Curves and then smoothed Jacob's skin with Skin Smoothing (15). Finally, I brightened the entire photo with a Levels adjustment. All in all, it was a very successful retouching job.

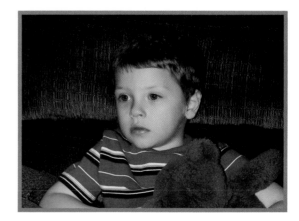

Figure 9.18
Those blue eyes are sparkling now.

Photo Study 42: Whitening Teeth

THIS IS A FUNNY PICTURE OF ME and my daughter Grace (see Figure 9.19) from 2006. She's wearing lots of pink, which was common for her. She's trending toward purples and teals lately. She's got pink glamour shades, a pink jacket, pink pants, and I think that's a light pink top she has on. The furry thing around her neck isn't a cat (although when it was on the floor at night it would freak me out because it looked just like our predominately black cats). It's a detachable faux fur neck that goes on an old coat. We keep it around to play with, and she's hamming it up as I hold her.

My teeth are really yellow in this photo. I don't want to resign this nice picture to the stack that we never show anybody, however, so I will whiten my teeth as I enhance this photo.

Whitening Teeth

Whitening teeth is another retouching job that can go a long way toward making a photo better. The simplest method is to choose the Makeover tools from the Tools toolbar and then choose the Toothbrush from the Tool Options palette. Enter a Strength and click on the yellow teeth.

Easy does it. Most of us don't have absolutely white teeth, and teeth that look too white can appear unnatural. To prove my point, look at Figure 9.20. I've applied the Toothbrush to my teeth and put the Strength up to 100. That's overkill!

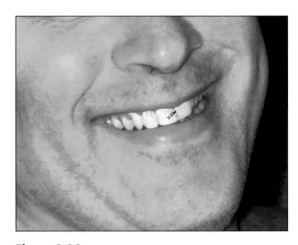

Figure 9.20
Overdoing it.

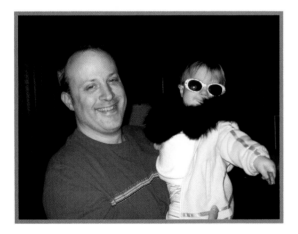

Figure 9.19
Daddy with his princess.

A better technique is to tone down the Toothbrush and apply multiple levels of whitening until you get the desired result. I've chosen a Strength of 30 for my teeth in Figure 9.21 and the result is more realistic. You'll notice that I pulled back the zoom quite a bit when compared to Figure 9.20. I get a better sense for how the whiter teeth will blend in with the rest of my face that way. Too much will stand out like a sore thumb, and too little is rather pointless.

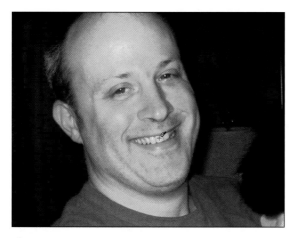

Figure 9.21
Realistic is better.

Teeth and Gums

If a person's teeth aren't touching (that sounds odd, but the gums may be separating the teeth), you may have to click multiple times on teeth in different areas to apply the Toothbrush successfully. The Toothbrush works partly like the Flood Fill tool.

Handling Blemishes and Skin Tone

If you look carefully in Figure 9.22, you can see that I've applied the Blemish Fixer to a spot in my eyebrow. That's a bad thing. You shouldn't be able to see it. The problem is that the tool can blend the area around the blemish too much. In this case, that surrounding texture is my eyebrow hair, which makes blending obvious. It would be better to use the Clone brush in this area.

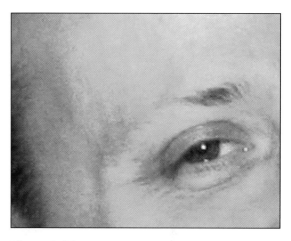

Figure 9.22
Blemish Fixer softens focus on brow.

The next few figures illustrate my efforts to even my skin tones. I've got some red areas (probably dry skin) on the bridge of my nose and other parts of my face. There are several possible ways to fix this problem.

I could use the Hue Up/Down brush to change the hue. I could use the Saturation Up/Down brush to lower the intensity of the red color in those areas. I could even try to use the Clone brush to clone areas of my skin that are a more pink color over the red areas. If you're thinking along those lines, that's great. Those are all good ideas.

I tried them, however, and wasn't happy with any of them. It was after I switched to the Change to Target brush that I got the result I was after. I used the Change to Target brush in Hue mode to change the hue of the red areas of my face to match that of another, less red, patch of skin. If you ever wonder why there are tools like this in PaintShop Pro, and why they have all these different modes, this should help answer that question. This tool and this mode will fix this problem easily.

I chose the tool first (the Change to Target brush, in this case). Then I pressed Ctrl while I hovered my mouse over an appropriate color (see Figure 9.23) to load a color into the Foreground and Stroke Properties box on the Materials palette. That changed the cursor to the dropper, which I clicked to load the color. I went for a nice pink that wasn't too red.

Next, and this is pretty important, I made sure the Mode (seen on the Tool Options palette) was in Hue. My goal was to match hues with another area, not lightness or saturation. With a more muted pink loaded into the right-sized brush, I started brushing away the red, as shown in Figure 9.24. If you're doing this and it looks terrible, Undo and find another shade of skin tone from your face and try it again. Trial and error is critical for finding the right color sometimes.

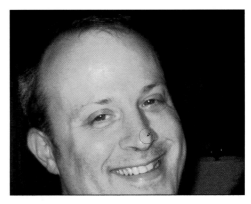

Figure 9.24
Taking the red out.

Other Touch-Ups

Before I close this photo study, I have a few more touch-ups to show.

First, as seen in Figure 9.25, I softened Grace's sunglasses. They were smudged, and the softening effect reduced the smudginess and kept it from being too obvious. Look to make touch-ups like this in your photos. It wasn't a big deal, but it *was*, if you know what I mean. If you're going to retouch photos, use all the powers of your perception and imagination to make them better!

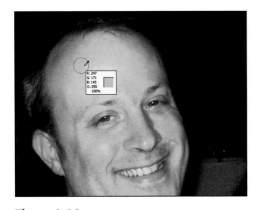

Figure 9.23
Select color for replacing hue.

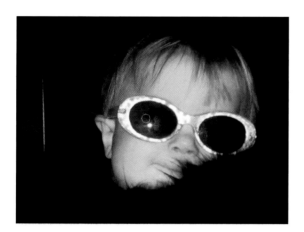

Figure 9.25

Softening smudged shades.

Finally, I liked the levels of the subjects, but I wasn't happy with the background. I isolated us from the background by performing a merged copy. (Remember, I did some cloning on my eyebrow, and when I clone I use a separate layer.) I pasted that as a new layer and then I duplicated the merged copy layer. One of the duplicate layers served as the Background layer (that I lightened) and the other held us. I am erasing us out of the Background layer in Figure 9.26. (A mask would work, too.)

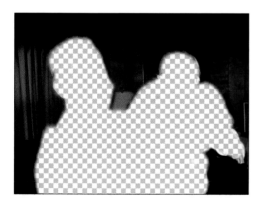

Figure 9.26

Preparing to adjust background only.

With that done, I could apply whatever color, brightness, or contrast change to the Background layer (the one I erased us out of) I wanted, and the foreground layer (myself and Grace) was left unchanged.

Finishing the Photo Study

To finish this photo, I applied a Histogram Adjustment to lighten up the background (the layer without us), and then I copied the merged photo, pasted that as a new layer, and made an overall levels adjustment. There's a subtle sheen to the background (look at the paneling) that wasn't there, and the contrast is much better. I made a Curves adjustment to brighten us up, masked Grace's clothes out so they wouldn't get too bright, and finished with Skin Smoothing. The final photo is shown in Figure 9.27.

I almost forgot to tell you, I cloned my thumb out. It's not a huge difference, but I think it makes the photo better without the distraction.

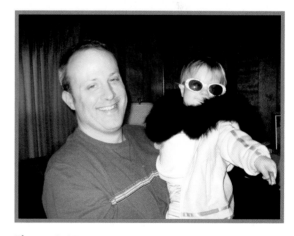

Figure 9.27

Daddy looks better now.

Photo Study 43:
Teeth, Eye, and Skin Touch-Ups

FIGURE 9.28 IS ANOTHER PHOTO of my wife, Anne, and son, Sam, from 2007. If you've got a digital camera and newborn children, you should be able to relate to this. We carried around the camera constantly, looking for opportunities to take more pictures. The great thing about digital photography is being able to take thousands of digital pictures and keeping the best.

If you take more pictures than you need, you're bound to capture the right moment.

I will use this photo to polish Anne's teeth a little differently than if I were to whiten them with the Toothbrush. I also want to show you a technique to brighten someone's eyes and use Skin Smoothing. She's in for a day at the spa!

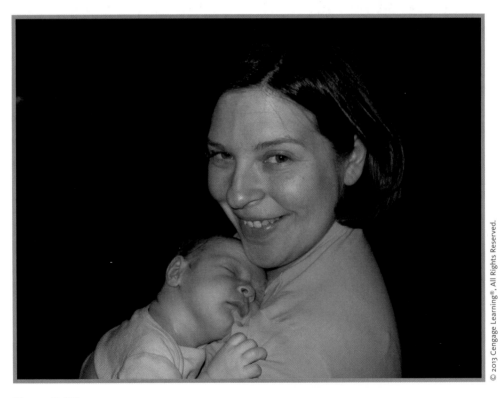

Figure 9.28
Looking good, but worth touching up.

Whitening Teeth

In this photo of Anne, I just want to polish her teeth a bit. It's more of a subtle approach than using the Toothbrush, but it makes teeth glow with a healthy radiance when you finish, instead of just being whiter.

To begin polishing, select the Lighten/Darken brush from the Tools toolbar and select an appropriate size. I like to make mine smaller than the tooth, but not by much. If it gets too small, you'll see all the little brush lines (unless you set the Step to 1 and have Continuous selected in the Tool Options palette). I also set the Hardness to 0%. For 99% of the time, you'll make your opacity something less than 100%. I am gently polishing Anne's teeth in Figure 9.29 and have completed one of her incisors and moved on to another.

I'll polish each tooth separately, changing my brush size if I need to. Do I need to mention that you should be doing all this on a duplicated layer (or otherwise copy-merged and pasted as new layer)? I didn't think so.

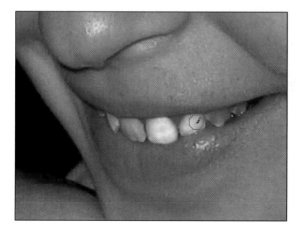

Figure 9.29

Lightening teeth.

Now that her teeth are whiter, there are yellowish areas between Anne's teeth in her gum line that should be pinker. I will use the same technique on her gums that I used in the previous photo study where I evened my skin tone.

I've selected the Change to Target brush, made sure it's in Hue mode, adjusted the size to very small (4 pixels), pressed Ctrl and clicked to grab a good pink color from somewhere else on her gums, and changed the hue from yellow to pink, as shown in Figure 9.30.

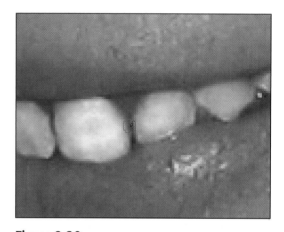

Figure 9.30

Changing hue of gums.

Retouching Eyes

People don't have to have red eyes for you to retouch them. You can use this technique to change their eye color or strengthen the existing shade. In this case, I reinforced the existing green color.

Select Red Eye Removal from the Adjust menu to get started. Draw the eye selection and then choose your settings. Essentially, I pretended she had red eye and added a green color over her iris, as shown in Figure 9.31.

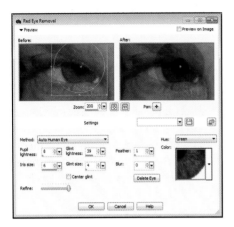

Figure 9.31

Deepening green eyes.

I used the Auto Human Eye method because I could select a different Hue and Color to apply over her eye. There are a number of different shades and intensities of green to choose from. I tried to get a pretty good match to her original eye color.

Since I applied her "new" eyes on a duplicate layer and erased the extra (see Figure 9.32), I didn't need to use the Refine control. Erasing, rather than using Refine, gives you more control over the area that is retouched.

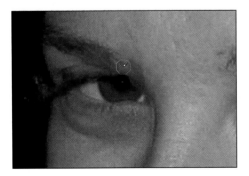

Figure 9.32

Erasing extra.

Finally, I lowered the opacity of the new eyes layer to 30 to preserve most of the original hue (see Figure 9.33).

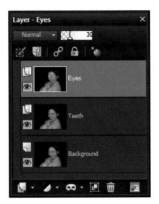

Figure 9.33

Lowering layer opacity to blend.

Skin Smoothing

This is turning into a real makeover. Anne has beautiful skin, and she takes good care of it. But she's human, and this is the real world. Unless you're a full-time supermodel with your own personal skin smoother, you're not going to have perfect skin. Besides that, models rely on digital artists to retouch their photos. Did you think those magazine close-ups were unretouched?

Figure 9.34 shows the Skin Smoothing dialog box. Select the person's face or skin you want to smooth and choose Adjust ❯ Skin Smoothing. Choose a strength that looks good in the preview window and apply the filter.

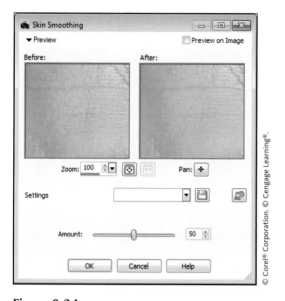

Figure 9.34

Smoothing Anne.

For some photos (this is a good example of one), select the area you want to smooth before you start the process, rather than applying the effect to the entire photo. Sam's skin doesn't need any smoothing, so there's no point in applying it to him. He's only a few months old, and his skin is about as smooth as humanly possible.

If you need to be more precise than using a rough selection, use a mask and mask out what you don't want smoothed.

Finishing the Photo Study

I finished the photo study by increasing the brightness by 15 and the contrast by 10 through Adjust ❯ Brightness and Contrast ❯ Brightness/Contrast; then I bumped up the saturation by 5 through Adjust ❯ Hue and Saturation ❯ Hue/Saturation/Lightness. The photo was a little dark and had a gray sheen to it. The brightness and contrast adjustment took care of that, and then the saturation gave more vibrancy to Anne's face. After looking at it closely for a while, I realized I could still improve the photo by cloning some imperfections from Anne's face and using the Smudge brush very lightly on the brighter areas to tone them down. After this, I finished with another brightness adjustment. This time: Curves.

This is one of those photos with bright subjects and a dark background. I could have separated Anne and Sam from the background and adjusted their layer differently than the background. I decided against that, as I liked the dark background in this instance. Figure 9.35 is the final photo.

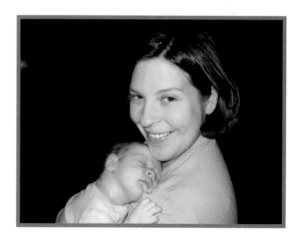

Figure 9.35

Much better.

Photo Study 44: Glamorous Skin Smoothing

I TOOK THIS PHOTO (see Figure 9.36) of my wife, Anne, in 2009, on my birthday. It's a great shot of her being playful, but when you look closely, her skin looks a little rough. That's the problem with good cameras and lenses—they show everything, whether complimentary or not—with 10 or more million pixels of detail.

I'm going to give her a glamorous skin-smoothing makeover for this photo study. It's actually not as hard as you might think, especially when the photo is great to start out.

The Treatment

Skin smoothing is a challenging endeavor to undertake because you risk smoothing away important details that make up a person, to say nothing about the rest of the photo. In that way, you face the same challenges when smoothing skin that you do when deciding how much noise reduction to apply to a noisy photo. The trick is to smooth a person's skin in such a way that you don't lose details in other areas of the photo.

Thankfully, there is a specific skin-smoothing adjustment in PaintShop Pro that targets skin. How well it does this in every circumstance is up to you to decide, but in general, the answer is very good. The trick is to only apply what you need, and if the going gets rough, mask out everything but a person's skin so you don't blur the entire photo.

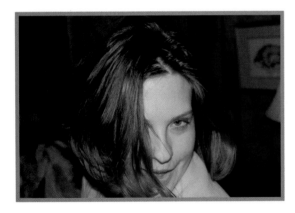

Figure 9.36
Lookin' sassy.

Testing on Other Areas

To get a sense of how much skin smoothing affects the parts of the photo that aren't skin, perform a "Max Effort Skin Smoothing" test. Here's how I do it:

1. **Duplicate the Background layer or the last fully opaque working layer you have so there are two identical layers you can use to compare.**

2. **Select the top layer and then choose Adjust > Skin Smoothing.** This launches the Skin Smoothing dialog box, which is so simple I don't need to show it here. You only have to set the Amount.

3. **Max the Amount and choose OK.** No sense in playing around. You want to see where details are going to be lost the most.

   The result is a layer with the most skin smoothing you can get from this tool on top of a layer without any.

4. **Zoom in and out, pan around, and toggle the skin smoothing layer on and off to compare with the unsmoothed layer beneath it.** Pay attention to where you lose the most detail outside of the skin and note these areas in case you need to return later to mask them out.

   Figure 9.37 shows one side-by-side comparison of an area with lots of edge detail—Anne's hair. Remember, I applied the maximum amount of skin smoothing to the photo. The result is a loss of detail, but not as much as you might expect. It looks like some of the highlights were smoothed.

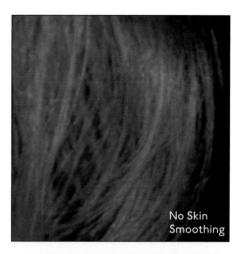

No Skin Smoothing

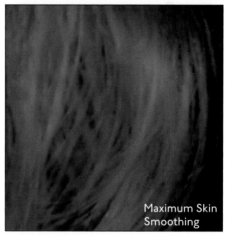

Maximum Skin Smoothing

Figure 9.37
Comparing maximum skin smoothing.

I find that toggling layers on and off is a very effective way of comparing results, even though it isn't as convenient as looking at the Preview windows in most adjustment dialog boxes. That's one reason why I don't conduct this test for every photo. Knowing the right questions to ask and how to conduct tests to provide your own answers is pretty important, though.

Finding the Right Amount

Finding the right amount of skin smoothing for each photo is pretty simple. Just open up the Skin Smoothing dialog box and either use the Preview window or the main image window. The things you want to look for here are the following:

▶ **Skin:** The main effect. Look at areas of the skin to see how smooth they are and increase or decrease the Amount accordingly. Figure 9.38 shows her cheek with too little Skin Smoothing applied to make much of a difference. The Amount was 20.

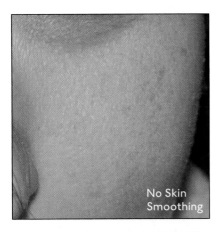

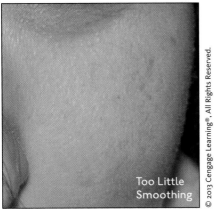

Figure 9.38

The top swatch has no skin smoothing while the bottom has too little.

▶ **Facial Hair:** Examine areas where there is facial hair, such as mustaches, beards, sideburns, eyelashes, and eyebrows. Figure 9.39 shows the area around one of Anne's eyes with the Amount at 100. This is too strong. Note the loss of detail in and around the hair follicles.

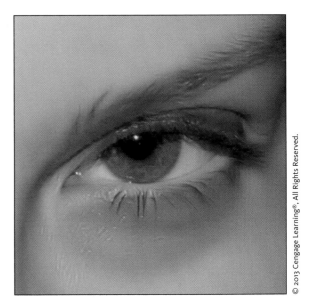

Figure 9.39

Oversmoothing eyelashes and brows.

▶ **Hair Boundaries:** Check out parts, cowlicks, and other areas where the hairline begins. Pay attention to where wispy hair extends over the skin, as you will likely lose it there. Figure 9.40 shows a close-up of where some hair is covering Anne's nose. In these cases, the amount of Skin Smoothing to use can be a tough judgment call. If you're going for a glamorous effect, I wouldn't worry about losing it.

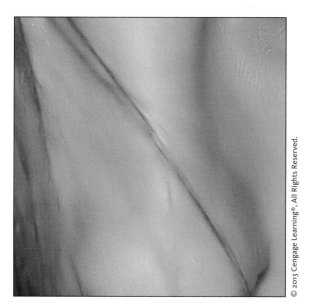

Figure 9.40
Oversmoothing here doesn't really matter.

At this point, you should have looked around and increased or decreased the amount of skin smoothing to suit your artistic purpose and not taken away the details you want preserved. If you have a tough time balancing things out, create a mask and apply skin smoothing to the photo layer below the mask layer. (They will both be in the same layer group.) Then mask out overly smooth areas. Don't forget, you can also lower the opacity of the smoothed photo layer and blend it with the unsmoothed layers below.

Smudging

I settled on a final strength of 75, which sounds pretty strong, but was a bit undersmoothed for this image. I wanted a definite glamour look, but didn't want it to look too airbrushed.

I wasn't done, though. After applying skin smoothing to the working layer, I duplicated it and hid the original. I then chose the Smudge brush, made it reasonably large, lowered the Hardness to 0 and opacity to 50, and smoothed the rest of Anne's face manually using gentle, circular brush strokes. (Hint: The larger the brush, the lighter your touch needs to be.) Figure 9.41 shows this in action.

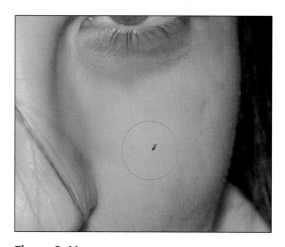

Figure 9.41
Smoothing by smudging.
© Corel® Corporation, All Rights Reserved. © 2013 Cengage Learning®, All Rights Reserved.

I tried using the Soften brush, but it didn't actually smooth away the details. The Soften brush softened edges, but didn't make her skin look smooth. The key is to choose the Smudge brush and lower the opacity to get a good smooth look. I varied the size of the brush and worked it over any areas that I thought could use more smoothing.

Next, I lowered the opacity of the "smoothed and smudged" layer to blend it with the normal layer beneath, as shown in Figure 9.42. Use your judgment here. The key is to balance realism with glamour.

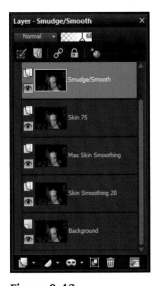

Figure 9.42

Blending the extra smoothing.

Next, I performed a copy merged to lock all the changes into a single layer. (This is important when you're working with semi-transparent layers that blend together and you want a single opaque working layer to continue with.) Then I used the Clone brush and Blemish Fixer to remove any remaining imperfections in her skin.

Finishing the Photo Study

After all that, I corrected the photo's brightness and contrast problems with Levels and boosted the Vibrancy a bit. I then experimented with the Glamour effect in Effects ❯ Photo Effects ❯ Film and Filters. This gave Anne a healthy glow about her that I liked. I also experimented going the opposite direction and tried sharpening the photo with Unsharp Mask.

Figure 9.43 shows the final result. I'm happy with the balance of skin smoothing that resulted in a glamorous effect and yet doesn't look overly done. I ended up using the Glamour filter, but toned it down some by lowering that layer's opacity and blending it with the first working layer beneath the Glamour filter layer.

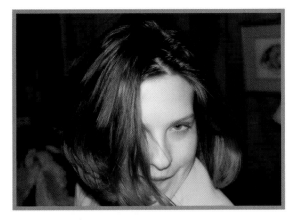

Figure 9.43

Glamorously smooth but not fake skin.

Photo Study 45: Complete Body Makeover

I'M HAPPILY MOWING THE LAWN in Figure 9.44, dressed in my lawn-mowing sneakers and shorts. The year was 2007. I like getting air and sun while I mow, so I dress minimally. It's an hour or so that I get to be outside doing something physical.

I've been an outdoor person and athlete most of my life, although it's been much harder to find the time the last few years. When I was at the Air Force Academy, physical fitness was regular and intense. Mandatory gym classes ranged from wrestling, boxing, judo, and unarmed combat, to water survival, which included a jump off a 10-meter platform in fatigues like you were bailing out of an airplane into the water.

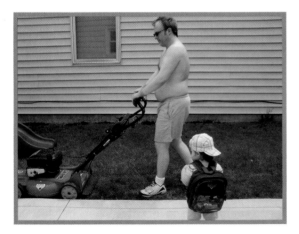

Figure 9.44
You don't have to say a thing.

Well, that was some time ago. I'm pale and flabby in this photo. But that makes it the perfect candidate to give myself a complete body makeover with the Warp brush.

Tummy Tucking

Conceptually, once you get the hang of what's going on here, it becomes a matter of execution.

First, I duplicated my Background layer so that I had a working layer to manipulate. Next, I started on the most obvious feature in need of repair, my tummy. (You talk funny when you've got four children under eight years of age—I would have never called this my "tummy" before I had kids.)

I tried to warp it in, but after several tries I realized it wasn't going to work. I needed to think outside the box. The solution was to copy and paste my stomach, rotate it to a new orientation, and then flatten it.

I selected it in Figure 9.45 with the Freehand Selection tool (Point mode). I made a rough selection with a little more than I needed because I will erase the extra and blend it in later.

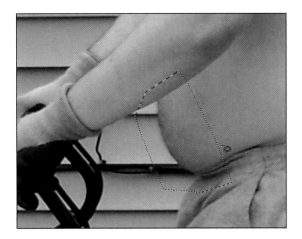

Figure 9.45
Select the offending bulge.

I copied and pasted it as a new layer, and rotated it to a more vertical orientation in Figure 9.46. I hid the other layers so you could see the rotation. When you do this, make whatever you're transplanting semi-transparent so you can judge the rotation in relation to the background.

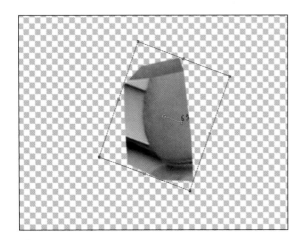

Figure 9.46
Rotate to desired angle.

I used the Warp brush in Push mode to flatten the bulge, as seen in Figure 9.47. Take your time with these warps. They are very important. Don't get tripped up by selecting too small a brush. Sometimes, a smaller brush works worse than a larger brush. In this case, a good large brush size (150) allowed me to push the center of my stomach in as a cohesive whole, rather than making several small, disjointed pushes.

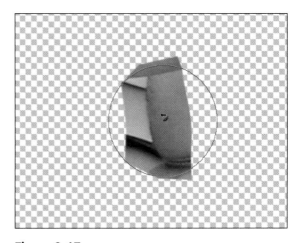

Figure 9.47
Flatten with Warp brush.

With the new tummy prepped and ready, I moved on to erase the bulging original. I used the Clone brush (see Figure 9.48) to push my stomach in and make it flat. I'm not worried about the outer border of the original stomach not looking perfect because the flattened version will serve that purpose. I just need to get enough of the old tummy out of the way so that it doesn't stick out from under the new, flatter one.

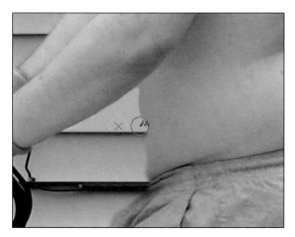

Figure 9.48

Clone away excess original tummy.

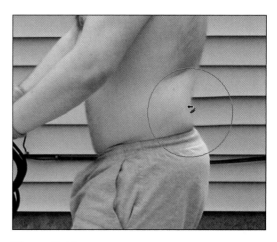

Figure 9.49

Warping those love handles.

I placed the rotated and warped tummy in position and toggled it on and off so that I could judge the right amount of cloning I needed to do. You will see the flatter, composite stomach in the next figure.

More Cosmetic Warping

With the new stomach in place, it's time for more cosmetic warping. I kept with the Warp brush in Push mode and alternated the size so that I picked up enough material in my warps to make steady, integrated pushes.

I am warping my "love handles" and pushing my back inward in Figure 9.49. This accentuates the curve of my back and will round the top of my buttocks. If you're still looking at my back, notice the shadow between the hair on my back and where I am pushing in. That's a good candidate to use the Lighten/Darken brush to take out some of the shadow (i.e., lighten it) to reduce its visual dominance.

Next, I worked my way up to my arms. First, I added some muscle to the back of my arm, or triceps, as seen in Figure 9.50. I'm clicking and dragging the arm toward my back to get the right bulge. Be careful with Undo and the Warp brush. Take one area at a time (like I'm doing here) and then apply the warp. After you apply, move on to another area. That way, if you have to undo something, you won't lose all your warps.

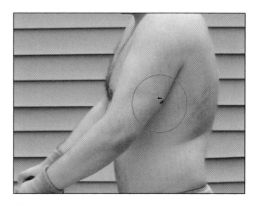

Figure 9.50

Adding triceps.

To balance my arms, I decided to add mass to my biceps. It's a simple operation of clicking and dragging toward the front, as seen in Figure 9.51.

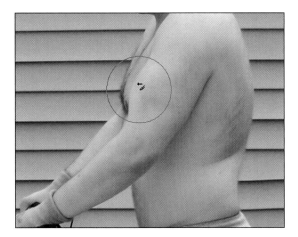

Figure 9.51
Bulging biceps.
© Corel® Corporation, All Rights Reserved. © 2013 Cengage Learning®, All Rights Reserved.

Warping my biceps out had the side effect of increasing my chest, and I didn't like that, so I decided to push the chest (not the arms) back in, as shown in Figure 9.52. I also accentuated the biceps by making my elbow look a little tighter. Pay attention to things like the siding on the house behind me. Those lines and shadows forced me to push material in line with them (or clone out problems later). If I weren't careful, you would see a bunch of wavy siding around me, giving something away.

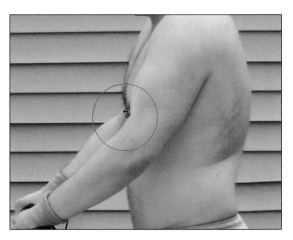

Figure 9.52
Accentuating biceps.
© Corel® Corporation, All Rights Reserved. © 2013 Cengage Learning®, All Rights Reserved.

I said that once you got the concept down, this was easy. As you can see from Figure 9.53, I continued finding different parts of my body that needed to be enhanced or minimized, and then I applied the desired warp effect.

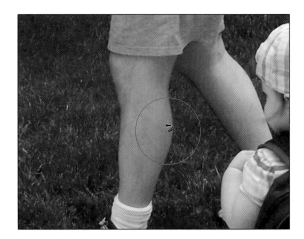

Figure 9.53
Boosting calves.
© Corel® Corporation, All Rights Reserved. © 2013 Cengage Learning®, All Rights Reserved.

Finally, I tightened up my neck and chin in Figure 9.54. There is less margin for error working around the face and chin, and I had to be careful here because the facial hair complicated the texture of my neck. If I just squished it in without thinking, I would make myself look much worse. To avoid that, I used smaller brushes and strokes.

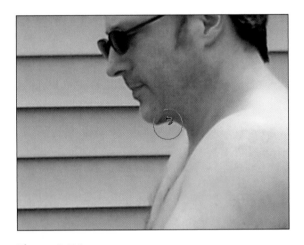

Figure 9.54
Tucking chin.
© Corel® Corporation, All Rights Reserved. © 2013 Cengage Learning®, All Rights Reserved.

Tanning

Last, but not least, I need a tan. The greatest challenge with the Tanning tool is to tan what you want without darkening your clothes or anything else. In cases like this, use a mask to mask out what you don't want to tan.

First, I copy merged and pasted that as a new layer. I then duplicated that merged layer to work with my mask. Then I moved on to creating the mask.

I created a "Show All" mask in Figure 9.55 and hid everything but the skin I wanted to tan. I also set up a white layer and a black layer underneath so that I could see where the borders were. I used those layers to help me see what I needed to mask. Without those helper layers, I would see either one of my merged layers underneath (which would make it impossible to tell where I was masking) or, if they were hidden, the transparent background.

This is like painting or erasing. Modify the size and hardness of your brush and make a few passes around your subject. You're not adding to or removing anything but the mask. You can paint the mask right back (or remove it, as the case may be) if you make a mistake. The important point is to make sure that you're working on the mask layer, not a photo layer.

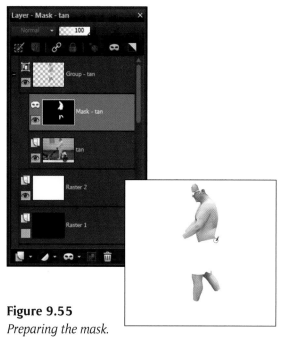

Figure 9.55

Preparing the mask.

The purpose of the mask is to set up a complicated selection—namely, my skin, and *not* to include my hair, sunglasses, clothes, or any other background. Here's how to make that selection and apply the tan.

1. **Finish the mask.**

2. **Duplicate the photo layer and put it above the mask.** This isn't absolutely necessary, but it's how I like to work. This is the layer that I applied the tan on.

3. **Select the Mask layer (this is very important).** It is contained in the layer group that gets created when you first create the mask and has a little mask icon next to its thumbnail in the Layers palette. In my case, the Mask layer is mostly black because I'm hiding most of the photo.

4. **Next, choose Selections > From Mask.** This will be active only if you've got the Mask layer selected in the Layers palette. This makes a selection based on the mask you created, and in this case is the purpose for creating the mask in the first place. With my skin selected, I can apply the tan liberally and not worry about it bleeding into other areas of the photo.

5. **Now, click on the layer in the Layers palette where you want to apply the suntan.** In my case, it was the layer I put above the mask group.

6. **Finally, select the Makeover tool and choose the Suntan mode.** Resize it if necessary and apply the suntan, as seen in Figure 9.56.

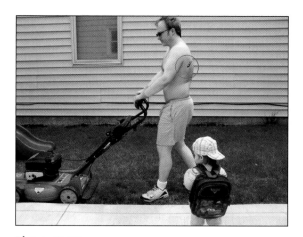

Figure 9.56

Applying suntan.

The suntan was a little dark on me, so I took that layer and lowered its opacity to blend it with an untanned layer beneath. This allowed me to set the tan's strength exactly where I wanted it to be.

There Are Always Alternatives

I chose to use a mask to make a selection in this photo study and then apply a tan to the area within the selection on a separate photo layer. That "tanning" layer wasn't a part of the mask group. An alternate method is to apply the tan to the photo layer in the mask group and let the background show through from beneath. I did it this way mostly to show (or remind you) how to make a selection from a mask.

Finishing the Photo Study

That's really all there is to it. I copied and pasted a few areas (my tummy and one small area of my waistband that I didn't have room to show you), warped them, and blended them in with the Clone brush. I used the Warp brush again to give myself some extra bulk in the muscle department and minimize my chest and chin. Then I created a mask of my skin so that I could apply the Suntan tool and blended that layer with an untanned layer to get the right strength.

To wrap it up, I made some brightness and contrast adjustments and ran the photo through the Smart Photo Fix. The finished product is Figure 9.57.

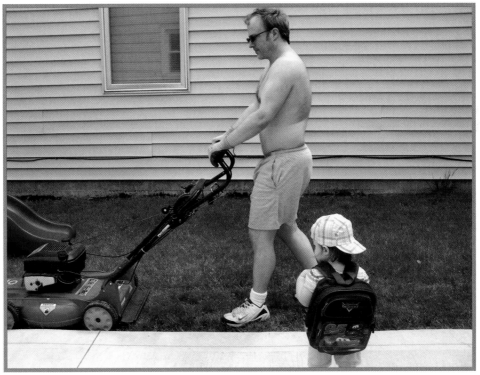

Figure 9.57
This is what I should look like.

Photo Study 46: Hiding Hair Loss

CAMPING IS FUN, and camping with your kids is even more fun. Ben, Jake, and I are setting up our tent in the backyard in Figure 9.58. (This was in the summer of 2006, about six months before Sam was born and while Grace was still just a wee babe.) I'm giving Ben a turn hammering the tent stake in, while Jake watches intently, ready for his turn to come next.

And there's my head. You can clearly see my thinning hair and balding spot. Rather than try to darken my scalp or thicken the existing hair, I want to show you how to perform a hair transplant.

First, I needed to find a suitable hair replacement. I scoured our digital photo collection and found a decent photo of my son Jacob from the back. He was looking out the front door (see Figure 9.59), and his hair looks great. I made a selection of the hair I wanted to take and copied it.

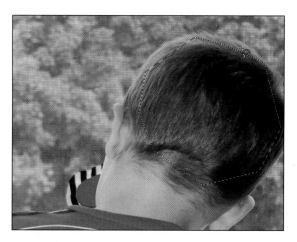

Figure 9.59
Copying Jake's hair.

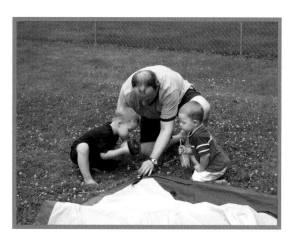

Figure 9.58
Remind me not to look down again.

Next, I pasted that hair as a new layer into the photo I wanted to modify, as seen in Figure 9.60. I used the Pick tool to shrink it down to the right size and match the two hair textures. It wouldn't look right if I had hair that was as thick as ropes!

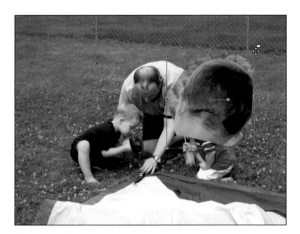

Figure 9.60
Paste, resize, and position.
© Corel® Corporation, All Rights Reserved. © 2013 Cengage Learning®, All Rights Reserved.

After resizing it, I positioned it over my head and trimmed it down to fit (see Figure 9.61). Because Jake's hair is lighter than mine, I had to use the Burn brush (Limit set to Highlights) to darken his hair to match mine.

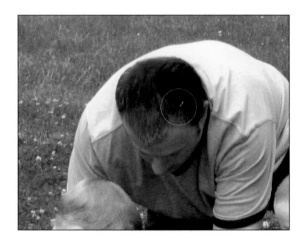

Figure 9.61
Burn to match darkness.
© Corel® Corporation, All Rights Reserved. © 2013 Cengage Learning®, All Rights Reserved.

Because I didn't want it looking like a toupee, I trimmed Jacob's hair transplant to match my basic hairline in Figure 9.62.

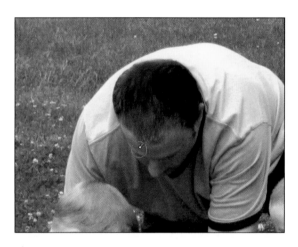

Figure 9.62
Trim to desired hairline.
© Corel® Corporation, All Rights Reserved. © 2013 Cengage Learning®, All Rights Reserved.

For the same reason, I reduced the opacity of the hair transplant layer to 57. This blended it with my balding head and made it look more natural, as shown in Figure 9.63.

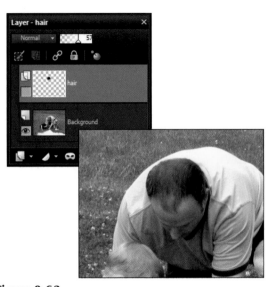

Figure 9.63

Blend using layer opacity.

Finishing the Photo Study

This study has surprised me by how natural the new hair looks. After selecting all, copy merged, and pasting as a new layer, I increased the contrast and ran the photo through a filter. I used the Effects ❯ Photo Effects ❯ Film and Filters menu to access the film filter effects and applied the Vibrant Foliage (because there's a lot of nice green grass in this photo) filter to get the final effect. Figure 9.64 shows the result.

I want to point out that I didn't just copy and paste someone else's hair on my head. I worked it. I chose someone I'm related to, carefully burned the transplanted hair color, erased it to fit a realistic hairline, and then blended it into the photo by making it more transparent. This approach is very effective.

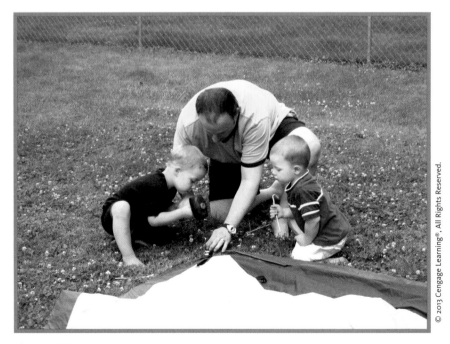

Figure 9.64

A very good hair transplant.

Photo Study 47: Cleaning Up Nostrils

I'M HOLDING MY SON, BEN, in Figure 8.67. It was in the spring of 2003, and we had our jackets on.

What's the first thing you notice when you look at this picture? Is it Ben, his smile, his eyes, his monkey, or is it the hairs coming out of his Daddy's nose? Once you spot them, you can't stop looking at them. One relatively minor blemish in a photo can overwhelm the positive things that are present.

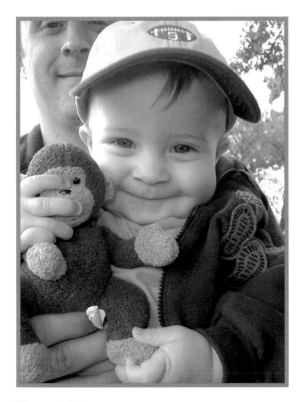

Figure 9.65
Funniest photo study title ever.
© 2013 Cengage Learning®, All Rights Reserved.

Fixing Noses

To fix the problem, I first cloned away the nose hairs on the outside of my nose, as seen in Figure 9.66.

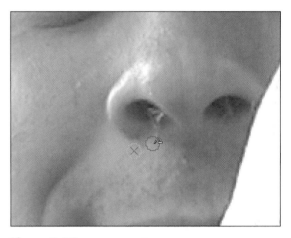

Figure 9.66
Clone hairs outside of nose.
© Corel® Corporation, All Rights Reserved. © 2013 Cengage Learning®, All Rights Reserved.

Since there wasn't enough darkness in my nostrils to clone over the hair that was still visible, I used the Burn brush to darken the light pixels (which is the hair), as shown in Figure 9.67. I switched the Limit parameter (look to the Tool Options palette to find it) to Highlights to burn only the brighter values.

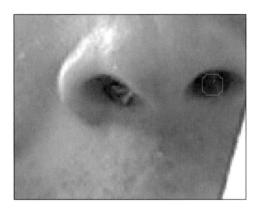

Figure 9.67

Burning nostril to darken.

When I got one good, dark nostril, I cloned that over to the other side, as seen in Figure 9.68.

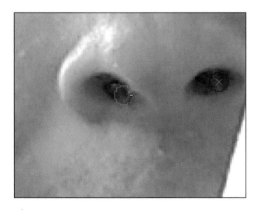

Figure 9.68

Cloning dark nostril to the other.

I wanted this to be an unobtrusive part of the photo, so I used the Soften brush to ensure that there were no sharp pixel borders to draw anyone's eyes to. I was careful to gently soften the nostril, as seen in Figure 9.69.

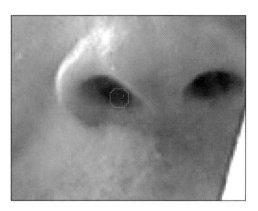

Figure 9.69

Soften to blend.

Finally, I tackled some extra blemishes on my neck and on Ben's nose, as shown in Figure 9.70, using the Blemish Fixer. Always be on the lookout for things like this to fix. Even small improvements can make a difference.

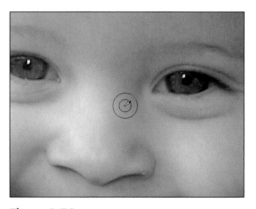

Figure 9.70

Taking out extra blemishes.

Finishing the Photo Study

This is an example of a photo that didn't take me more than 15 minutes to retouch from start to finish. I spent the most time at the end, deciding on which method to use to enhance the brightness and contrast.

In the end, I used Smart Photo Fix and then altered the levels. The final result, as seen in Figure 9.71, is free of extraneous nose hairs and blemishes.

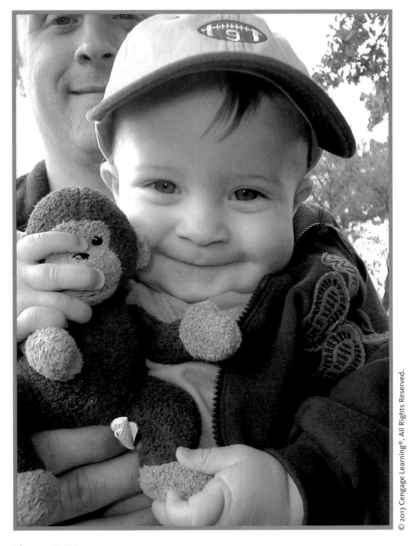

Figure 9.71
Nose hairs safely trimmed.

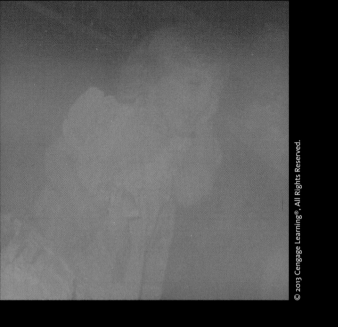

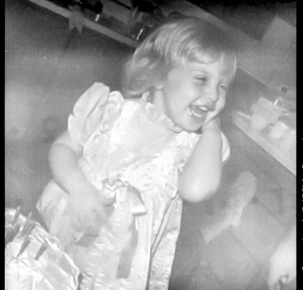

The Good, the Bad, and the Artistic

10

THIS CHAPTER ENDS THE BOOK ON THREE creative and challenging notes: the good, the bad, and the artistic. First, we all love good photos, but do you know that even good photos can be improved? Professional photographers do. That's one thing that makes a pro successful. They take great photos and use software to make them even better. If they can do it, you can too!

Second, if you're like me, you've got a bunch of photos either in albums, in shoeboxes, or on your hard drive that you can't bear to throw away or delete. There's something about them that you love and don't want to part with. The problem is, they're "Prognosis Negative." By that I mean there's something so wrong with them that you can't bring yourself to put them in a frame or post them to your Facebook page. Maybe they're badly out of focus, overexposed, or wildly bright, or maybe it's a fuzzy photo taken by a child. Despite these problems, you may be able to partially save them.

Finally, you don't have to make every photo turn out realistically. I don't! There's a time and a place for all sorts of artistry, and PaintShop Pro is a fantastic tool to use to empower your inner artist.

 ▶ **Photo Study 48: Lipstick, Please**—This is a good casual snapshot of my wife, taken in 2006. It doesn't look like it needs any fixing. However, after we took some time to look at it carefully (an important part of photo retouching and restoration), we realized she could use some lipstick!

 ▶ **Photo Study 49: Dude**—This study puts together some of the fairly straightforward techniques you've learned in the book to make this decent photo of my uncle, taken in 1958, even better.

► **Photo Study 50: Prognosis Pink**—This is a poorly exposed print of my wife at her third birthday party. It's so pink that you can barely make out any details. Learn how to tackle even the hardest photos and save what you can in this study. I think you'll be surprised.

 ► **Photo Study 51: Deblurrification**—My youngest son, Sam, took this photo of my wife as she was getting ready to change his diaper. This photo has great potential, but it's out of focus and blurry. You'll learn that you don't always have to use Sharpening to sharpen a photo, even a very bad one.

 ► **Photo Study 52: Pen and Path**—Learn how to use a photograph as a vector art template.

 ► **Photo Study 53: HDR Exposure Merge**—High Dynamic Range photography brings out details in scenes that traditional photos miss. Learn how to use PaintShop Pro's HDR Exposure Merge tool to create a moderately artistic rendering of a scene in this photo study.

Photo Study 48: Lipstick, Please

FIGURE 10.1 IS ANOTHER PICTURE of my wife, Anne. We bought the black, child-size cowboy hat at the local supermart, and she's playfully tipping it at the camera. Ben, who had just turned five years old, took this photo.

I stumbled across the idea for this photo by accident. I was looking through all our digital photos, and this struck me as being a beautiful picture of Anne. Then, with a critical eye, I started looking for things I could fix. I didn't come up with much of anything, but when I saw that her lips were devoid of any lipstick, I was struck by the notion of adding it.

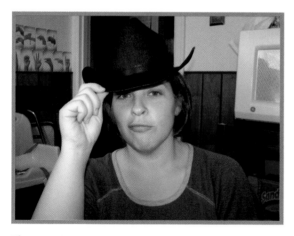

Figure 10.1
Great photo, but missing lipstick.

Applying the Lipstick

Step one is deciding what color the lipstick should be. The Material Properties dialog box (see Figure 10.2) is a good place to start. To open it, click the foreground color in the Materials palette. Browse through different hues by first clicking on the outer circle. That establishes the hue. Next, click in the color square to fix the saturation and lightness. I decided on a nice, dark red.

My Lipstick Expertise

I know nothing about lipstick, so Anne was looking over my shoulder coaching me as I retouched this photo. It pays to have an expert tell you what's what!

However, and this is an important caveat, what you're seeing is *not* my first attempt to get the color right. I had to go through the technique a few times to be able to get the right color by the end of the process. I would choose a shade, finish the technique to see what it looked like, and then come back to recalibrate if the color looked off. In the end, I was able to choose the right *beginning* color, knowing that the *ending* color would be slightly different.

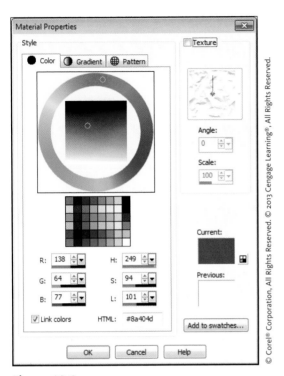

Figure 10.2
Choosing a base lipstick color.

Next, create an empty raster layer to apply the lipstick on, and then select an appropriately sized brush to paint it on with. I'm applying Anne's lipstick with a brush 50 pixels in size and a hardness of 0 in Figure 10.3. It goes on rather thick!

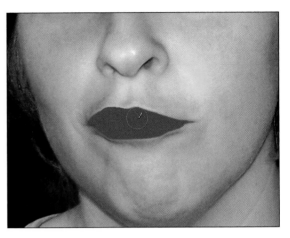

Figure 10.3
Painting it on.

You don't need to be too picky when you're applying the lipstick because the next step is to switch to the Eraser and trim away the excess, as shown in Figure 10.4. Soften the eraser so there are no hard lines that would look artificial.

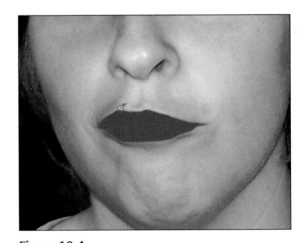

Figure 10.4
Erasing to fit.

The next step relies on one of those features of PaintShop Pro that separates beginners from more advanced users: Blend modes.

Ah, the Journey

When I first started using graphics programs, including PaintShop Pro, I didn't understand blending. To me, Normal was good enough and that's what I used. I didn't even want to learn about the other modes because they seemed too complicated and fussy.

Over time, I realized Blend modes were a powerful feature that helped me achieve effects I couldn't otherwise get. It doesn't take much to understand them, and they really increase your creativity.

Blend modes are the rules a layer follows to determine how it will blend in with the layer(s) below it. Normal is based on opacity. If a pixel is opaque and on top, it covers all pixels beneath it. If it's semi-opaque, you can partially see through it to the layer below. Some Blend modes are based on color, hue, saturation, or other ways to compare pixels. Overlay (which I am changing to in Figure 10.5) allows the color of the lipstick to "stick" to the detail of Anne's lips.

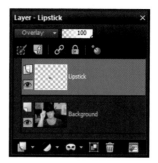

Figure 10.5
Blend mode changed to Overlay.

After changing the Blend mode, the effect was almost there, but the lipstick was too bright. I lowered the opacity of the lipstick layer to blend it in better (see Figure 10.6). In effect, I'm blending the Blend mode. Double blending like this results in a very realistic lipstick effect.

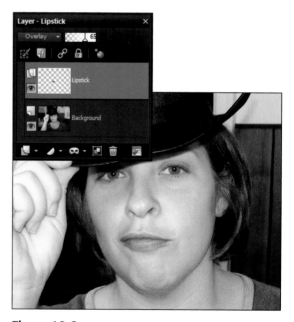

Figure 10.6
Lowering opacity for final effect.

Other Adjustments

With the lipstick done, I looked around to see if there were any other improvements that could be made. I consolidated the changes to a merged layer and then made a very small Histogram adjustment, as shown in Figure 10.7, to brighten the photo.

After this, I bumped up the vibrancy of the photo by 20. You can see the effect on Anne's lips in Figure 10.8. They are slightly more colorful. Perfect!

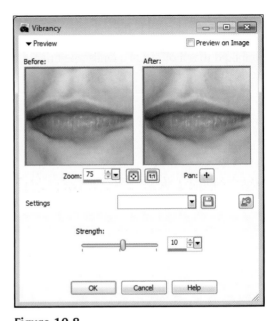

Figure 10.8

Strengthening colors a tad.

© Corel® Corporation, All Rights Reserved. © 2013 Cengage Learning®, All Rights Reserved.

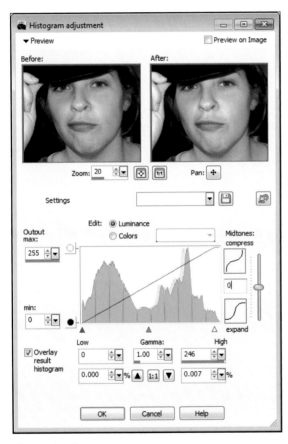

Figure 10.7

Tweaking overall Histogram.

© Corel® Corporation, All Rights Reserved. © 2013 Cengage Learning®, All Rights Reserved.

Finishing the Photo Study

After reviewing the photo (for the umpteenth time), I made a few fairly significant changes. First, I smoothed her skin using Skin Smoothing at a strength of 80. Next, I decided to use the Depth of Field command to blur the background, and then I recomposed the photo from a landscape orientation to portrait.

Figure 10.9 shows the Depth of Field dialog box (Adjust ❯ Depth of Field). I've selected the area I want to be in focus with the Freehand selection tool and have altered the settings to produce a nice blur in the background that transitions nicely to the foreground.

Afterward, I used the Crop tool set to a 4×6 aspect ratio (then oriented vertically) and cropped the photo. This had the effect of removing all the background distractions and making Anne truly the center of attention. One consequence is that the background blurring is not so prominent, but that's okay. That effect still blurs the areas you can see behind the person. Figure 10.10 shows the final result.

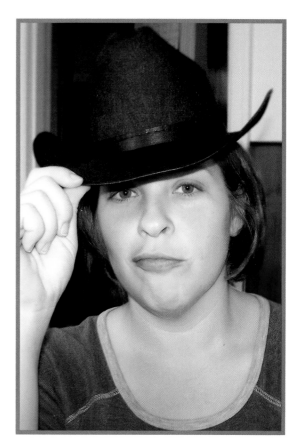

Figure 10.10

Lipstick and other improvements.

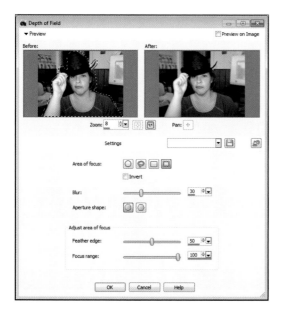

Figure 10.9

Limiting the depth of field.

Photo Study 49: Dude

FIGURE 10.11 IS A PHOTO of my Uncle Tom, taken at his parent's house in 1958. He is a year out of high-school here. The thing that strikes me about this photo is his confident pose. He was all that, and more. He was fun-loving, unafraid, and competitive. I remember him coming to visit one time. (He was in the Air Force and flew into a base near us on business.)

We fished, joked around, and had a blast. We must have played a hundred games of backgammon as I tried to beat him.

Tom passed away last year. Finding this photo of him to restore was a blessing. For its age, this photo appears to be well preserved. It still looks good, and is a great candidate for this chapter. Photos like this are great to work with.

Making the Changes

First, it's a good idea to clone the small stuff out when things are already looking good. There are numerous scratches and miscellaneous specks throughout the photo. I'm beginning to clone the photo in Figure 10.12.

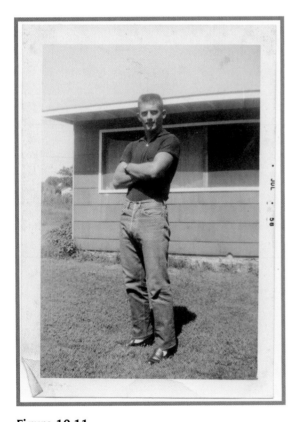

Figure 10.11
Great photo of a working man.

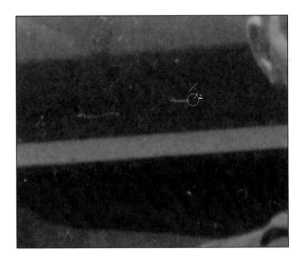

Figure 10.12
Cloning away minor issues.

The cloning stuff should be old hat for you by now. Create a blank layer (my technique) to clone on, grab the brush, adjust its size, make sure Use All Layers is checked, right-click to set the source, and you're off.

One of the bigger problems with the photo is a bent-in, lower-left corner. Although you can dodge this area to whiten it, I chose to clone the edges of the photo to re-create the corner (see Figure 10.13).

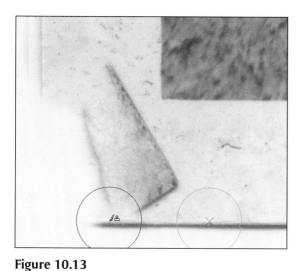

Figure 10.13

Cleaning up the corner.

Following this, it was time to fix the photo's brightness and contrast. In this case, I first used a Curves adjustment layer, shown in Figure 10.14. I clicked on the house trim to establish the white point.

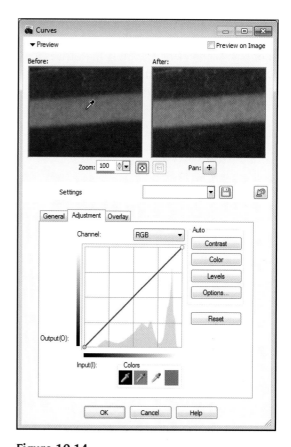

Figure 10.14

Establishing the white point.

I followed that up with a Levels adjustment layer. In this case (see Figure 10.15), I drug the left slider upward, strengthening the dark region in the photo. The contrast is much better.

Next, the photo could use a little sharpening. I used High Pass Sharpen to bring out some details in Tom's face, shown in Figure 10.16, without increasing the noise level. There's not much point in trying to solve one problem when you create more.

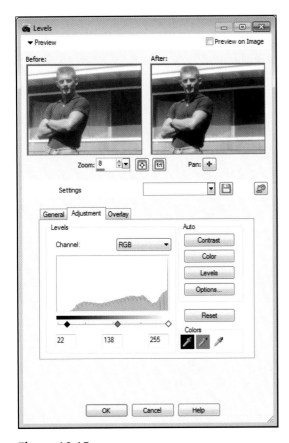

Figure 10.15

Improving the contrast.

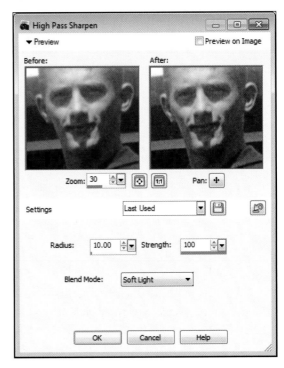

Figure 10.16

Sharpening without elevating noise.

Finally, there were still numerous small specks in the darker areas of the photo. At times like this, the Salt and Pepper filter can eliminate them much more quickly than you can clone them out. If you are gentle with it, as shown in Figure 10.17, you can reduce the effect of the specks without otherwise damaging the photo's sharpness.

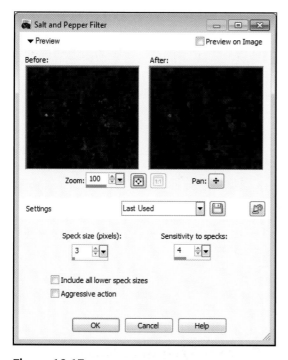

Figure 10.17

Automatically removing specks.

Finishing the Photo Study

The funny thing about this photo is that I actually did a lot of stuff to it. I made contrast and brightness changes, cloned out blemishes, cleaned up the border, sharpened the focus, and cropped out a bit of the border. The moral of the story? Even good photos can be improved upon. Figure 10.18 shows the final result.

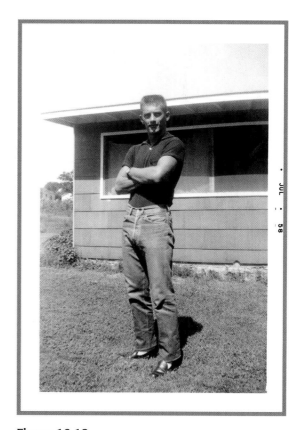

Figure 10.18

The result is a much bolder photo.

Photo Study 50: Prognosis Pink

FIGURE 10.19 IS AN UNSALVAGEABLE
photo if I've ever seen one. You can barely tell, but
this is a picture of Anne at her third birthday party.
You can see part of her birthday cake in the lower-
left corner of the photo. She is laughing and has a
big smile. Something happened to the film when it
was in the camera, or it was processed incorrectly.
Her mother says every photo on the roll turned out
this way when it was developed: Prognosis Pink.

Taking the Pink Out

First, I decided to take a look at the Red, Green,
and Blue channels to see where the most data was.
Figure 10.20 shows that Green and Blue provide
the most information. Red is almost a complete
washout. I can use this to help me blend information from the channels to create the best looking
black-and-white image.

There's an important point to note about the Red
channel. It has good information at the top, which
shows the counter and sink behind Anne. If I reject
the Red channel entirely, I will lose this. Since Green
has the most detail and Red has missing detail, I
can use a combination of the two to arrive at the
best black-and-white image. I'm using the Channel
Mixer in Figure 10.21 to do just that.

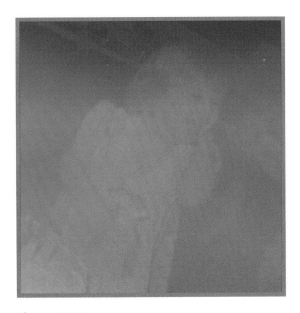

Figure 10.19
One of the worst photos I've seen.
© 2013 Cengage Learning®, All Rights Reserved.

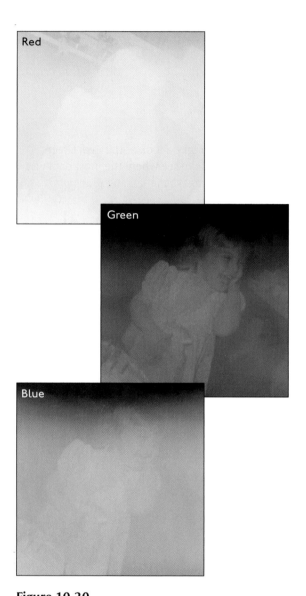

Figure 10.20

Examining the color channels.

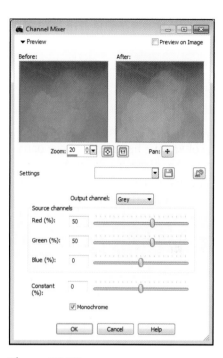

Figure 10.21

Taking the pink out.

Favorite Methods

Over time, you will find your own favorite methods for tackling problems. The funny thing is, they change periodically. That's one reason why I've been careful to avoid telling you a particular method is "The Way" to do something. I've tried to expand your thought processes, your imagination, your horizons, and your creativity by sharing how I do things, telling you why, and at the same time letting you know that you have the power to make up your own mind.

Next, I start correcting the levels. The Levels dialog box is shown in Figure 10.22.

Next, I decided it was time to sharpen the photo, as shown in Figure 10.23. Notice that I've not cloned the imperfections out. This is another case where fixing the other problems takes precedence.

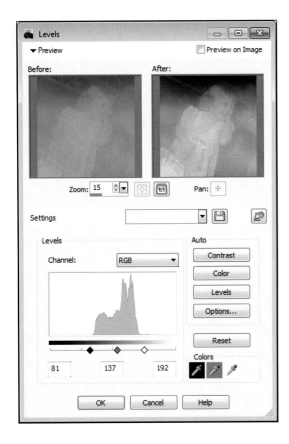

Figure 10.22

Correcting levels.

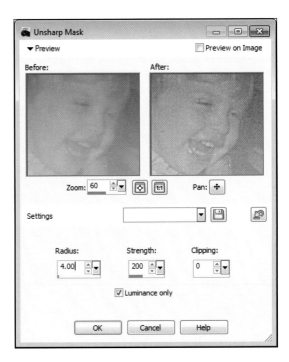

Figure 10.23

Sharpening, but not too much.

After this, I took the bold step of applying fill light and clarifying the photo. Notice from Figure 10.24 that the settings for Clarity are pretty high. I thought that these settings combined to reveal more detail in the photo and make the edges in the photo stand out more.

Next, I wanted to see what a good dose of Digital Noise Removal (see Figure 10.25) would look like. I think it does a good job of smoothing out the image. I'm almost done.

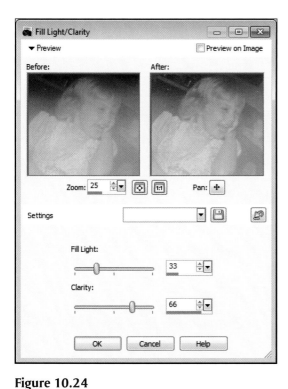

Figure 10.24
Revealing detail and adding clarity.

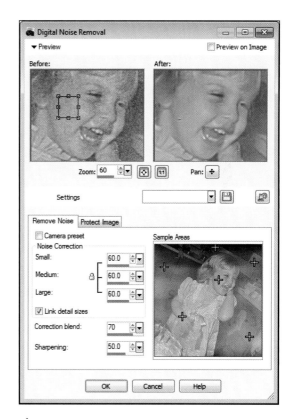

Figure 10.25
Smoothing with digital noise removal.

Finally, now that the specks and scratches are visible and the rest of the photo is in its final form, I can clone out the problems without worrying about tone or texture mismatches, as shown in Figure 10.26. At this point, if you can't match things very easily with the Clone brush or Blemish Fixer, don't sweat it. You've already saved the photo.

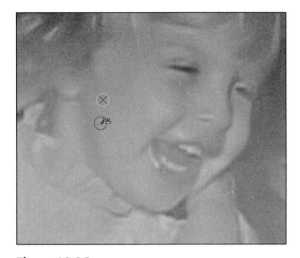

Figure 10.26
Time to clone.

After laying this aside for a while, I came back and performed a Histogram Adjustment to lighten the photo and then did another round of light sharpening with Unsharp Mask and Digital Noise Removal. It may sound like overkill, but I thought I could get her a bit clearer and smoother.

Finishing the Photo Study

This photo was a challenge. Its original state was Prognosis Pink. There was no way to restore it to what it was intended to capture, but with PaintShop Pro I was able to rescue a surprising amount of detail from the beautiful photo of a young girl having the time of her life at her third birthday party (see Figure 10.27). That makes it all worthwhile.

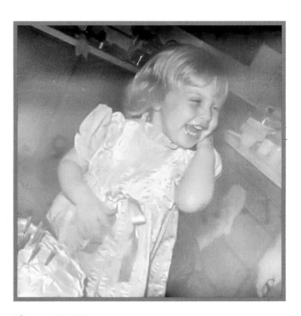

Figure 10.27
Priceless rescue.

Photo Study 51: Deblurrification

THE PHOTO IN FIGURE 10.28 was taken by our youngest son, Sam, while Anne was getting ready to change his diaper. He was just over two years old when he took this. The composition is great, and he caught Anne with a cute smile—she's having fun with him taking her photo.

The problem is, of course, that Anne is completely blurry in this photo. That isn't necessarily Sam's fault. We don't give the kids $1,500 cameras to run around with. This photo was taken with a Panasonic DMC-LZ8, which sold for around $100 in 2010.

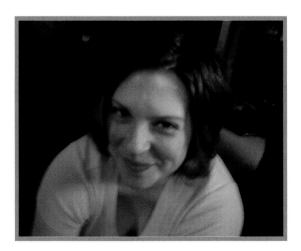

Figure 10.28
Another really blurry photo.
© 2013 Cengage Learning®, All Rights Reserved.

Although it is a very capable camera, it is still a budget compact digital camera with no anti-shake or image stabilization features. When you combine that with the inevitable lag between the time you press the shutter and when the picture is taken, the photographer and subject often move, which makes the photo blurry.

You might think this photo is unsalvageable, but quite by accident, I realized I could make something of it. I was looking at a small thumbnail of the photo and thought it was a good one. When I opened it up, I realized it was so blurry that it was basically useless. This happens a lot if you're looking at the LCD screen on the back of your camera to tell if photos are good or not and you don't zoom in. The small size fools you into thinking the photo is sharp when it is in fact badly out of focus or blurry. To fix this photo, I'm going to do the same thing: reduce its size.

Shutter Lag

I hate shutter lag—the time between pressing the shutter release button to take the picture and when the camera "clicks" and tells you it has it.

It's possible to anticipate and work around shutter lag, but it's a pain. Unfortunately, shutter lag is a fact of life in some compact digitals and super zooms.

Reducing

First, I'll reduce the size of the photo, which is the whole point. It gives me a sharper image that I can then retouch. As with many things, deciding the right size is largely a matter of trial and error. The original photo was taken with an 8-megapixel camera and has dimensions of 3624×2448. This photo was so badly blurred I didn't think there was any chance of saving it anywhere near that size. I'll have to find out how small it needs to be by reducing it and looking at it.

I'll do this by using my mouse wheel to gradually zoom out and make the photo smaller. This simulates reducing the size on-screen so I don't have to continually resize the photo and undo. When you see the picture turn from something blurry to something that looks reasonably sharp, stop and take note of the magnification. As you can see from Figure 10.29, it's 8%. That gives you the number you need to start with.

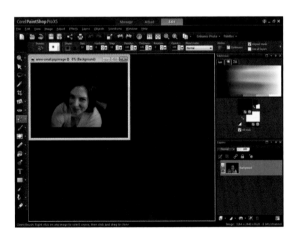

Figure 10.29

Zoom out until it looks better.

Next, choose Image ❯ Resize and resize the photo to the percentage you just decided looked the best. In this case, that was 8% (see Figure 10.30).

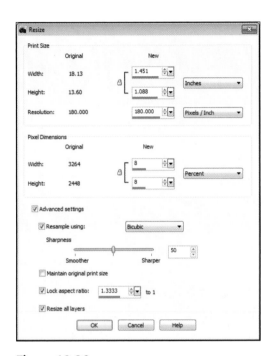

Figure 10.30

Resize.

Examine the photo at 100% (see Figure 10.31) after you've resized it to your initial target percentage. If it looks good, continue on. If the photo doesn't look good, undo and choose a smaller percentage. You may need to try this process two or three times to come up with the best size, and you may even need to come back to this step later in the process. Don't let that throw you—it has happened to me.

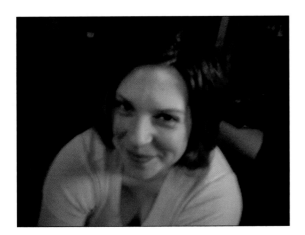

Figure 10.31
Examining at 8%.

This Actually Works

I showed my wife this technique, and we had a good laugh about the circumstances of the photo (the diaper). She told her mom, who ended up doing the same thing (the photo, not the diaper) not too long thereafter to put a blurry photo in her church newsletter. She was able to use a photo that wasn't very sharp by reducing its size.

The reverse is also true. I often run into photos that look fine displayed on the camera's small LCD monitor only to find out they are blurry when I view them on my much larger computer monitors.

Finishing the Photo Study

I settled on a reduction to 7% of the original size, which resulted in a photo that measured 228×171. That's a pretty big reduction, but it turned a really blurry photo into something usable.

After finding where the best reduction was, I made some additional adjustments to give the photo more life. I used Smart Photo Fix and accepted the suggestions, and then I used Color Balance to cool it down some. (The original photo had too many yellows.) I sharpened with Unsharp Mask and smoothed with a light touch of Digital Noise Removal.

The final result, shown in Figure10.32, is a great little photo—certainly good enough to put in a newsletter or online on Facebook, MySpace, Twitter, or another site where you can use small photos to customize your pages.

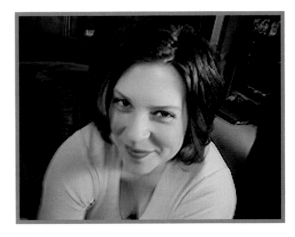

Figure 10.32
Deblurrification.

Photo Study 52: Pen and Path

MY WIFE IS A MASTER OF FOAM board art, and she loves putting together wall hangings for the kids' birthdays. They are made from layers of foam board that you can buy at your local mega mart or craft store. She designs a pattern, cuts the pieces out, and glues them on a background the day or so before the birthday. We hang them up in the kitchen the day of their birthday, and the kids get to put them on the wall by their beds afterward.

I took the photo in Figure 10.33 on Sam's birthday in 2009 (he turned two). Anne put together a wonderfully cute dump truck for him and taped it up on the kitchen wall the whole day. You can use photos like this to create vector art files from.

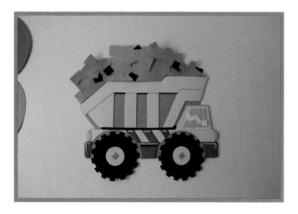

Figure 10.33

A cute birthday wall hanging.

© Corel® Corporation, All Rights Reserved. © 2013 Cengage Learning®, All Rights Reserved.

Prepping the Photo

Although there wasn't any need to retouch this photo in the traditional sense, I decided to quickly touch it up so that it would be a better pattern. First, I lightened the photo to make it easier to see, so I could match the colors better. I used Smart Photo Fix, as shown in Figure 10.34.

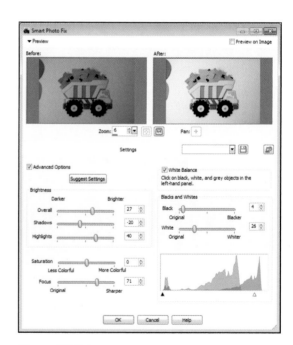

Figure 10.34

Lightening to work.

© Corel® Corporation, All Rights Reserved. © 2013 Cengage Learning®, All Rights Reserved.

Next, I rotated the working layer to straighten the truck. I used the bottom of the truck frame, as shown in Figure 10.35, as the guide.

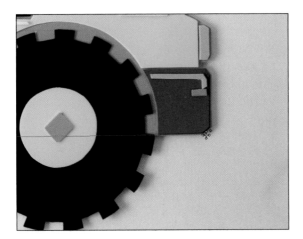

Figure 10.35
Straightening before starting the vector work.
© Corel® Corporation, All Rights Reserved. © 2013 Cengage Learning®, All Rights Reserved.

With those two simple adjustments, I was ready to begin work on the vector shapes.

Strategizing

Mechanically, this study is easy. Use the photo as a pattern to create vector shapes with the Pen tool; then color and adjust those shapes according to the photo. Keeping things organized is harder. In fact, I jumped right in before thinking about it and eventually had to start over. Based on that experience, I came up with a strategy for how to approach this type of vector work, because it's going to get complicated:

▶ Create a separate vector layer for each color. In my case, I created eight color-based layers in all: orange, yellow, dark blue, light blue, highlights, brown, light brown, and black.

▶ Consolidate identical colors at the same depth into the same vector layer group. For example, I created the different yellow shapes that made up the truck bed on the same layer.

▶ Work from the bottom up. I created different layers based on depth and function. For example, I created the truck frame layer at the bottom level.

▶ Use strokes and fills at first. It was very hard to work with an outline only, so I created each original shape with a black outline and a white interior color. This helped me see and select each shape. I also lowered the opacity of the layer to be able to see through the shape to the photo.

Creating Vector Shapes

Creating the shapes is like washing your hair. Wash, rinse, and repeat. Therefore, I'm not going to illustrate every shape I created. I'll use several to show you specific points.

Basic Shapes

The orange truck frame is the background for everything on the truck, such as the yellow and blue details, plus the wheels. The dirt and rocks in the back are underneath this layer.

To create any of the shapes associated with the truck, follow these steps:

1. **Create a new Vector layer and rename it, as shown in Figure 10.36.**

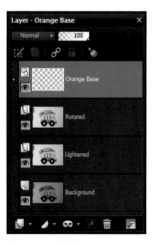

Figure 10.36

Creating a vector layer.

2. **Lower the layer's opacity so you will be able to see through it.** I set it between 50 and 60.

3. **Select the Pen tool from the Tools toolbar.**

4. **Enter Draw Point to Point—Bézier Curves mode.** Make sure that Connect Segments and Show Nodes are selected.

5. **Make sure that the Line style is solid and enter a width that will enable you to see the line.** I used a value of 5 to 10.

6. **Select the preliminary stroke and fill colors.** These can be the final colors, but I like using black as the stroke and white as the fill color (see Figure 10.37) until I'm ready to finalize the image. You could choose not to make the layer semi-transparent and instead set the fill color to transparent, but I think this makes selecting the shapes and moving or working with them harder down the road.

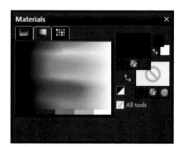

Figure 10.37

Setting up initial materials.

7. Zoom in so you can set the nodes precisely; then click to start the shape.

Vector shapes are based on points you create. The program connects the points you create with lines and fills the shape. Therefore, what you're actually doing is outlining a shape.

Nodes that connect straight lines are easy, as shown in Figure 10.38, where I'm creating the basic truck shape. Straight lines connect the points I have clicked to create. You can see the shape is being filled as I create it. That's why it's important to make it semi-transparent. Thankfully, most of the lines of this truck are straight, so it's an easy process of clicking on each corner.

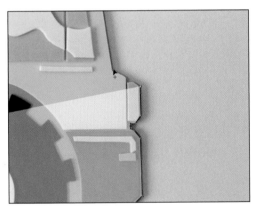

Figure 10.38
Creating straight lines to make this shape.
© Corel® Corporation, All Rights Reserved. © 2013 Cengage Learning®, All Rights Reserved.

8. When you reach the last node, select Close Selected Open Contours from the Tool Options palette. This automatically connects your last point to the first point and closes the shape.

That does it for the orange truck base. I didn't need to start a new shape on the same layer, so the shape and the layer it's on are done. If you need to edit any of the nodes, first, zoom in and make sure you're in Edit mode. Click a node and drag it to fine-tune its position (see Figure 10.39). I am moving a node that I purposefully misplaced back to where it belongs. Be careful not to move the entire shape; it's easy to accidentally select the shape and not the node. The cursor looks like an arrow with movement arrows if you're above the node. If you're above the shape, it looks like the cursor with a wavy line.

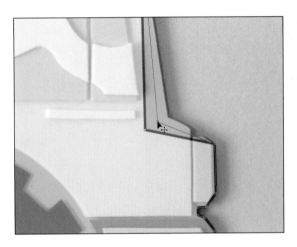

Figure 10.39
Moving a node in Edit mode.
© Corel® Corporation, All Rights Reserved. © 2013 Cengage Learning®, All Rights Reserved.

Creating More Layers

The next step was to create the other layers and populate them with the appropriate shapes. It's easy to get confused as you work with vector objects. Pay attention to the layer you have selected in the Layers palette to ensure that you're drawing on the right layer.

You could conceivably create all these shapes in one vector layer group (see Figure 10.40).

I prefer to work with different groups.

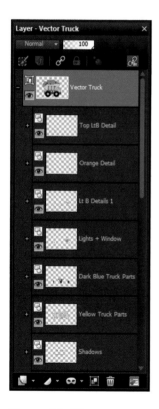

Figure 10.40
Working in a single vector layer group.

Creating Curves

The process for creating curved shapes is similar to that of straight lines, except that you draw midpoints of the line that you use to specify the curve. For example, the wavy lines on the window are curved shapes. I clicked to establish an initial sharp corner point and when I clicked again I held the mouse button down and dragged it to establish the shape, as shown in Figure 10.41.

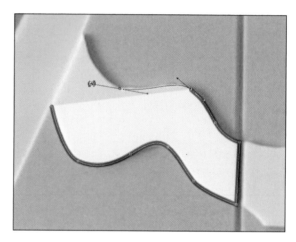

Figure 10.41
Drawing a curved shape.

You can come back and edit these nodes just as corner points, and you can use the extra handles to modify the curve as well.

Colorizing

When all my shapes were created, I went through each Vector layer and set the final colors and opacity. It's not hard, once you get the hang of it. Until you do, it can be dicey.

1. **Hide the other Vector layers that you aren't working with, so you can see what you're doing.**

2. **Hide the Vector layer you want to change the color on.** Trust me, you need to do this so that you can choose a color from the photo. Otherwise, the vector object will get in the way.

3. **Select the Vector layer you want to color and expand it.** Double-click the path layer to open the Vector Property dialog, as shown in Figure 10.42. It will contain the materials you used to create the initial path. In this case, black and white.

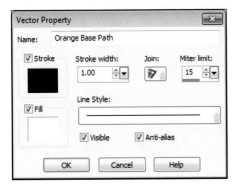

Figure 10.42

Preparing to colorize.

© Corel® Corporation, All Rights Reserved. © 2013 Cengage Learning®, All Rights Reserved.

4. **Based on the pattern you're copying and your artistic goals, populate this dialog with the properties and colors you want.** For this object (the orange base of the truck), I turned off the Stroke property, as shown in Figure 10.43, because I didn't want the shape to look outlined.

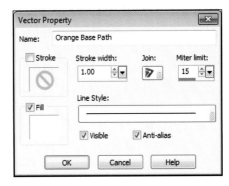

Figure 10.43

Turning off the Stroke property to avoid having an outlined shape.

© Corel® Corporation, All Rights Reserved. © 2013 Cengage Learning®, All Rights Reserved.

To choose a new fill color based on one of the colors in the photo, click the Fill color swatch. This opens the Materials Properties dialog box, which you can ignore. If you need to, move it out of the way. Next, click on a color in the photo you want to use, as shown in Figure 10.44. This is a really convenient way to match the colors of the actual object.

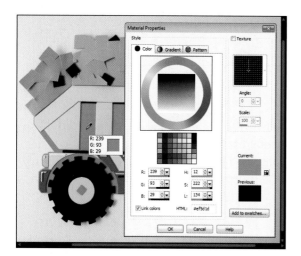

Figure 10.44

Selecting a color from the photo.

With the new color loaded into the Current swatch of the Materials Properties dialog, close the dialog box by selecting OK. That loads the new color into the Vector Property dialog and automatically updates the shape.

5. **Continue turning off layers that you aren't working on and turning on those you want to color until you're finished.**

Finishing the Photo Study

When you're done colorizing, turn all the layers back on and examine your work. If you want, you can convert the Vector layers to Raster layers and create cool drop-shadows from the Effects menu. I would duplicate the Vector layer first, convert the copy, and then hide the original. That preserves your choice to come back and edit the vector object's properties later. You can add drop shadows to vector layers through Layer Properties. (Double-click the layer from the Layers palette to open this dialog box.) However, putting more than one object on a layer complicates this.

In the end, I created a white Raster layer above the photo layer to serve as a new background and then exported a JPEG for desktop use. Figure 10.45 shows the final result.

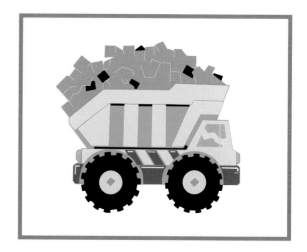

Figure 10.45

Big wheels are meant for turning.

Photo Study 53: HDR Exposure Merge

FIGURE 10.46 SHOWS THREE exposure-bracketed photos I took from a bridge in 2012. This area is normally under water. I love shooting exposure brackets with scenes like this, and then merging them into a single High Dynamic Range (aka HDR) image, because you can get much more color and detail from several photos than you can from one.

You do this by mounting your camera on a tripod and taking three or more differently exposed photographs of the same scene by altering the shutter speed and keeping the aperture and ISO constant.

The shots, as seen in Figure 10.47, run the gamut from dark to light. The point is to get at least one photo that has the bright areas of the scene under control (so they don't *blow out* or turn completely white), one photo where the dark areas aren't so dark that you lose all the detail, and one photo in the middle.

After you take the photos and download them onto your computer, use PaintShop Pro's HDR Exposure Merge feature to combine the exposures together.

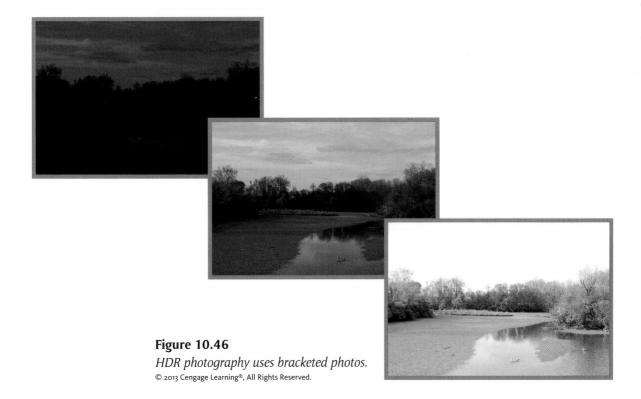

Figure 10.46
HDR photography uses bracketed photos.

The Merge

HDR Exposure Merge is an effective tool to create HDR images. The first task is to collect your bracketed photos.

1. **Take the bracketed photos and download them to your computer.** If you want to use your own RAW editor like I did to convert the photos from RAW to another format (TIFF or JPEG), do so now. You can just as easily use JPEGs.

2. **Open PaintShop Pro.** You can be in any of the three workspaces.

3. **Select File > HDR > Exposure Merge.** This opens the HDR Photo Merge dialog box.

4. **Your first task is to add your exposure bracketed photos.**

5. **If any other photos appear, click the minus sign at the bottom of the dialog box to remove them.** To add photos, click the plus sign (see Figure 10.47). Navigate to the photos you want to use with the Open dialog box, select them (see Figure 10.48), and choose Open. I have selected three photos, which is how many exposure brackets I photographed for this scene.

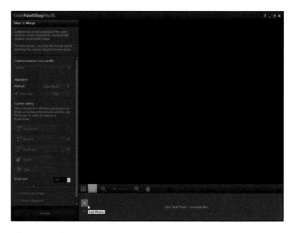

Figure 10.47

Click the plus symbol to add photos and start the process.

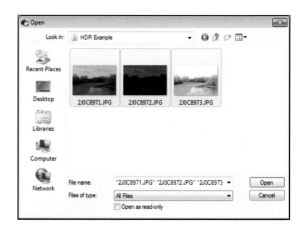

Figure 10.48

Choosing bracketed photos.

The photos appear in the bottom of the Merge dialog box, as shown in Figure 10.49. You're ready to start working.

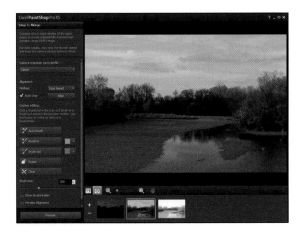

Figure 10.49
Photos loaded.
© Corel® Corporation, All Rights Reserved. © 2013 Cengage Learning®, All Rights Reserved.

6. **Although there are many subtleties to this dialog (I'm going to ignore the custom editing feature), the least you need to do is align the photos.** Choose Edge or Feature-based from the alignment method area of the screen and then choose Align.

   This makes sure that each bracket you shot lines up with the rest. Do this even if you've used a tripod.

   Preview how well the alignment works by clicking Preview Alignment. If the method you chose isn't working very well, try the other.

7. **Next, select Process.** This combines the photos together and gets you ready to tone map the result, which PaintShop Pro calls Step 2: HDR Adjustments (see Figure 10.50).

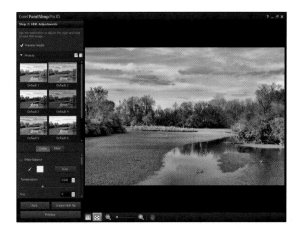

Figure 10.50
Merged and ready to make adjustments.
© Corel® Corporation, All Rights Reserved. © 2013 Cengage Learning®, All Rights Reserved.

8. **I find it helpful to choose a preset first (Default 2 and Default 5 are good to start out with), as shown in Figure 10.51, and then tweak the controls at the bottom.** You may also save and load presets. In this case, preset Default 4 looks pretty good.

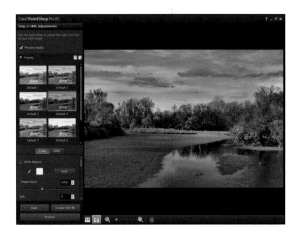

Figure 10.51
Choosing a Preset.
© Corel® Corporation, All Rights Reserved. © 2013 Cengage Learning®, All Rights Reserved.

9. **Next, make any adjustments to the individual options to make the photo look better.**

   - Use White Balance to correct color balance problems. You may choose Auto, slide the Temperature control yourself, or click the Dropper and then click a black, white, or gray area in the photo.

   - Increase or decrease Contrast, Highlights, Midtones, and Shadows to achieve the look you want. These controls are fairly self-explanatory, but the effect they have is hard to describe. Use these controls to alter the photo's brightness and contrast in the various tonal regions.

   - Adjust Vibrancy to increase the saturation.

   - Choose Natural detail and adjust the controls to achieve a more natural look to the photo.

   - Choose Creative detail and play with those controls to achieve a more creative look, as shown in Figure 10.52.

10. **Select Process to continue.** PaintShop Pro generates the final image and will throw you into Step 3: Fine-Tune, as shown in Figure 10.53.

11. **The next step is to use the same controls you find in the Adjust workspace to fine-tune your photo.** I won't go into the details here. You should be familiar with these controls.

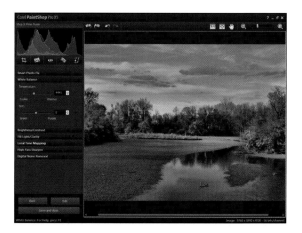

Figure 10.53
A challenging interior shot made possible with HDR.

12. **Finally, you have the options of selecting Save and closing or jumping directly into editing.** If you want to save the image first, you'll be able to choose a location, name, and file type. If you plan on editing this later, you should choose .pspimage or .tiff.

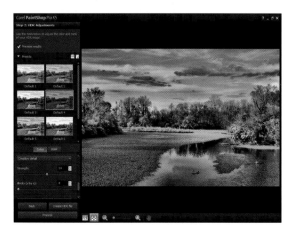

Figure 10.52
Changing preset parameters to experiment.

At this point, you can be done, or not, depending on what you want. If you want to finish here, you can. I normally retouch my tone-mapped HDR images just as I would a normal photo out of the camera. In Figure 10.54, I am working with Curves and White Balance adjustment layers to tweak the image.

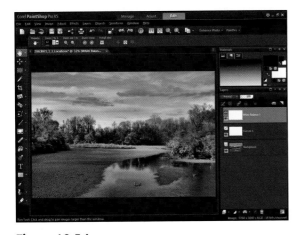

Figure 10.54
Continue editing if desired.

Finishing the Photo Study

Figure 10.55 shows my final results. I brightened the water and sky a bit and actually reduced the image's vibrancy a bit to make it look less garish.

There you have it: HDR plus a bit of editing at the end. Remember, HDR is composed of two very important, yet different, tasks. The first is photography. You have to go out and take the bracketed photos. That requires a bit more investment than normal photography, but the results can be astonishing. The second aspect of HDR is in the software. Without merging the brackets, you've got nothing.

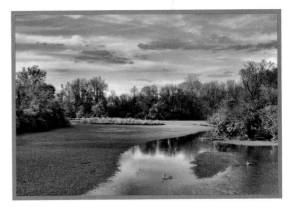

Figure 10.55
This photo is bursting with artistry and creativity.

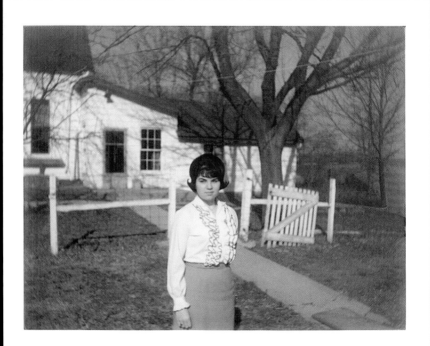

More Useful Information

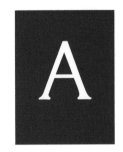

THIS APPENDIX HAS A LOT OF USEFUL information in it that directly and indirectly touches photo restoration and retouching. Scanning, for example, is how you transform photo prints into computer files. You'll also find helpful tips on using a pen tablet, not to mention organizing, printing, and archiving your photo collection.

Using a Pen Tablet

I USED TO USE A MOUSE for all my computer pointing and clicking needs, but that changed after I spoke with a friend of mine who is a radio, TV, and film professor at a college in California.

We were talking about his experiences as an animator for Disney when I brought up the fact that I had seen a behind-the-scenes segment on Disney animators. This "DVD extra" showed the animators using their pen tablets to draw actual animations from the movie. I asked him about tablets, and he said he used one all the time.

I was sold. I did some research and budgeting, and then bought a Wacom pen tablet (*www.wacom.com*). I love it. My wife loves it. Our kids love it. The tablet integrates perfectly into PaintShop Pro and is very easy to use.

You can choose different sizes to suit your needs and budget. Wacom (pronounced "wok-um") also offers larger and more expensive models priced for professionals.

Practice That *Thang*

A pen tablet takes some getting used to. Your mind and muscles have been indoctrinated into *mousing* so much that you have to retrain yourself. It's worth it. Once you get the hang of it, you will have more control than you did using a mouse. As an added bonus, you can use the pen tablet in many other applications besides PaintShop Pro.

Make sure that you look at tablet specifications to ensure that it's compatible with your system and that you read and follow the installation instructions. When your system recognizes the pen tablet as a valid pointing device, you'll be off and running.

Scanning Photos

SCANNERS ARE WONDERFUL. I love them. I've filled up many gigabytes of hard drive space with scanned photos, pictures from books, maps, patches, and more. You can even scan negatives and slides. Scanners are the only way to digitize (strange how old-fashioned that sounds) material that exists in the physical world and make it available to use on your computer.

If you scan a photo print, you can view, edit, and archive it using PaintShop Pro.

Scanner Types

There are many types of scanners. Aside from the flatbed scanner (the most common, and the subject in these sections), there are hand-held scanners, rotary, drum, planetary, 3D scanners, and probably more. They all have different strengths and weaknesses.

How Scanners Scan

Scanners shine a powerful light through a clear glass plate onto something reflective, such as a photo. The light bounces off the photo and is captured by photo-sensitive receptors in the scanner. These are called *charge-coupled devices*, or CCDs. Your typical flatbed scanner has three arrays of CCDs, each of which senses a different wavelength of light that corresponds to the colors red, green, and blue. After the scanner scans the photo, it saves the information as an image file.

Choosing the Right Resolution

Scan resolution for the typical flatbed consumer scanner is measured in dots per inch (dpi). Dpi is a measure of how many discrete color and brightness measurements the scanner makes per inch. When it comes to scanning, more dots per inch capture finer details. Fewer dots per inch capture less information.

The trade-off to higher quality and detail is space. Greater scan resolutions produce much larger files (more dots means more data, which takes up more space). They push your system and PaintShop Pro to their limits as you edit them because the sheer number of pixels changing or being displayed is tremendous. They also take up more space on your hard drive.

It is reasonable, therefore, to choose a scanning dpi based on what you're doing. Think along these lines:

- **Typical photo work: 200–300dpi.** I use 300dpi regularly. Scanned at 200dpi, a 4×6 photo has 800×1200 pixels, which is just shy of a megapixel. Scanned at 300dpi, the same photo consists of 1200×1800 pixels, or over 2 megapixels.

- **Small photos or higher quality scans: 300–1200dpi.** If the photo is on the small size, you can use a larger dpi and not end up with too large a file. Scale the dpi to the size of the photo. A 4×6 photo scanned at 600dpi has 2400×3600 pixels, or well over 8 megapixels.

- **Very small photos or ultimate quality scans: 1200–2400dpi.** Use as much dpi as you can muster to scan your most treasured photos and save them as permanent, archival quality files. It's harder to work with them, but you can resize them and save a smaller working copy using PaintShop Pro. Very high dpi is also useful for very small photos.

One adverse effect of higher scan resolutions is that you start to scan the surface details (and defects) of the photo, not just the photo itself. Sometimes, it's good *not* to know all the pits, specks, and microscopic dust that are present on a photo. You'll be tempted to want to restore things that, to be honest, won't be caught if you scanned the photo in at 300dpi. Figure A.1 shows the difference between a photo scanned at 300dpi versus 2400dpi.

Notice the trade-off that occurs. At 300dpi, the photo is clearly not as sharp as at 2400dpi. However, there are far more scratches on the 2400dpi version.

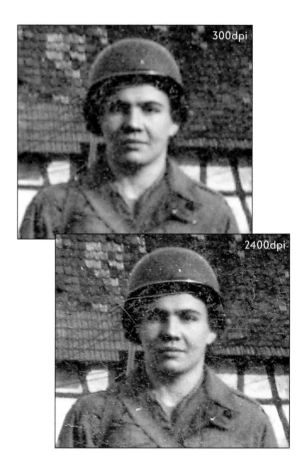

Figure A.1
The visible difference between 300 and 2400 dpi.
© 2013 Cengage Learning®, All Rights Reserved.

You'll have to experiment to find the precise resolution you prefer working with. I've found that the resolutions I use the most are those that my computer can handle without choking. That's somewhere between 300 and 1200dpi, depending on the photo size. There are times when I scan at 2400, but for the most part this is to save a high-res scan for archival purposes only. I reduce the resolution when I plan on restoring the photo.

Don't Forget About Bit-Depth

We tend to focus on dpi as the single measure of scan quality. While it is very important, don't forget to use an appropriate bit-depth. This ensures that you scan the photo with enough colors (or levels of grayscale detail). For the highest quality, scan at 48 bits and save your files as 16 bits/channel TIFFs (16 bits per channel times three channels equals 48 bits). While less capable than 48 bits, 24-bit scans (also called 8-bit images, because 8 bits per channel times three channels equals 24 bits) are acceptable in most instances. If your scanner has the ability, experiment with each type and examine the trade-offs between image quality and file size (48 bits will be much larger).

Not All Scanners Are the Same

We bought a printer some time ago that's one of those "all-in-one" types. It wirelessly prints, copies, scans up to 1200dpi, and connects to the Internet. It's incredibly versatile. I copy things all the time. Our kids print coloring and activity pages using the built-in touch screen. My wife prints plans and school schedules from her computer. I routinely scan things I have signed and need to email.

Despite the fact that it is more than adequate for all these tasks, it is not up to producing high-quality photo scans that I can use to retouch or restore. Figure A.2 shows a small portion of a 1200dpi scan of my wife's grandmother sitting in a yard. It looks terrible. The edges look fuzzy and sometimes "jumpy." (I think this is due to oversharpening that I can't disable, which creates harsh edges that seem to jump back and forth.) This type of scan limits your effectiveness as a photo retoucher.

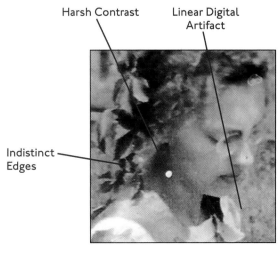

Figure A.2
A poor scan from an all-in-one printer/scanner.
© 2013 Cengage Learning®, All Rights Reserved.

Figure A.3 shows the same photo scanned in with our new scanner, the Canon CanoScan 9000F. It's what I would call a mid-range consumer scanner. It's not the cheapest scanner out there (try and avoid these, for the most part), nor is it the most expensive (professional scanners can cost well over a thousand dollars). The results are clearly better. At the same resolution (and with auto enhancements off), this scan has more detail, fewer artifacts, and a much better tone to it. It may not appear as sharp, but that's part of the point. You should see the photo as it is, not something that you can't keep from being artificially enhanced. Although the photo wasn't perfect to begin with, this scan is a much better source to work from.

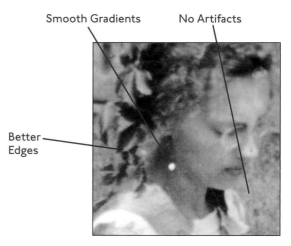

Figure A.3
This is more like it.

Scanning Photos and Other Objects

ALTHOUGH I MOSTLY REFER TO PHOTOS, this information applies to other objects as well. Don't forget about old newspaper clippings, obituaries, baseball cards, postcards, letters, patches, maps, diplomas, and other historical objects. Be creative with objects that are larger than your scanner bed. Try scanning a small portion at a time and putting the pieces together like a puzzle using PaintShop Pro.

Cleaning Your Scanner

Be fanatical about cleaning your scanner. Clean it before every use. I use a popular brand of glass cleaner and unused coffee filters to wipe with. Coffee filters are lint-free and neater than newspapers. Experiment with the filter size to find out what you like best. Smaller ones get dirty and there isn't much to fold over to use a new section. On the large side, there are commercial coffee machines that take huge filters. Those filters are big enough to clean sliding glass doors with.

Cleaning Photos

If your photos need to be cleaned, consult a professional or research photo cleaning on the Internet and follow the advice that best suits your problem. To dust photos off, I use a dust blower and brush I bought to clean my digital SLR cameras.

▶ Don't use anything that will scratch the photo, such as a rough paper towel.

▶ Don't rub or buff vigorously, or you'll scratch or fade the photo.

▶ Don't use a cleaner that could chemically interact with the print and destroy it.

▶ Be careful with "canned air," as it can condense water out of the air and blow it all over the photo. Make sure to get a variety that says "moisture and residue free." Regardless, be careful and do some test runs with plain paper on humid days.

Handling Photos

Handle all of your photo prints with care. Clean your hands prior to touching old photos, or better yet, wear protective gloves. The oil your skin naturally produces will damage photos over time. If you decide not to wear gloves (or don't have them with you), handle the photos by the edges and support them from beneath. This will prevent your fingerprints from getting all over the photos.

Be very careful when you handle photos or other documents that are in albums. Older albums are especially prone to grabbing onto photos and not letting them go. The first step in restoring an old photo is often rescuing it from a poorly designed storage environment. (If the photo sticks, scan it in while still in the album.)

Be Careful How You Treat Other People's Photos

If you plan on restoring or retouching other people's photos, especially if you are going to do it for money, take every possible safety precaution to protect the photos and yourself. Wear gloves when you handle the photos, scan them carefully, put them in a rigid sleeve, and get them back to their owner safely and quickly.

The plastic "protective" sheet (or sleeve, as the case may be) may stick to the photo, or the sticky paper of the album may be sticking too much. If this is the case and the photo is important, you should seek the assistance of a professional conservator or photographer with this type of experience. If you are going to remove the photo yourself, carefully try to peel the protective sheet back, but if you feel the surface of the photo starting to give way, stop immediately. Never try to peel the photo off the page. You may bend and damage the photo.

Running Your Scanner Software

Make sure that your scanner is plugged in, powered on, and connected to your computer or network. You must have installed the scanning software that came with your scanner.

Here is a general scanning workflow. Use it as a baseline to fit your situation and to jog your memory so you don't forget things:

1. **Open the lid and clean the scanner bed.**

2. **While the scanner glass is drying, gather the material you want to scan.** Make sure that the scanner bed is clean and dry before continuing.

3. **Place your ruler or other straightedge on the scanner bed to give yourself a square, straight photo placement helper.**

   It's quite hard to place a photo or other object on the scanner perfectly straight. If you put your photo at the edge of the scanner bed, you're very likely going to lose a little bit of your photo because it's outside of the scanning area. Try it and see. That's why I use a plastic ruler that rests against the bottom or any side of the bed. It gives me a straight offset from the border of the bed, and I can crop it out later.

4. **Place the photo against the rest.** Make sure that it doesn't go under or over it.

5. **Close the scanner lid.** If the ruler or straightedge you use keeps the scanner from closing properly and securing the photo to the glass, you may have to put the photo in by hand and straighten it later in PaintShop Pro.

6. **If you haven't started your scanner software, do so now.**

7. **Depending on your software, you may have different options here, but you'll probably want a preview or overview scan of what is on the scanner bed.** This is done very quickly at a much lower resolution than the final scan.

8. **Select the area you want to scan.** When you are scanning small photos, this really helps keep file sizes down. For sizes of 8×10 or so, you won't save on file size, but it will keep cropping down to a minimum. I like to leave a little border around each side that's larger than the photo itself so I can decide later exactly how I want to crop it.

9. **Select a scan resolution and bit depth (sometimes called *image type*).**

10. **Make sure that automatic corrections are turned off.** The thing is, you're scanning in photos so that *you* can restore them, not the scanner.

11. **Scan.** You can normally select to scan to a file or image type. If you choose .jpg, make sure that the image quality is set to "highest," or 100%. I always choose uncompressed .tiff, which is a high-quality image format.

12. **Bask in the glow of a job well done.**

Choosing a Commercial Solution

Believe it or not, you don't have to scan everything yourself. You can choose to have photos commercially scanned at a fairly reasonable rate. This would be most cost-effective if you were restoring and retouching photos as a small business and could offset the expense by including scanning costs in your quotes, but in small batches, paying a professional to scan your photos isn't too costly. If you're working on family photos, take up a collection from your relatives if it gets too costly. You can also take your photos to photo-printing kiosks, but this is no better than scanning at home (unless, of course, you don't have a scanner).

I use a local print and copy business that I became familiar with when I was freelancing in the marketing and design industry. We would send them quite a bit of professional printing business and had a good working relationship. When my wife's grandfather died, we used them to scan in several old photos so that the family could concentrate on other, more important matters.

Search your local area for print and copy companies that might perform this service, call them up, and ask for their rates. If you plan on using them a lot, ask for a discount. Verify what dpi they are capable of scanning and what format you want the files to be saved in before closing the deal.

Organizing Your Digital Photo Collection

WE'VE GOT MANY THOUSANDS of digital pictures that we've taken over the last several years. They pile up like crazy with one digital camera. If you have more than one camera and more than one photographer in your household, you've got some serious managing to do.

Organization is the key to being able to access, edit, and not lose them. There is a long-term component to organization as well. When it's time for you to pass your family photos down to your children or other family members, how are they going to make sense of things? Are things logically organized so that generations to come can spend their time reminiscing and not fighting the system?

Folder and File Organization

I've gone through several organizational schemes over the years.

First, there was the "Throw the photos in subject folders" idea. It seems ridiculous now, but those were the days of 8MB memory cards. Digital photos were a new thing, and I don't think my wife and I averaged taking more than 25–30 pictures in a month. We just didn't think about it the same way. At that time, we organized our pictures in subject folders within one overall digital photo folder and left the names alone.

Digital Photo Downloading Options

Programs that automatically download pictures to your computer from your digital camera normally come with the camera you have. These programs can also be associated with a graphics application or photo-editing program, such as PaintShop Pro.

When we had our first child. I decided to try and organize things a bit because the subject folder scheme was getting too complicated. When I took a picture of my wife and my son and the cat all together, did the file go in the "Robert" folder, the "Anne" folder, the "Cats" folder, or the "Ben" folder? That's when I implemented my "Year-Month-Day" scheme on the folders, and it seemed natural to start renaming the files, too.

Therefore, I created folders by year and month, and then downloaded the photos into them, renaming each photo afterwards.

I really liked this system because I could look at a photo and tell you exactly when I took it from the name.

Know Your Digital Camera

Check the documentation that came with your digital camera and see what file-naming options you have. You might have several to choose from, find one that fits your needs, and never have to manually name a file again.

Again, the reason this worked was the fact that we had one camera and took maybe 50 photos a month.

When we got a new, 3MP camera, I changed organizational schemes again. By this time, I was tired of naming every single file, so I dropped that. I was also tired of putting photos by month into folders. So I just copied the folder the camera used on the memory card over to the computer and left it alone. I call this my "I give up" scheme. The problem with this scheme is that it gave me no usable information.

Today, I have several dSLRs, compact digital cameras, and super zooms with more on the way. I also rent cameras for certain shoots. I don't have time to spend messing around overorganizing and renaming. However, to keep things straight, I do need some form of organization.

Therefore, I use the following process:

1. **I have dedicated an entire drive to photos.** I download new digital photos here. I keep them separate from scanned photos that I am retouching or restoring.

2. **I create a folder for each camera.** You only have to do this once, each time you get a new camera. I put the manufacturer and mode. For the Canon EOS 5D Mark III, I would use "Canon 5D3."

3. **I create folders as needed when transferring photos from the camera's memory card to the computer.** My particular naming scheme is to put the camera name, year (so the folders sort by year), month, day, and a sequence number. I separate the month and day to make them easier to spot when I'm looking at the folders.

Here's an example of how I would name a folder to receive the first batch of photos from a Canon 5D Mark III taken on May 27, 2012: 5D3-2012-05-27-01.

4. **I then manually transfer the photos from the memory card to the folder I just created.**

5. **If I have more than one download that day, I create more folders and assign new sequence numbers (02, 03, etc.), as required.**

6. **I then make a copy of the download folders to remind myself I need to archive them to an external drive.** This preserves a temporary copy in case I accidentally delete a photo or do something I can't undo. Over time, I move the original folder to an external hard drive for long-term storage and protection and delete the copy. (The space the copies take up prompts me to quickly archive the originals and free up the space.)

You can load the original folders into whatever organizational software you use. Then edit, tag, and continue to organize to your heart's content.

Protecting Your Files

Unlike physical photo prints that are developed from negatives, digital photos have no negative. The image file is the original source. Protect it at all costs!

I made the mistake of changing my original photos a few times when I got my first digital camera. I rotated, cropped, or resized a photo, then saved it, only to realize that I had just overwritten my master copy. My original source was gone forever. It was as if I had held up the negative and burned it, leaving me with a resized print that would never be as good as the original. I learned my lesson.

My wife will attest to my rigorous efforts to protect one copy of our digital photos from ever being edited, resized, cropped, or otherwise tampered with. I suggest you get into the habit, at least for important pictures (weddings, births, birthdays, and so forth), of always making a "Do-Not-Edit" copy of the photos you transfer to your computer and placing all of those files into one folder that is clearly marked. Leave them in there for safekeeping and later archive them away.

Printing Photos

PRINTING PHOTOS THAT you've worked on is one of the most rewarding aspects of photo retouching. Hang them on your wall, put them in new photo albums or scrapbooks, or sell them.

You can do this from the comfort of your own home using your own printer or seek out other professional or commercial solutions. There are quite a few ways to print your material. This is an idea section meant to help you choose which one is right one for you.

Printing at Home with the Right Printer

With the advent of affordable color inkjet printers, printing photos at home has become the new normal.

Most of us now have high-quality inkjet printers that can print 1200dpi or more. You can even buy specialized photo inkjet printers for under $100. Because there are so many types, it can be confusing about which one to select. There are general printers, as well as those that are specifically targeted at a particular user group, such as photo enthusiasts. Some photo printers print only a few specifically sized prints, such as 4×6 or 5×7. If you need to print 8×10 or other sizes, you should note that and buy a printer with that capability. Many printers now are all-in-one printer/scanner/fax–capable. You can also buy a combo digital camera and printer dock!

From a technical standpoint, you should focus on at least four different areas: type, compatibility, connectivity, resolution, and "other."

▶ **Type** is type. Is it just a printer or is it a photo printer? Is it an inkjet or laser printer or an all-in-one contraption? Personally, I think inkjets are fine if they are high quality, and if you buy the right ink and paper for the specific model of printer you have. Photo inkjets tend to have features that make sense for photo restorers, like border-less printing, panoramic photo printing, and color photo ink cartridges. Color laser printing can get really expensive. If you have limited funds, I would buy the best scanner you can and save the printer for later. You can always take your file to a print shop to get the job done, but the scanner will enable you to get prints into your computer to edit. If you work totally with digital photos, you won't need a scanner at all.

▶ **Compatibility** is whether or not your printer is compatible with your computer and operating system version. Most are, but you always want to make sure, especially when new operating systems hit the market like Microsoft Windows 8 (especially if you're running 64-bits). Another consideration is whether or not you are running Windows on an Intel-based Mac with Bootcamp. Always confirm compatibility.

▶ **Connectivity** is how you send data to the printer to print. Most often, this will be USB, although wireless network printers are now available (we just bought one). Make sure that your printer is up to the latest specification if you want to take advantage of the highest speeds.

▶ **Resolution** is how detailed your prints will be. In most cases, the printers you will be looking at will have more than enough. Non-photo printers, however, might have less.

▶ **Other** is a catch-all category of points to ponder. Do you need auto red-eye removal in a photo printer? No, not if you are going to do it yourself. Do you want an automatic 5×7 photo paper tray? Maybe. Do you need Bluetooth? Possibly, but Bluetooth is not really necessary for photo restoration and printing. Find a printer that has only what you need. You're paying for a lot of stuff you don't need otherwise. If the printer has RAM slots to upgrade its memory, go for it! I would soup it up as much as I could. Printing 1200dpi 8×10 photos is very memory intensive.

There are so many printers out there today that you almost can't go wrong. They are very capable. The key is to know what you want and get the printer that meets your needs. Spend time on the Web or in a store looking at printers and comparing prices.

Retail Outlet Printing

Printing your photos at retail outlets is a viable option, even for high-quality restorations. Today, you can stop by your neighborhood supermart and drop your digital photos off to be printed and picked up in an hour. Just like the old days of dropping off negatives.

There are a ton of places that develop (I mean, print) digital photos: Wal-Mart, Meijers, Walgreens, Sams Club, Target, Kmart, CVS Pharmacy, and Sears (just to name a few) all offer digital photo printing services. Take your digital photos to the store on a memory card or CD-ROM and have them printed while you shop. For a pretty reasonable price, too. Most places give you the option of sending your files over the Internet and then picking them up or having them mailed to you when they're done. Talk about convenient!

Whether you use a kiosk or hand things over to a person behind the counter, ask whether the prints will be glossy or matte. At some places, your options change based on how fast you want the prints or their size. Don't be surprised (like we were).

We take advantage of these services when we print a large number of digital photos. Anne loves putting together and sending photo albums, especially for my dad and other long-distance family and friends. The albums catch everyone up on what's been happening in our lives. You can also put together theme albums that cover events like birthday parties or holidays. Dare I mention scrapbooking? There's something about having a real photo album to look through that's nice.

The benefits of having someone else print your photos are obvious: fast, cheap, timely, and hassle-free. It's far cheaper for us *not* to use our own ink and photo paper for large-scale operations. The store prints are normally very good quality.

Look around at the stores you frequent and ask for their prices and printing options. Some may not be able to print .tif files. Others may. JPEGs should be universally accepted. You probably won't be able to take a .pspimage in to have it printed. Make sure to save a copy of your work in a format the store will accept.

You can decide for yourself whether or not you like sending your files over the Internet. The store doesn't even have to be in your town. Kodak has services that are entirely Internet-based, and they will mail you the prints.

Anne has one more thing for me to add. We had an experience at one store where the overall product was very different, depending on how fast we wanted the prints. If we wanted them done in an hour, they printed them in-house—without making any adjustments whatsoever to the photos. We learned that we had to tweak the lighting ourselves the next time to make the photos better. If we ordered them to be picked up in a few days, the printing was done in a different city, and they made lighting adjustments. If you've restored a photo and everything is exactly the way you want it, you probably don't want someone else changing it. Ask and test. Send some test photos to be printed and evaluate them critically. Printing is a funny thing. What you see on your monitor has to be calibrated so that you're seeing what is present in the photo, and then it has to be translated from ones and zeros to ink and paper.

Professional Printing

Even if you've got a fantastic setup at home, I doubt you'll be able to match the equipment that a professional print company has. The professional printing avenue is the solution that will achieve the highest quality printouts.

Yes, it costs money, but even if the per-page printing costs are more than what you would pay at your local supermart, it's offset by two factors. You're going to have a reasonably low volume, which means you should be able to afford to pay more per copy. Secondly, the quality and features a print and copy business have are astounding.

Here are a few of the products and services available from the print and copy company I use:

- ► Booklets
- ► Brochures
- ► Calendars
- ► Catalogs
- ► Digital Copies
- ► Note Pads
- ► Binding
- ► Cutting
- ► Folding
- ► Lamination
- ► Offset Printing
- ► Pickup and Delivery
- ► Shrink Wrapping

Call a marketing or design agency (whoever you think needs a good printer) in town and see where they get their printing done. Ask around. Talk to people.

Visit them on the Web first and then call them. Tell them what you're doing and what sort of production you'll need (numbers, sizes, format). Ask them for a price list or quote. Before you send anything in, make sure you've asked what format they require and be clear on what sort of output you want (mainly size, but also paper, cutting or folding, and finish).

I'm sure you can develop a good relationship with someone. These people know a lot about printing. They may even have some suggestions that you can use to prepare your work to be printed. Send them a file and try them out. Evaluate the product and your experience, and then go from there.

Archiving

WHEN I SAY "ARCHIVING," I'm talking about preserving your photos electronically and then protecting those digital backups. Your photos could have been digital to start with, scanned photos that are now graphics files, scanned film or negatives, and, of course, the PaintShop Pro files that you generate as you work on restoring and retouching your photo collection. The whole shebang.

For this edition of the book, I can only recommend one approach: buy external (or swappable) hard drives. They're the cheapest and most reliable media. They hold tons of data, and external USB, FireWire, and eSATA drives can be swapped easily. I have several external eSATA/USB drives that I swap as if they were floppy disks.

I've looked into all the alternatives: tape backup (too clunky, proprietary, and expensive), DVD/CDs (far too little capacity, although BluRay discs are promising), and online storage (for my purposes, this would take far too much Internet bandwidth). No other solutions are as inexpensive, reliable, and compatible. You copy files normally—nothing to decode to reverse the process.

Don't lose all your great work because you didn't think about this. Don't lose your family's history because you never backed anything up!

Index